My Non-Political
FBI
From Hoover to a Violent America

BOB PENCE

FULCRUM
GROUP

Wheat Ridge, Colorado

The opinions expressed in this book are those of the author
and not of the FBI.

ISBN: 978-1-56373-199-0
Library of Congress Control Number: 2020944591

0 9 8 7 6 5 4 3 2 1

Fulcrum Group
3970 Youngfield Street
Wheat Ridge, CO 80033
800-992-2908 • 303-277-1623

Contents

Preface

RETIRED AFTER NEARLY THIRTY YEARS of service, I can honestly claim that I found, with very few exceptions, that "Bureau" personnel were truly the cream of the crop. Inside the FBI we normally referred to our agency as the "Bureau" or sometimes just the "B," and I hold up our employees as among the highest quality American patriots I have ever met. To honor them and herald their efforts are some of the main reasons for my writing this book. Certainly, without them, most of the adventures and successes I will mention could not have occurred.

It should come as no surprise that FBI employees are certainly not robots and present themselves in all types of personalities – loud, quiet, flamboyant, reserved, conservative, and liberal. Some work fast and efficiently while others are equally efficient, but work slower and more deliberately, putting in long hours. Among the gun-and-badge carrying Special Agents (SAs), some are interested in advancing in the Bureau and will subject themselves to office transfers and other processes, while others prefer to forgo the family moves and other personal inconveniences, trying to apply their investigative talents as much as possible without relocating.

With regard to personalities, the most important point I would like to make is that in all my years with the Bureau, there was really only one person, I repeat only one person, out of the hundreds I worked with, for whom I lost total respect and with whom I regret having had any relationship or association. About that single, solitary person, I would only answer as the articulate Forrest Gump might have put it, "That's all I want to say about that." However, I think it speaks volumes about the nearly thirty-eight thousand other employees of the FBI.

For me, personally, I believe the root reason for my attraction to the FBI had a "sociological" genesis, and the book will explain in detail the how and why of my interest. Clearly my service in the Bureau from 1962 to 1992 allowed experiences during some of America's most tumultuous and challenging times, both during the civil rights movement in the South and the Vietnam War unrest ravaging across our home front. Not only did I witness the problems firsthand but also actively participated in efforts to help resolve them. Through my eyes and memories the book will recapture some of those times and incidents.

I doubt that few readers have not at least heard the name FBI (Federal Bureau of Investigation), which will be my main focus. However, for those not familiar with the agency, we will start with a brief overview of the Bureau's history as well as the ensuing course of events and directions the book will take.

The FBI is the principal investigative agency of the US Department of Justice and has jurisdiction over more than two hundred federal statutes, which cover both major crimes in and the security (counterespionage and counterterrorism) of the United States. In addition, the FBI is responsible for providing extensive and detailed background investigations of candidates for security clearances to obtain a variety of high level and sensitive government and private sector positions. With the criminal investigations by the FBI, all prosecutive decisions are left to US attorneys' offices or attorneys of the US Department of Justice. In some cases, decisions by prosecutors might lead to FBI personnel providing their testimony in state or local courts.

The Bureau started in 1908 as the Bureau of Investigation numbering a few hundred investigators described largely as political hacks. It changed dramatically, however, in 1924 under the leadership and iron-clad rule of J. Edgar Hoover who "reigned" as Director until his death in 1972 (interesting to note that during that period the Bureau's name changed to the FBI in 1935). This book outlines the lasting improvements through the years that occurred under Mr. Hoover's leadership. Also included are some of my personal experiences at FBI Headquarters involving Mr. Hoover during his tenure.

Readers can get a taste of FBI policy, procedures, and actual cases worked as the book tracks my various assignments to Field Offices and FBI Headquarters. A couple of chapters will feature my "forty-thousand-foot" appraisal of FBI transitions in personnel, communications, and investigations through the years – partly from my personal observation and experiences and after retirement through contacts with active FBI personnel.

There then follows a series of individual chapters examining special topics, including the FBI hiring of female Special Agents (SAs), the FBI's age-old relationship with bank robbers, understanding and working with the media, and the close partnership with the US military.

The next chapter deals with the question I get most often – what does it take and what are the requirements to become an FBI Agent? This is important to me, and I dedicated an entire chapter to the complete answer.

An important question faces most SAs (and probably most law enforcement officers) as they approach and close in on retirement – what will I do after retirement? Three chapters follow with how that was handled in my case. In short – not to worry, there seemed to be plenty of options!

One of those chapters deals extensively with the period of time and effort I spent learning so much from a wonderfully dedicated group of professionals in the pursuit of fair and equal Juvenile Justice.

The last three chapters are actually three parts to a problem that should concern every American. One, how serious is the problem of violence in America? Two, why do we have the problem? and Three, what can we do about it? I used the opportunity to put forth for consideration my personal effort to analyze a major problem and include some of the possible solutions.

Finally, while I believe it is important and purposeful to identify at the outset what this book is about and what it hopes to convey to its readers, I think it just as important to lay out what it does not propose to accomplish. Books and writings appear every day crafted by former organization insiders for the express purpose of exposing embarrassing realities or alleged wrongdoing inside the organization by its employees. Sometimes the ink or "dirty laundry" is designed to "get even" or bring retribution against a boss or other employee or employer who committed a real or perceived wrong against the writer in the past. Quite clearly, this book claims no such motives.

Actually, I can probably summarize my career with at least some of the lyrics of the late American singer Frank Sinatra in his iconic ballad *My Way*. He sang the words, "Regrets I've had a few, then again too few to mention; I did what I had to do and saw it through without exemption." The only exception for me would be instead of doing it "my way," I always tried to do it the "Bureau way." I retain an immense love, loyalty, and respect for the agency, and I hope that many of my fellow Americans will have an interest in learning more about the Bureau through my memories, perspectives, and experiences. Hopefully, this book can accomplish that goal.

CHAPTER 1

Decisions, Decisions ...

Cowboy, Mountie, Soldier or FBI Agent?

BORN THREE DAYS AFTER CHRISTMAS in 1938 into a small, God-loving family of very meager economic means, I had no thoughts or realization that I would be a poster child for what a celebrated sociologist would write and teach many years later. Dr. Morris Massey is now a retired sociologist, highly regarded in his field, and the recipient of numerous awards. During the 1960s and 1970s, he was an associate dean and professor of marketing at the University of Colorado in Boulder. He is well known for his work in determining when and how a person's values are developed. In his work, I think he summed it up succinctly for me in one phrase: "What you are, is where you were when." When I eventually heard of Dr. Massey and his work, I was well into my career but instantly realized that my early life fit almost perfectly into his philosophy.

My hometown is Brookville, a small rural community of about four thousand folks in western Pennsylvania. Since few people have ever heard of it, I normally answer the question of where Brookville is located with the explanation that it is very close to where the groundhog emerges in February of every year and almost always sees its shadow, forecasting six more weeks of winter. Due to nationwide media coverage, nearly everyone seems to have heard of Punxsutawney Phil in Punxsutawney, Pennsylvania.

Being born at the onset of World War II, I grew up listening to news accounts of war, watching movie newsreels showing airplanes dropping their racks of bombs, hearing air raid sirens wailing and practicing for the real thing, and greeting block wardens knocking on our door, ordering a blackout of all lights in practice drills to prevent enemy aircraft from locating our town. Taken together, events in those years instilled in a young mind a certain element of fear, and cultivated a strong respect for safety and security.

Although our family had no television in those days, radio shows were replete with tales and exploits of law enforcement agencies fighting and winning against the criminals. I clearly remember my favorite program was called *The FBI in Peace and War*. On Saturday afternoon, the local movie theater matinee normally started with a segment of a continuing serial film showing cops fighting robbers, followed by a feature film in which a cowboy star like Roy Rogers or Gene Autry fought against the likes of stagecoach robbers and cattle rustlers. The good guys not only always prevailed, but they also won all the pretty female hearts. Furthermore, they normally did it without killing anyone, usually shooting the gun out of the bad guy's hand or, at most, "winging" him with a shot to the arm or leg. Other superhero models for justice, like Superman, Batman, and the Lone Ranger, were also prominent in comic books, movies, and later, TV screens. They, too, represented moral and ethical heroes in the war against the evil empire. So for me in those years, it was reassuring that both safety and security were considered extremely critical, and that the various entertainment media correctly portrayed right winning over wrong and good being victorious over evil. When I came to understand that I probably would never be a singing cowboy or a flying superhero, I began to focus on the heroes who were real and actually fighting genuine criminals and spies in America. When my parents finally convinced me I was not Canadian and could not become a Mountie (Royal Canadian Mounted Police) with a horse, a smart red outfit, and a beautiful husky dog, I believe at that point I began my desire, consciously or subconsciously, to become an FBI Agent.

The one fact that became crystal clear to me early on was that due to my family's financial situation, I would need to take personal responsibility for ensuring my future education. I knew that the FBI Agent position required a college degree and probably a law degree. Most nights during high school I studied well into the midnight hours and was rewarded ultimately with a grade point average close to the 4.0 level and a speaking role at my high school graduation ceremony. The hard work and grades led to a number of college scholarship offers and eventually admission to Dickinson College in Carlisle, Pennsylvania. A combination of scholarships as well as employment through the college food service as a waiter in one of the girls' dormitories, allowed me to complete my college years with a bachelor of arts degree with a major in political science.

Through my high school and college years, the importance of the rule of law grew even stronger in my mind, along with respect for those who are charged with enforcing it. Since my early life was centered in the state of Pennsylvania, the law enforcement agency I admired most was the Pennsylvania State Police. Their flat-brimmed campaign hats, dark-gray uniform with britches and boots, latest fully equipped vehicles, all topped off by their professional demeanor, left me totally impressed. However, growing up and riding with my parents, it was not always so enjoyable to see the troopers up close and personal, when they pulled my parents over occasionally for creeping a bit above the speed limit. Fortunately, later in my FBI career and even after retirement, it was very satisfying for me to be able to personally inform the then-current Pennsylvania State Police Commissioner and other command level troopers of the very strong influence their agency had in my decision to enter a law enforcement career.

Curiously, after retiring from the FBI and having more time to review some old personal documents from my high school days, I was reminded of my early interest when I located a very detailed research report that I had completed on the FBI for my high school civics class. All things considered, I remain truly convinced, as Dr. Massey taught, that my destiny was in safety and security mainly because of "where I was when." As I was growing up, security was, and still is, more than a job or even a career for me. It is an essential pillar of our society, and I've always wanted to be a part of it. In retirement, I still do a fair amount of public speaking and frequently open a speech with my personal analysis that there are only four basic and essential needs for life on Planet Earth (given the fact that the Creator has provided the air to breathe), and these are:

1. Food and nourishment;
2. Shelter, whether a cave, tent, or a million-dollar mansion, and clothing to further shelter the body, especially when away from the cave, etc.;
3. Safety from any of the natural, animal, or human threats to you and your continued survival;
4. Good health (I added this as a fourth by popular demand, after a speech to employees at a large Denver metropolitan hospital);

It seems that most, if not all, of our occupations, skills, and business efforts have a nexus in some way in either accomplishing, enhancing, expanding, improving, or supporting these basic needs.

I suspect that many conscientious readers, upon careful contemplation, can themselves relate to the philosophy of Dr. Massey, when looking back at their lives and the choices they made. Obviously, for me the answer was number three.

Looking back through my college years, one decision stands out as having tremendously influenced the direction of my life and career, probably more than any other, and that was enrollment in the Reserve Officers' Training Corps, at Dickinson College. The college had an army ROTC program, and successfully completing the program led me to a two-year active duty tour as a commissioned officer in the US Army. I thoroughly enjoyed the military science program and studiously applied myself, earning upon college graduation the *Chicago Tribune* Medal for outstanding ROTC efforts. The lessons surrounding military discipline, responsibility, and strategy and tactics proved particularly helpful to me, not only in ROTC courses but also in understanding and achieving real objectives in my college years and well beyond.

Upon completion of college in 1960, I served my two-year military obligation from 1960 to 1962, receiving my initial officer training at Fort Benning, Georgia. I was then reassigned to Fort Dix, New Jersey. Fortunately, I did very well during the training at Fort Benning, and successfully finished the course near the top of my class. Shortly after arrival at Fort Dix, New Jersey, I was promoted from second lieutenant to first lieutenant and given command of an infantry training company at Fort Dix. Each class of army recruits assigned to my training company numbered a few hundred, and the training lasted for several weeks. If ever I could claim any leadership and management skills gained for my future life, it was undoubtedly during, and due in large part from, my sustained exposure to literally thousands of young army recruits, mainly from the greater New York City area, for the several-week basic infantry training course at Fort Dix. Many of the recruits had medical, drug dependency, and other disciplinary problems and presented daily challenges during the several-week period. However, working with an excellent cadre of officers, some well-experienced sergeants, and a truly extraordinary first sergeant, this young, immature country boy from Pennsylvania learned and matured rapidly during his years at Fort Dix.

Not only did I experience successes and failures dealing with so many different types of people at Fort Dix, but, to my incredible and lasting benefit, found myself located almost adjacent to McGuire Air Force Base (MAFB). Through some personal connections, I was able to take advantage of another type of valuable experience due to the

First Sergeant LLoyd Pool

proximity of MAFB. During recess periods, after my troops had graduated and I was awaiting the fill of the next class, I was able to acquire military assignments as a courier officer, leading a security detail of sergeants and escorting classified materials on missions, normally flying out of MAFB to destinations throughout the world. These experiences, along with my command experience at Fort Dix, provided me with knowledge of both army and air force policies, procedures, and operations.

As the last few months of my active duty tour neared completion, I gave more thought to applying for my ultimate dream job. I wanted to determine all of the qualifications necessary to become an FBI Agent, and wrote a letter to the FBI Field Office (FO) located in Newark, New Jersey, not far from Fort Dix. I explained my interest and my current position as a US Army Infantry company commander at Fort Dix and was invited to visit the Newark FO for a personal interview. To my surprise, upon arrival I was met by the Assistant Special Agent in Charge (ASAC) personally for my interview. I learned there were just under six thousand Special Agents (SAs) in the FBI at that time, but due to increasing tension with Russia and the possible positioning of missiles in Cuba, the FBI was hiring additional SAs, and my interest in applying might be very timely. He explained that the requirements at that time did include a law or an accounting degree, but, under the circumstances, certain highly qualified exceptions were being considered. I vividly recall being asked about salary and responded that I would consider $3,000 annually, since as a first lieutenant in the US Army

I was making a little more than $2,000 a year. The ASAC responded, "How about $7,000 per year?" (since the entry SA salary at that time, as I recall, was $6,995). Of course, I was very pleased to agree to this figure. The ASAC then asked me to fill out an extremely detailed application, took a set of my fingerprints, and told me they would be in touch with me later.

Several weeks later, separation day from the army finally came. Without really knowing my future, I packed my belongings, along with my personal German Shepherd, Wolf, who was also the company mascot, and headed back to my family home in Pennsylvania. I left the army with very mixed emotions, since I truly loved and respected the military and the service it provides our country. All during the long drive home, I could not stop wondering if I had made the right decision to leave and pondered what really might be lying ahead for me.

My dog Wolf, also the company mascot for Company F, 3rd Training Regiment.

CHAPTER 2

Joining Hoover's FBI

AS I RETURNED HOME TO PENNSYLVANIA after completing my tour of duty in the US Army, my dream job of becoming an FBI Agent was still a dream. I had submitted my extremely detailed, many-paged application several weeks prior, but upon arriving home had still heard nothing. Then, with almost perfect timing, after just a few days the telephone in my parents' home rang and the operator wanted to speak with me. I'll never forget her noticeably excited but apprehensive voice, as she told me she had a telegram for me and asked if it was okay if she

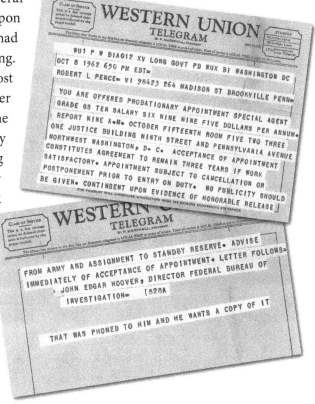

read it. Noting that was a rather strange request, I answered something to the effect that reading it to me would be the best way for me to know what it said, "so please proceed." The telegram contained the dream come true. It offered me a probationary appointment as a SA of the FBI, cautioning that no publicity should be given to this appointment, and instructing me to report to Washington, D.C., by a closely approaching specific date for further instruction and training. The telegram was signed "J. Edgar Hoover." Frankly, it sounded like the telephone operator was as pleased and awestruck as I was.

Having barely unpacked my military uniforms, I realized I needed to rapidly purchase a couple of civilian business suits and other items of clothing, and prepare to leave home again. Fortunately, my parents agreed to care for my dog, Wolf, and I very quickly got packed up and took off for D.C.

After reporting to FBI Headquarters in the Department of Justice Building on Pennsylvania Avenue, I was immediately sworn in as an FBI Agent. Then, for the next day or so, we handled insurance and other administrative matters. Finally, the class of approximately fifty new SAs were issued what seemed like a mountain of manuals, books, and other instruction materials, and then led to waiting FBI buses for transportation to the FBI Training Academy at Quantico, Virginia. For the next sixteen weeks, we were schooled in firearms, defensive tactics and arrest techniques, physical training, legal matters, and, for the purpose of this introduction, the especially broad jurisdiction of the FBI. Near the completion of our New Agent Training, we received two weeks of what was probably the most interesting and valuable segment – the opportunity to return to Washington, D.C., and pair up with an active SA assigned to the Bureau's Washington Field Office (FO). I was privileged to work with an SA assigned to a bank robbery squad. It was nearing Christmas, and we responded to a number of such robberies, as well as covering some leads developed from past robberies. Parenthetically, I knew FBI SAs were down-to-earth human beings when I first met my Washington FO SA, and he sheepishly confided that it was nearly Christmas, and he needed to do a little Christmas shopping. He asked if it was okay with me if we stopped a couple of times to purchase some presents for his family while we were out covering leads during the next two weeks.

So, after two weeks and the actual exposure to real field investigations under our belts, we returned to Quantico for the completion of our very intensive and demanding training program. Finally, we prepared for graduation back in Washington, D.C., at the Seat of Government (later renamed FBI Headquarters), and the highly anticipated personal meeting with the Director. From there, we would leave directly and immediately for travel to our first field assignment.

Now, before moving on to describe some of my own personal adventures, I would like to share a bit of background information relative to the organization I had just joined and its storied first Director, who unofficially, but actually in real life, became Director for the rest of his life.

The FBI

With daily exposure in a variety of TV series, movies, and the mainstream news media, the name "FBI" is probably familiar to most, if not every American – young and old. However, for the benefit of all readers, I think it appropriate to include at this point a brief descriptive portrait of America's FBI, short for the Federal Bureau of Investigation.

Established in 1908, and named at that time the Bureau of Investigation (BOI), the agency was reported to be full of politically appointed hacks and littered with inefficiency and corruption. However, everything changed in 1924, when the then-current US Attorney General Harlan Stone persuaded a young BOI attorney, named John Edgar Hoover, to become Acting Director of the BOI. Shortly thereafter, President Calvin Coolidge appointed Mr. Hoover to be the BOI's sixth permanent Director. Despite the fact that it did not receive its current name as the FBI until 1935, I believe the real FBI was born when Mr. Hoover agreed to take the BOI Director's job on the principal condition that his agents, to be called Special Agents, would only be selected on the basis of merit.

Administratively, the FBI is located in the US Department of Justice (DOJ), under the supervision of the US Attorney General. It is the principal criminal investigative agency of the DOJ, and probably the best known federal investigative agency in the United States. Moreover, it is arguably one of the most prominent crime-fighting organizations in the entire world. It has widespread jurisdiction, which includes more than two hundred separate federal criminal classifications or violations. In this century, probably the most important classifications involve the FBI's leading jurisdiction in the areas of counterterrorism, foreign counterintelligence or counterespionage, and cybercrime. Essentially, FBI jurisdiction includes most crimes that involve some interstate connection. Other important jurisdiction involves bank robbery, organized crime, and civil rights violations. Beyond criminal and security-type investigations, the FBI is also responsible for a wide variety of background investigations when individuals are being considered for several different high level or classified appointments to offices throughout the US government and for security clearances in connection with sensitive assignments in the private sector.

Throughout the years, the only significant loss of jurisdiction came in the late 1970s and early 1980s, when the resources of the Bureau were committed to work along with the Drug Enforcement Administration in the worldwide war against illegal drugs and their traffickers. It was at that time military deserter apprehensions were returned to the military, and most of the general fugitive classifications were turned over to the US Marshals Service, for the purpose of freeing the FBI to work on higher priority matters.

Subsequent to the catastrophic terrorist attack on the United States on September 11, 2001, commonly referred to as 9/11, Congress acted to better coordinate national intelligence activities, and established the Office of the Director of National Intelligence. By virtue of its position as a key member of the US intelligence community, the FBI has a dual responsibility now to report to both the Attorney General and the Director of National Intelligence (DNI). In fact, each of the FBI FOs has an SA designated to represent the DNI.

Operationally, in addition to the Headquarters of the FBI located in Washington, D.C., the Bureau operates throughout the United States from fifty-six strategically located FOs headed by a Special Agent in Charge (SAC), and more than four hundred smaller regional offices called Resident Agencies, which, in turn, respond to the FO covering their state or region. Understanding that crime and security problems have become truly global, occurring throughout today's world, the FBI has established nearly seventy offices (with the number increasing), staffed with a growing number of FBI SAs, in embassies and consulates around the world, called Legal Attachés. They are there not to conduct independent investigations but rather to coordinate requests and activities with law enforcement and security agencies in their host countries.

At this point it is important to note not just what the FBI is, but, perhaps more importantly, what it is not – and that is a national police force. From the beginning, Mr. Hoover made it abundantly clear that his agency was there to investigate specific federal criminal statutes. Beyond that, the role of the FBI would be, and always has been, to support, in every way possible, the efforts of the local, county, state, and federal law enforcement agencies in the United States.

J. Edgar Hoover, the FBI's First Director

When Mr. Hoover accepted the position of BOI Director in 1924, it could well have come with the title of "FBI Director for Life" since indeed that was how it turned out.

He was still Director when his life ended peacefully during the night of May 2, 1972. He had been Director for forty-eight years. For several senior retired SAs living throughout the United States today, he remains the "Director" since he was the only Director for whom they ever served. Since then, there have been seven additional permanent Directors, with Christopher Wray assuming the position on August 2, 2017.

One of the questions I got during my career, and still frequently field in retirement during speeches is, "What was it like to work for the FBI and J. Edgar Hoover?" The reality that underlies the answer began to hit me the day I received the telegram offering me a position as Special Agent and signed "J. Edgar Hoover."

I had just been contacted by one of the most revered or feared (depending on your circumstances), powerful, and well-known figures in our country. From this introduction, I continued to work under his directorship for the next ten years, until his death in 1972.

Indeed, he was a very demanding leader who seemed to be the genesis of the phrase "don't embarrass the Bureau," which was widely attributed to him. For those who stepped over the line, either purposefully or accidentally, and sometimes for rather minor infractions, bad things could happen quickly. I personally knew of SAs who got transferred to, at the time, rather unpopular assignments such as Butte, Montana, or Buffalo, New York, and were directed to be there the following Monday. Letters of Censure were also common and placed in many a personnel file.

The Director required a professional appearance and quality product from all of the SAs. It was rumored that he considered a person's sweaty palms as a sign of nervousness and weakness. That might well have been true! When my New Agents Class assembled to graduate and meet the Director for the first time, our two experienced SA counselors squirted talcum powder into our palms and instructed us to rub them together so they would not be sweating. As we moved into the Director's Office, one by one, and shook the hand of J. Edgar Hoover that day, there was not an embarrassing sweaty palm anywhere to be found.

However, the dry palms notwithstanding, the stress of that single brief meeting was felt by all, since one negative comment from the Director could have cut short and terminated, then and there, the career of a brand-new, freshly trained FBI SA. Further, the careers of the two experienced SA counselors were also in jeopardy, since any incidents or failing by a graduating SA up through the time of meeting Mr. Hoover could also adversely impact their careers. For me, successfully meeting Mr. Hoover in my dark suit, white shirt, and conservative tie was a great relief, as he greeted me warmly and wished me well in my new assignment. Then, dutifully as directed, I immediately prepared to leave Washington for New Orleans, Louisiana, my first field assignment. Little did I realize then that I would get to learn a lot more about the iconic Mr. Hoover, up close and personal, upon my transfer back to FBI Headquarters, not too many years in the future.

CHAPTER 3

The Big Easy
Was Not Always Easy

WHEN I LOOK IN RETROSPECT AT MY FIRST office assignment to New Orleans, Louisiana (NOLA), I'm reminded of the line from Charles Dickens's *A Tale of Two Cities*, written in 1859, describing the life in London and Paris before and during the French Revolution – "It was the best of times, it was the worst of times." The reminder and quote comes primarily because the New Orleans Field Office (FO) covered two states, and what I found in one was dramatically different from what awaited me in the other.

It was great to learn a few weeks before graduation from the FBI Academy that my first assignment would be the exciting and glamorous Crescent City of NOLA. I had never traveled farther south than my temporary assignment to Fort Benning, Georgia, during my military training days, and NOLA had the reputation of being a fun city with lots of FBI-related work. The New Orleans FO in those days covered both the states of Louisiana and Mississippi, with smaller offices called Resident Agencies (RAs) in both states that responded to supervisors in the headquarters city of NOLA. I was assigned to a criminal squad, but being a brand-new first office Agent and not married, I understood I would be tapped for a variety of assignments, at all hours day and night, and anywhere in either state.

In the 1960s, the Bureau policy found SAs being transferred about every two years to experience large and small FOs, while also experiencing cross-assignments to allow familiarity with cases involving criminal, security, civil rights, and a wide variety of other investigations within the FBI's jurisdiction. Almost immediately, I found myself being called out at all hours to respond to anything from bank robberies or bank burglaries along the Gulf Coast of Mississippi in locations like Gulfport or Biloxi, Mississippi, to investigations of an administrative type such as car accidents involving FBI vehicles.

Although I was very satisfied with my assignment, it was later that I learned that my NOLA destination was not simply chosen at random.

Whether or not it was an official Bureau policy is unknown to me, but the rumor circulated at the time that Mr. Hoover had dictated that new SAs from northern states should be considered for assignment to southern offices for a very important reason. He and other senior staff at Headquarters were anticipating pressure for the FBI enforcement of civil rights and voting rights legislation coming from Congress and wanted to avoid any criticism from voices that might suggest SAs already assigned to southern FOs might have a racial bias. Well, regardless of whether there was any such official policy, nearly all SAs in the NOLA FO would experience the battle, which was to come, to enforce our new civil rights laws.

The Best of Times

For a new FBI SA interested in gaining a wide variety of criminal investigative experience, there was probably no better venue to be assigned in the early 1960s than NOLA. My first opportunity to make an arrest occurred very shortly after I arrived.

In those days, jurisdiction for investigating, tracking, and arresting military deserters rested with the FBI. One day an urgent teletype was received from another FBI FO with information reporting a tip that a fugitive US Navy deserter, using a specific alias, was working with a certain plumbing company in New Orleans. The fugitive desk supervisor assigned another new SA and me to check it out.

Contact with the company verified that a plumber's helper with the alias name was indeed employed by them and was currently on a job in one of the suburbs. We checked our .38 caliber revolvers and handcuffs and proceeded to the address of a small business in the suburb of Metairie, Louisiana, near the Mississippi River. There, we quickly located our young fugitive working with a pipe wrench under the sink in the men's room. He was easily identified from the description furnished us and arrested without a struggle.

I didn't know about the SA with me, but between the deserter and me, I couldn't tell who was shaking more as I fumbled with the handcuffs. However, as we stood him up and turned him facing us, my confidence quickly returned, and I knew we had won the challenge. The front of his pants was thoroughly soaked and not from anything in the sink overhead. This was my baptism of fire, so to speak, and I was ready for my next arrest.

In my opinion, jurisdiction for the FBI to handle and work military deserters, as part of our fugitive program, proved an excellent vehicle for newer SAs to get trained and experienced in fugitive investigations. It allowed familiarity with paperwork, investigative techniques, and arrest procedures, while engaging lower-risk fugitives who were usually unarmed and not excessively violent.

That said, I recall a US Army deserter in one of my later assignments who was not to be taken that easily. We had intelligence information that he visited his home in San Jose, California, frequently, but every time we visited, his mother swore she had not seen him. After a number of visits, we set up surveillance in the neighborhood and finally observed him enter the house. With his mother denying he was home and vowing he would not hurt a fly, he suddenly bolted from a closet, and it took three of us to eventually wrestle him down and effect the arrest.

Unfortunately, as deserter investigations were valuable for training FBI SAs to handle much more complicated and more dangerous fugitives, many of us were upset, after a few years, when a high level decision was made to transfer these cases back to military authorities in order that FBI SAs could deal with matters of a higher priority.

In NOLA, much of the classic criminal activity revolved around life and activities in the notorious, infamous, and wonderful French Quarter. The strippers and showgirls of the joints along Bourbon Street in the French Quarter were excellent informants, and normally knew very well who was in town and who might be wanted by law enforcement. I had a number of informants among these women, and remember debriefing them during the day, when they weren't dancing, in their apartments and rooms located on the second floor above a number of the joints or bars along Bourbon Street.

During the days of my assignment in NOLA, the strip clubs were even more open than they are today. One would merely have to walk down the middle of Bourbon Street and look left or right to see the nearly naked women inside the open doors of the clubs. Now patrons usually need to actually go into the establishments and pay cover charges or buy drinks to see the show. I remember the sights, sounds, and smells of the French Quarter with its fragrance of stale beer and liquor everywhere. Frequently, broken glass and pools of dried blood

On Bourbon Street in the Big Easy.

were left from earlier fights and falls. Common were the sights and the smell of what heavy drinkers' stomachs rejected and ended up on the sidewalks of the French Quarter. I remember the hot dog carts for Lucky Dogs that existed on almost every street corner in the Quarter. (In recent visits, I noticed that they still prevail, and that the prices have not really increased that much since the early 1960s.)

I remember the excellent cuisine and the locals' and tourists' custom of stopping by the famous Café Du Monde for the beignets and chicory coffee at all hours of the day and night. In recent visits, I have noted that the Café Du Monde is still as active as ever with large crowds waiting to be seated. Of course, the highlight of the year remains the famously attended Mardi Gras, which brings throngs of thousands of people to the French Quarter every year the week before Lent, where you can still see girls flashing their chests by lifting blouses and tops. They are begging for Mardi Gras beads being thrown from the balconies of the French Quarter, and also from the floats that are in the many Mardi Gras parades.

On one occasion during the Mardi Gras, I recall walking down the middle of Bourbon Street through crowds of hundreds and noticed that in front of me was a young woman. There was a light, misty rain falling, and I noticed the woman was wearing a transparent raincoat.

As I got closer, I noticed that it was all she was wearing – it was literally a naked woman walking, covered only by a transparent piece of plastic. I have to admit out of amazement I walked a little further down Bourbon Street on that occasion than I had intended, but eventually turned around and proceeded to my destination.

During Mardi Gras, all the police were out in every vehicle, no matter how old, that bore the words "New Orleans Police Department." Frequently, I noticed the arrests for drunkenness and/or disorderly conduct were so numerous that the police, on occasion, strung cable along Canal Street bordering the French Quarter, and handcuffed some of those being arrested to the cable until the bus arrived to take them for booking.

I distinctly remember my favorite showgirl in those days was the star performer at a club called The Sho Bar on Bourbon Street. I don't remember her name, (if I ever knew it), but I knew she was supposedly a girlfriend of the owner. She was a beautiful young lady, normally wearing only a mini leopard-skin outfit. Sometimes, when in the French Quarter and walking along Bourbon Street, I would stop by to say hello. I mention her here mainly to express my regret as to how women in these situations are used and abused.

Fast forward for a moment now to the late 1970s, to my assignment in the Louisville, Kentucky FO, and our efforts at that time to clean up corruption in the Newport/Covington area of northern Kentucky. One evening while getting briefed by FBI SAs of our Covington RA regarding the investigation, and checking some different strip joints along the Ohio River at Newport, I was noticing bizarre activities, including actual sex acts in the back booths of one of the clubs. I happened to be walking through the club when one of the dancers stumbled out on the stage from behind the curtains, obviously intoxicated, and showing her advanced age. As we were walking by, she literally fell off the stage into my arms. Incredibly, to my great surprise and disbelief, I recognized her as the leopard-skin star from my earlier days in NOLA. One of the bouncers from the club quickly grabbed her from me and carried her backstage.

Now thinking back to my very early days in NOLA as a brand-new FBI SA, I recall an incident that could have been embarrassing, but, fortunately, turned out well. As a strong advocate for the rule of law and with my new badge and authority, I reacted on one occasion to a local law breaker without really thinking it through. Suddenly finding myself driving behind a speeding, weaving, and apparently reckless driver, I reacted by activating my lights and siren and pulled over the vehicle. Stopped behind the traffic violator with no evidence whatsoever of a federal violation, I mentally asked myself, "What have I just done?" Gathering my wits, I got out of the Bureau car, walked up to the other vehicle, and merely suggested he slow down a bit and drive more carefully. Noticing the odor of alcohol, I then returned to my car and radioed the Louisiana State Police, furnishing the vehicle description and location, and advising them that the occupant appeared to be driving carelessly and might need to be checked out. All worked out well, and I was thanked by the state trooper.

Parenthetically but interestingly, the only other time I recall using an FBI car for a non-FBI-related car stop occurred later, in the early 1980s in Raleigh, North Carolina. As the Special Agent in Charge (SAC) in North Carolina, I was riding with Bill Moran, the Supervisory Special Agent in Charge of our Raleigh RA, en route to a business appointment. While driving on an interstate highway around Raleigh, we noticed a vehicle ahead literally weaving back and forth and bouncing off of tractor trailers and guard rails. We activated the emergency equipment and gradually forced the driver off the interstate. He exited and continued to proceed at a slower speed along a residential street, driving over lawns and mowing down mailboxes. We finally got him stopped and, assuming he was intoxicated, radioed the North Carolina State Highway Patrol. We waited for a unit to arrive, and the responding trooper quickly determined that the elderly gentleman was not drunk but suffering serious diabetic insulin shock. He took immediate action to revive him and requested an ambulance. In that particular incident, our action could well have prevented a serious auto crash, and possibly saved the life of the gentleman.

Although I had no additional unofficial car stops, I do admit to a tactic, on occasion, when I witnessed a dangerous speeder or a reckless driver in a car or truck. I found that by coming up behind them and placing my rotating blue or red emergency light on the dash, without activating it, I could normally induce a therapeutic corrective effect on the offending driver.

My recollections of life in NOLA would have to include the tremendous heat and humidity. In those days, our FBI vehicles were not equipped with air conditioning, since Director Hoover did not permit the Bureau's budget to be used on such luxuries. Parking the car in the French Quarter, or for that matter, anywhere in NOLA for any length of time, meant a punishing return to the vehicle. Door handles were almost too hot to handle, and all doors and windows had to be opened to let the air circulate before you could even get in and drive the vehicle.

Today, in my visits to NOLA and the French Quarter, I note that a number of things have not changed. They both still fascinate and entertain the visitors who come by the thousands to enjoy the experience and some of the best food in our country.

The Worst of Times

Working in NOLA and throughout Louisiana was exciting and provided the kinds of criminal cases most FBI SAs enjoyed and expected to be working, but the New Orleans FO also covered the state of Mississippi. Clearly events were unfolding there that were to test the resources, commitment, and capabilities of the FBI to its very limit. During the latter 1950s, efforts commenced to correct the segregation of races, mainly in our southern states, and institute equal rights policies for all our citizens. The protests, demonstrations, and marches ultimately resulted in Congress passing a slew of legislation, including such laws as the Civil Rights Act of 1957 and the Civil Rights Act of 1960. These, in essence, made it a federal crime to prevent minority citizens from registering to vote and voting. The FBI had the jurisdiction to investigate violations and enforce the laws. This, along with other similar legislation, and its enforcement action, was not accepted well by many in the South, to say the least. Violent opposition was promised and executed by the leaders and their klaverns of the infamous Ku Klux Klan (KKK), who were intent on maintaining at all costs the status quo for African American communities.

I mentioned earlier that my first assignment, being from Pennsylvania and going to NOLA, was probably not handled in a random manner. One rumor for the policy had it that Reverend Martin Luther

King, Jr. had complained to Director Hoover that SAs living in the South couldn't be trusted to enforce the civil rights laws, since they would be biased against minorities. Supposedly, to avoid such criticism, the order was given to send a number of new SA graduates, whose homes were in northern states, down to the South. So with that backdrop, I arrived in NOLA at the very beginning of 1963.

Although assigned to a criminal squad in the headquarters city of NOLA, I would be dispatched as needed to assist SAs assigned in Mississippi, and it nearly always involved civil rights–related projects and investigations. The atmosphere between metropolitan NOLA and the entire state of Mississippi was as different as night and day. Signage in Mississippi announcing "whites only" and "colored only" seemed to be visible everywhere, for drinking fountains, public transportation, public restrooms, and so on. It made it easy for the violent KKK activity, because it appeared to be part of the general mindset and way of life for most of the population in that state. Seemingly, dismantling segregation would take a sea change in thinking, as well as positive action on the part of white and black citizens.

FBI SAs were viewed almost as an invading army, with the agency referred to by many (including other local law enforcement officers) as the "Federal Bureau of Integration." You could feel the cool reception and resentment on the part of waitresses in restaurants, and by many other customer-service representatives. Visits to law enforcement offices were not always warmly welcomed or met with full cooperation. In fact, later investigation found a number of KKK members actually employed and embedded in local and county law enforcement. Roadblocks seemed to appear everywhere – SAs needed to identify addresses for victims and witnesses but usually had only post office box numbers, which made it difficult to determine the actual location of the witnesses. Frequently, SAs had to visit local post offices for help with these directions, and many postmasters personally refused to cooperate in providing the actual locations of the box holders. This refusal to cooperate was reported to FBI Headquarters (FBIHQ), and we heard that Director Hoover further reported the problem to then Attorney General Robert F. Kennedy. Reportedly, Attorney General Kennedy discussed the situation with the Postmaster General, and demanded that the postmasters in Mississippi and the South cooperate fully with the FBI. Whatever transpired back in Washington seemed to have worked because, shortly thereafter, we began to get at least acceptable, if not cordial, cooperation from postmasters and mail carriers.

Part of my standard equipment on all road trips into Mississippi was a huge camera with a long post or rod that barely fit into my Bureau car and extended from the front dashboard all the way back to the rear window. Its purpose was to photograph all voting registrations at county clerk offices in towns and cities I was visiting. You can imagine the reception I received from county clerks when they saw me coming for a visit.

As an aside, I vividly remember the many trips to Mississippi and how tired I would be driving back to NOLA late at night. Crossing the twenty-four-mile causeway bridge over Lake Pontchartrain on the way back into the city, and with no traffic in sight for miles, and no commercial radio with music to keep me awake, I would sometimes open all the windows and turn on the siren for a while just to keep me awake.

Despite the almost uniform reticence and reluctance to cooperate from much of the white population, FBI SAs moved forward with our mission, only to experience another frustration from an unexpected area. Black citizens, who were obvious victims or witnesses, were reluctant and did not often want to cooperate. Either out of fear of retribution or because they had become resigned to their roles in the segregated society, they just wanted to be left alone. They simply did not want to "rock the boat" in any way, shape, or form. I recall interviewing a probable victim of a physical beating, with obvious bruises and cuts, who did not want to be photographed and repeated to me a very familiar phrase, "It's okay boss, no problem." Witnesses to church burnings and bombings, lynchings, and cross burnings frequently and adamantly remained silent. Victims who were denied the right to register and vote usually disclaimed any interest in voting or possessing the right to register.

Unfortunately, as it became clear that the FBI was there to stay until all Mississippi citizens had equal rights under the law, the violence and the resistant activities of the KKK and their supporters began to escalate. Just about the time that the storm clouds were gathering, predicting the coming intensive battle between the KKK and the Bureau, I was summoned to the office of the SAC Harry Maynor in NOLA, who was a great leader and consummate gentleman. He held in his hand a "greenie" from FBIHQ (greenies were communications from Headquarters on green paper that were not as important as a teletype but more important than a regular letter on white paper). SAC Maynor explained that while I was in training school I took a battery of different tests, and asked me if I remembered that. I told him I remembered the tests, and he went on to advise that one test showed that I had exemplary potential for learning foreign languages. He then continued that Headquarters wanted to know if there was any reason I should not be ordered under transfer to California to attend a one-year course in Cantonese Chinese. He smiled and added, "Believe me, if Mr. Hoover wants you to go, you don't really have any reason not to go!" What a change of pace – within a few short weeks my conflict with the KKK would be in my rearview mirror.

Although I would be removed from the struggle, I certainly intended to (and actually did) maintain my interest, and kept in contact with my fellow SAs to stay up-to-date on what was happening back in Louisiana and Mississippi. As fate would have it, within just a couple of months after my departure, matters literally "hit the fan," so to speak. In June 1964, three young civil rights workers named Michael Schwerner, James Chaney, and Andrew Goodman, driving a 1964 Ford station wagon, disappeared in the vicinity of Philadelphia, Mississippi. Their burned-out vehicle was soon located, but there was no sign of the three occupants. The intensive search eventually located their bodies, and investigation into their murders brought a focus, from the eyes of the entire nation, on the civil rights issues in the South, and a massive response from the FBI, triggering a Bureau special investigation dubbed "MIBURN" (meaning "Mississippi Burning"). The Hollywood movie, with the same title of Mississippi Burning would later present a relatively realistic picture of what FBI SAs were encountering during that time period.

Scores of SAs, numbering well over one hundred, were sent to Mississippi. The KKK fought back, turning up the violence with church burnings, shootings, and threats. I was told that SAs were being bombarded with telephone death threats at home and even at their offices. Bureau cars were damaged with sand poured into the gas tanks, and reportedly, one SA's wife opened their residence mailbox to find a rattlesnake inside.

Director Hoover made it clear that the playing field would be leveled and that FBI SAs would not be intimidated. I heard that he sent reinforcements, on temporary assignment, in the persons of SAs from offices such as Chicago and New York, who were really more accustomed to encountering mob figures and other more violent criminals. Before the end of 1964, the FBI would open a new FO in Jackson, Mississippi, and Director Hoover traveled personally to open it. It was to be commanded by a widely respected and tough SAC named Roy K. Moore, and its primary and early mission was to focus the struggle against the Klan and others, who were intent on violating the newly passed civil rights laws. This move took some of the pressure off the New Orleans FO, and Jackson continues to be a permanent FO with its smaller RAs covering the state of Mississippi.

FBI efforts remained relentless in the investigation and solution of the violent crimes of the KKK against the African American citizens of the South. It is also important to understand that many of the killings and church bombings were felonies without any statute of limitations. While memories are fading and witnesses dying (as well as the perpetrators), as information is developed, FBI SAs continue to work leads and solve cases from that troubled era. Without question, working the civil rights cases in the South during the 1960s was difficult, tedious, often frustrating, and largely thankless. It is probably safe to say that most of the SAs would rather have been chasing fugitives or working bank robbery cases for the satisfaction of measurable and successful results. Nevertheless, FBI SAs persevered, stayed the course, and eventually the tide began to turn. The people of the South began to realize that life there had to change, and that all citizens needed to be respected and able to enjoy their freedom and rights, including the right to vote. Key informants were developed, and cooperation increased as the people allowed us to thoroughly, and decisively, penetrate the KKK's inner circles.

When I reminisce about the extreme challenges faced by the FBI SAs during those years and the results realized from their efforts, I honestly believe that period embodied some of our finest hours and produced some of the most significant contributions in FBI history. The challenges were met and overcome, and results helped effect the much-needed sea change toward equal rights and treatment in America. To be sure, America's work is not finished, and all too often outbreaks of racial hatred and violence continue to plague our progress. Still, when I reflect on how it was when I arrived in Louisiana and Mississippi in 1963, compared to how it is today, I remain very proud of the part played by the FBI.

So I wrapped up my assignment in NOLA and headed off to a very different challenge in Monterey, California. I treasured my good times and incredible experiences in that fascinating, crescent-shaped entertainment mecca, as well as the challenging lessons learned in the important civil rights investigations in Mississippi. Little did I know then, or expect, that future assignments would find civil rights challenges right back on my agenda.

CHAPTER 4

Learning Chinese

The FBI Foreign Language Program

I FOUND THAT IN THE FBI, as in every other aspect of life, you play the cards you are dealt and do the best you can with the results. As with most FBI Agents of my era in the 1960s, the assignments were many, varied, and required a number of geographical moves (several more than the average Special Agent in today's FBI). With me, I would look for the quality of life highlights in every locality I was assigned. Honestly and truly, I was determined that I would enjoy every one of them! Whether in the southern United States, the east, or the west, I would try to become an active part of my community and enjoy my time there. It is with that mindset and determination that I prepared to leave my first office assignment in exciting New Orleans and challenging Mississippi and head west.

First, a little background. Although unknown to me, Mr. Hoover and the FBI, in the early 1960s, had made arrangements with the military and the US State Department for SAs of the FBI to participate in a very active and aggressive program to receive specialty training in particular foreign languages. The languages would be those that Special Agents (SAs) might find helpful in conducting investigations (both criminal and security), involving individuals and organizations whose primary language was other than English. SAs selected would be chosen based on the results of a battery of tests taken to gauge their demonstrated aptitude to successfully learn a particular language. The language classes would be for a six-month or a one-year term with full-time immersion in the language chosen. Two schools were utilized, the Army Language School at the Presidio in Monterey, California, and a school run by the State Department in the Washington D.C., area.

Personally, I had only a vague recollection of taking the language aptitude tests, among the many other exams, during New Agents Training. So you can imagine my surprise when my Special Agent in Charge (SAC) in New Orleans called me in to give me the news that I was being transferred to the San Francisco Field Office (FO), and assigned to the Monterey Resident Agency for a one-year term to learn the Chinese Cantonese language. My initial thoughts were that I had no particular interest in China and couldn't recall that I had ever even eaten a Chinese meal. Probably, my main reluctance and concern centered on the fact that I was being plucked from my main dream of being an FBI SA, who carried a gun and badge and investigated cases, and was now going back to a classroom again for a whole year. Then, as I commenced the long drive to Monterey, California, my thoughts kept drifting back and forth between the total change in my life that surely lay ahead and more seriously, what was occurring in the deteriorating civil rights situation back in Mississippi.

Driving along, I also considered my luck, that although my class would last one year, instead of six months, I would get the chance for my first visit to California and the Pacific Ocean. Finally, upon arrival in Monterey, I must admit it was love at first sight. It exceeded my expectations in a major way, and made it clear to me instantly why artists and writers often describe the Monterey Peninsula as "the most beautiful meeting of land and water in the world." It became, and has remained, one of my very favorite destinations, and my arrival there commenced one of the most interesting and culturally satisfying years of my life (so precious to me that later when I met my wife-to-be, we flew back to get married in Carmel on the Monterey Peninsula).

The Presidio of Monterey, which was administered by the US Army, was in the process of changing its name from the Army Language School to the Defense Language Institute (DLI), West Coast Branch. It is perched atop the highest hill in the area with a breathtaking view directly down over the city of Monterey to the Monterey Bay and the Pacific Ocean. Although it is a closed military facility today, it was open and readily accessible from several entrances during my tour there. A few days after arrival, I successfully located an apartment in a newly constructed and reasonably priced apartment building, just down the hill and an easy drive away from the Presidio.

As luck would have it, my next-door neighbor turned out to be a captain with the Monterey County Sheriff's Office (MCSO), who was living in one of the apartments temporarily until a new house he was building was completed. We became fast friends, and he soon asked me how I would like to spend my Monterey year in a beautiful house in Pacific Grove, right along the Pacific Coast. I laughed and told him I could hardly afford the inexpensive apartment I had just rented. He explained it would be as a sort of caretaker for the second residence of a San Francisco insurance executive. The MCSO had been keeping an eye on the gated property located on the hill above Monterey Bay, separated from the rugged coast only by some cypress trees and lots of roaming deer. I jumped at the opportunity, and he was able to arrange a rental arrangement for the estate-like property for a mere $125 per month. My good luck was continuing, and I was off to a great year!

My "temporary estate" with a backyard to the Pacific Ocean.

Before classes started at DLI for the school year, all FBI SA students attending got a special briefing from the Senior Resident Agent of the Monterey RA, who would be our lifeline to the Bureau while at school. He advised us of the rules, policies, and administrative procedures while we were assigned there, and kept us informed regarding happenings in the FBI world. He was a wonderful gentleman and became a good friend and mentor to many of us. I never knew exactly how many SAs were studying at DLI concurrently, but I met several during coffee breaks, lunches, and other social events during the year. Some were learning other Chinese dialects, Russian, Spanish, Serbo-Croatian, and several other languages.

As classes started and we met our four native Chinese instructors, who would rotate for periods during the day, it was clear that learning Chinese Cantonese would be neither a walk in the park or piece of cake, so to speak. Instead, it was going to be a very difficult language. All day, five days a week, we would be inundated with memorizing an unending flow of vocabulary and dialogues, as well as reading and writing some extremely difficult Chinese characters. Chinese Cantonese is made up of nine distinct tones in voicing the characters in phrases and sentences. Unfortunately, using the wrong tone or mixing up the construction of the written characters can drastically, frequently embarrassingly, change the meaning of what you said or wrote. There was a heavy use of flash cards to remember vocabulary, and several books of dialogues to become familiar with common expressions. It required pure memory of all words, grammar, and syntax with very little, if any, similarity to English construction.

My class had nine students, including one other FBI SA named Joe Sparks, who was a more senior SA with several years' experience. The other seven were active US Army personnel from various units, and in ranks from lieutenant-colonel down to corporal. The one standout was a US Army captain, who was native Chinese and spoke fluent Chinese Cantonese. Graciously, he was extremely professional and a great help to the rest of us. Aside from wondering why he was there, we had no problem whatsoever with him finishing the year at the head of our class. Captain Larry Kee went on to complete a distinguished military career and served in some very sensitive assignments. He is now retired, and both he and his wife, Karen, remain close personal friends. Clearly, it was not that easy for Joe and me, and we frequently spent hours together after class, and in the evenings, practicing vocabulary and dialogues, which we would need to perform in class the following day. I would conservatively estimate, over the entire year, that I spent two to three hours every weekday evening studying and memorizing material necessary for the following day.

As challenging as it was academically during class and doing homework, the time away from class made it all worthwhile. Back home in my "estate," I realized the property had a doghouse almost as large as someone's garage. I missed my German Shepherd, Wolf, who was still living with my parents in Pennsylvania, and had him flown in to live with me. With Wolf at my side and a nice fire in my fireplace, I really didn't mind studying Chinese, as I glanced out my huge west-facing windows at the beautiful sun setting over the Pacific Ocean. To be sure, my house also found itself a popular host for some memorable weekend parties for my fellow students and friends.

My good fortune continued as it turned out one of my neighbors was raising a real law enforcement family. Clarence "Buck" Wardle had been a US Army Provost Marshal in Europe, and was now back home and working with the MCSO. One son was a probation officer in the San Jose, California, area, and another son was a motorcycle officer with the Los Angeles Police Department who would later transfer to the California Highway Patrol. The youngest son would eventually undertake a career with the US Coast Guard. Buck and his wife, Sally, practically adopted me as a member of their family and introduced me to all sorts of local activities and community leaders. One such leader was Dick Snibbe, a former police officer who was now professor of criminal justice at the Monterey Peninsula Community College (now the Monterey Peninsula College). Dick and his wife, Jane, became close personal friends, and Dick also became my golf partner. The Pacific Grove Municipal Golf Course was literally within walking distance from my house, with the back-nine holes curling right along the Monterey Bay coast. We ended up playing together there many a Saturday morning. Since Dick had taught courses for many of the law enforcement officers in the area, as well as the corporate security officers who were former law enforcement officers, we were also invited as guests to play all the golf courses in the area, including those at the world-famous Pebble Beach and Cypress Point clubs.

After a couple of months, I even had a chance to catch up first-hand on what had been happening back in New Orleans. By chance, I learned that Joe Coleman, one of the FBI support employees for my old squad, was doing an active duty stint with the US Army and was stationed in the Monterey area. We met up and found the time to comanage one of the little league baseball teams in the Monterey area for that summer season. Joe was an excellent FBI employee and later became an SA, assigned to our Atlanta, Georgia FO.

Interestingly, it was not just FBI SAs whom I met and then maintained contact with in later years. Small world as it seems, I met a soldier named Tom Brereton at one of the social events. It's fair to say we were both very surprised years later when I got transferred to take over the Charlotte, North Carolina, FO, and found Tom to be an SA assigned to our Greensboro, North Carolina, RA. Tom was an out-standing producer and almost a legend in his success against white collar criminals in North Carolina.

Getting back to language school activities, there were also some very valuable breaks from the tedious and difficult classroom rigors. To become thoroughly immersed in the Chinese culture, the class enjoyed several field trips to Chinatown in San Francisco. We visited many different restaurants, learned to use chopsticks, and sampled all types of food delicacies. I gained such a love and appreciation for Chinese cuisine that it remains my favorite today. In addition to the restaurants, we visited a variety of businesses and the Chinese newspaper office. Certainly, I believe these field trips brought all of us a real and special appreciation for the Chinese culture and daily life.

The Chinese newspaper office in San Francisco wrote about our visit.

Fortunately, for the FBI SAs there were a few other opportunities during the year for us to return, at least briefly, to more traditional FBI work. During those few occasions, around Christmas and Easter for example, when the DLI would break for more than a day or two, we would strap on our weapons and handcuffs, dress appropriately, and hit the streets. Working through the breaks, SAs would be assigned investigative leads to assist the Monterey SAs or others throughout the territory of the San Francisco FO. I recall that in those times most of my leads were around the San Jose, Santa Clara, and Salinas areas.

As expected, the year turned out much different from what an FBI SA might expect to be doing, and certainly different from what I had been doing before the California experience. As the end approached, both Joe Sparks and I took and passed the oral and written final exams, which would qualify us as acceptable Chinese Cantonese speakers. We eagerly awaited the transfer orders to our next assignment, and were not overly surprised when we got the word. We were both on our way to New York City – the FBI's largest Field Office.

In retrospect, it was both a very busy year and a very informative, culturally satisfying one. It was difficult to say good-bye to my classmates with whom a whole year had been shared in such a close, intimate fashion. It was particularly sad to hear from sources later that a few of my classmates never made it through the Vietnam War. It was just as difficult to leave some of my friends in the community outside of DLI, who had become very close to me during my months there. Certainly, as the final days and hours closed in, I knew I had to put Wolf on another airplane back to my parents in Pennsylvania, and reluctantly say farewell to my oceanside "estate." Fortunately, my departure would not be forever, since I have returned there for visits many times.

After final good-byes and in the car heading back east, my thoughts turned to the status of the war being waged against the Ku Klux Klan for equal civil rights in the South. I planned my route to New York to stop through New Orleans so I could catch up with progress since I had left. I had an opportunity to visit my former SAC, Harry Maynor, and observed that his physical appearance in my one-year absence had changed him to appear ten years older. The stress he experienced in leading the FBI investigations of several murders, church arsons, and other civil rights matters had indeed taken its toll. I heard that he retired shortly after my visit. It was reassuring to hear from some of my friends that the FBI was indeed persevering and turning the tide against the Klan. My visit there complete, it was back in the car and off to the Big Apple, and yet another major and exciting change of pace.

CHAPTER 5

Adventures in the Big Apple

Life in the New York Office

FOR THOSE OF YOU WHO HAVE not worked there and maybe never even visited New York City (NYC), its nickname, the Big Apple, dates back to the 1920s and did not come by accident. It apparently started as a reference to big rewards at the horse racing tracks in the NYC area, but went on to represent the "best and biggest" of American cities. When I was a kid growing up, TV and radio shows, movies, and news headlines constantly referred to NYC as the "naked city with eight million stories," or the "city that never sleeps," among other monikers that suggest its magnitude. Considering that NYC's five boroughs, Manhattan, Queens, the Bronx, Brooklyn, and Staten Island, are spread over only about three hundred square miles, and with its now more than 8.5 million population, you can easily understand why it reigns as the largest and densest city in the United States. It was in the 1960s, and still is, America's leading media, financial, entertainment, cultural, and commercial center. Although the diplomatic world officially revolves around Washington, D.C., with embassies from most countries in the world, most of those same countries also maintain a diplomatic presence in NYC, through their missions or consulates. Then to top off its role as the world diplomatic leader, the city domiciles the headquarters of the United Nations.

To add to its critical importance, its location, where the massive Hudson River meets the Atlantic Ocean, presents a strategic seaport stretching miles around the city, as well as key portions of the New Jersey coast. Vessels from all over the world patronize the ports of New York and New Jersey daily, under the supervision of the Port Authority of New York and New Jersey. Airports in the area, Newark Liberty, LaGuardia, and John F. Kennedy are among the busiest in the world.

With the foregoing as a brief thumbnail sketch of the city, it should not be surprising that NYC has the largest field deployment of FBI Special Agents (SAs) and support employees of all the FBI's fifty-six Field Offices (FOs). At the end of 1964 when I arrived, there were approximately a thousand SAs in the NY Office, which represented a significant percentage of total SAs deployed throughout the United States. The size and significance of the NY Office (NYO) at that time merited its commander to have the rank of Assistant Director (AD), the only one allowed by Director Hoover anywhere outside FBI Headquarters in Washington. During my assignment there, the AD was John Malone, who was held in high regard by Mr. Hoover.

The word around the field was that the NYO was different from any other FO, and the SAs there had a different attitude, the so-called New York attitude, which, in their minds, placed them in a world of their own. The NYO had squads seemingly for every kind of criminal problem, from bank robberies to hijacking, major thefts, massive white collar type frauds, and organized crime and the Mafia. They justifiably considered their cases among the biggest, most challenging, and complicated in the nation. On the security side, or foreign counterintelligence (FCI as we called it), there were squads to investigate espionage, terrorism, and other illegal activities against the United States, involving various nations or groups suspected of conducting these types of activities.

Having just completed an entire year immersed in studying the Chinese Cantonese language, upon arrival I was assigned to the NYO exactly where I fully expected to go – to the FCI squad investigating suspected espionage activities by the People's Republic of China (PRC), or commonly referred to as Chinese Communists (Chicoms). My squad was made up of several senior SAs with well-developed skills in conducting security investigations, as well as several younger, less experienced SAs like me, some of whom had native Chinese language skills and others who were recent graduates of the FBI Foreign Language Program.

It was a pleasure to note early on that this squad was highly motivated, with little problem or concern expressed when we needed to work seven days a week on occasion, and all hours of the day and night when necessary. As interesting as the work and cases were, unfortunately, due to the subjects involved and the sources and methods used to investigate them, the activities and nearly all the documents prepared were (and probably remain) highly classified and unavailable for my public discussion.

As much sense as my NYO assignment made, what happened to my fellow Chinese Cantonese graduate, Joe Sparks, upon his arrival in New York, left me scratching my head in disbelief for years to come. Joe did not get assigned to my squad, as logic might have dictated. Instead, he was immediately assigned to a squad investigating Latin American matters. Unknown to me, he had some prior skill and ability in the Spanish language. Whether by his own wish or due to the immediate needs of the NYO, he was assigned to utilize his Spanish language skills. It was difficult for me to accept how and why the hard work of an entire year, on Joe's part, to learn the very difficult Chinese Cantonese language, could be virtually wasted and never put to use. It did not seem reasonable, neither for the sacrifice Joe made, nor for the resources expended by the Bureau to train him. At any rate, our contacts after arrival in the NYO were not frequent, and we always commented jokingly to each other that, before long, all Joe could remember was how to greet me in Chinese, and ask how I was doing. Eventually, Joe was transferred to the FBI Legal Attaché (Legat) program and assigned into Mexico and the Caribbean area. Years later, when I was assigned to our Inspection Division and inspecting our Mexico City Legat Office, I was able to reunite with Joe in Guadalajara where he was then assigned. He was later transferred to the office in St. Thomas, Virgin Islands, where he eventually retired.

My squad in the NYO occupied a very key and interesting location there. Situated on the tenth floor, which also housed the main public entrance to the NYO, there were many opportunities to view well-known officials and celebrities paying visits to AD John Malone, who was a very well-known and respected public and community figure in NYC. His executive office was on our floor, and I recall on one occasion waiting at the elevator to leave the building, and as the door opened, world-famous bandleader Lawrence Welk emerged to pay a visit to AD Malone. Of course, occupying the public access floor also brought with it the responsibility of being the first armed responders in the event the receptionists encountered emergency situations that required their activating the panic alarm.

Situated adjacent to our squad, on the same floor, were members of the Liaison Squad. This squad was made up of both experienced SAs and special Investigative Clerks (most of whom were waiting for eligibility to become SAs). These individuals had the sole responsibility to maintain relationships, and cover a multitude of leads requiring contact every day, with the offices and agencies throughout NYC of the greatest continuing interest to the FBI. Some of these included the New York City Police Department (NYPD), Immigration and Naturalization Service (INS), New York Telephone Company, New York State Department of Motor Vehicles, US State Department Passport Office, and so on. This squad was of vital interest to nearly every SA of the NYO, and it was a real benefit to our squad having them as neighbors. For example, I recall one of the Liaison SAs as August "Gus" Micek. Gus sat very close to me and was the NYO's liaison with the NYPD. He spent virtually every day at NYPD Headquarters, which was one of our most important contact agencies. At one time or another, every SA would end up sending a lead to SA Micek for contact with the NYPD. Gus was a wonderful SA and human being, beloved by all of us at the NYO (and from lots of feedback, equally loved and respected by the NYPD).

Geographically, the NYO was located on Manhattan's fashionable Upper East Side in a renovated warehouse building at the corner of East Sixty-Ninth Street and Third Avenue. This was directly in the center of an upscale residential area, surrounded by fancy restaurants and coffee houses. Unfortunately, except for a few FBI vehicles (Bucars) reserved for the AD and the other executive managers, SAs had to hop a public bus on Third Avenue and ride up to a garage on Ninety-Second Street to access the Bucars, which needed to be returned there at the end of the workday. SAs then took a bus back down Second Avenue to the office. Unlike today, no Bucars were permitted to be taken home at night for possible emergency response after duty hours. The NYO had far more SAs assigned than Bucars, so it was important to reserve one in advance if needed specifically on any given day. Frankly, on most days, thanks to the excellent public transportation system in NYC, most SAs traveled to cover their leads either by bus or subway. In fact, travel by subway to cover routine leads throughout all the boroughs of NYC was faster and easier than by Bucar. To make things even simpler, a large bowl of free tokens was placed readily available on a desk by every elevator for SAs to grab a handful.

At this point, it might be interesting to mention an obstacle or road-block that SAs encountered in those days in the NYO, and probably throughout the FBI. It might be difficult for folks today, even FBI employees, to believe or comprehend, but the issue was coffee – yes, I said coffee. Director Hoover was a firm taskmaster, and believed that when FBI employees signed in each morning they should be actively employed without breaks, including coffee breaks, until their scheduled lunch hour. Hence, there was no breakroom, coffee machine, or any kind of coffee service in FBI space, and no allowance for stepping outside for a cup. Knowing how law enforcement, including the FBI, seems to run on coffee, you can imagine how difficult it would be to separate an SA from his or her morning coffee. In the NYO, AD Malone was apparently determined to take Director Hoover at his word, and was personally involved in enforcing the no-coffee rule. He was known to be out on the street some mornings, checking the neighborhood coffee shops to catch and/or deter SAs from partaking. In Mr. Malone's absence, other managers would be instructed to be out on patrol. SAs, not to be deterred, would find themselves drifting farther and farther down the street away from the NYO to grab a morning cup of coffee. Obviously, SAs heading out for the subway to cover leads could easily make a stop en route, but I am aware of a few occasions when innovative and determined coffee drinkers, not planning to leave the office on leads, would hop the bus to the Ninety-Second Street garage, check out a Bucar, and head to Queens to get their safe coffee break.

Logistically, many SAs made considerable sacrifices just to get back and forth to work in NYC. Unlike today, there were no cost-of-living subsidies provided to SAs assigned to high-cost cities like New York. SAs who could not afford to reside in Manhattan commuted from New Jersey, suburbs in the other boroughs of New York, and the eastern New York counties on Long Island. It was not uncommon for commutes to last more than two hours each way and involve several subway or train connections. I knew one SA who commuted by train daily from Philadelphia, Pennsylvania. Unfortunately, through my time in the FBI, I knew of many fine SAs who, despite the excellent work opportunities in the NYO, declined transfers there and resigned from the FBI, due to the high cost of living and the other hassles and struggles associated with just living in the NYC area.

For those who could see beyond the challenges of living in the Big Apple and working for the FBI, there were many benefits beyond experiencing the best cases to investigate. For starters, the NYO had a strong internal social organization. We enjoyed a very well-organized bowling league that brought SAs and support personnel together once every week in the evening, with excellent participation. Other activities included the FBI softball league, which had teams playing in Central Park in the evenings during the summer. In addition to league games, sometimes fun events occurred such as a softball game with the local Playboy Bunnies, who were working at that time as hostesses for Hugh Hefner's Playboy Club in midtown Manhattan. Beyond the internal relationships in the NYO FBI family, contacts outside the Bureau for all law enforcement made living costs a little more bearable for our employees. Scattered throughout the greater NYC area were outlets with law enforcement discounts for men's clothing, shoes, electronics, jewelry, furniture, vehicles, tires, and just about anything you needed or wanted.

Receiving the FBI league softball trophy for our team from Assistant Director John Malone.

On a personal note, I found that assignment to the NYO provided excellent opportunities for personal social outreach. Unfortunately, for many people, life among the eight-million-plus population in the big metropolis could leave you feeling lost, alone, and deserted. For an unmarried FBI SA in NYC at that time, the situation was very different, both from contacts made during official business events and through independent networking and associations with other single SAs in the office. For example, one such contact led to social meetings and a friendship with some members of the Radio City Rockettes, the famous female precision dance group, who perform regularly at the Radio City Music Hall in NYC. However, most importantly, I eventually made the contact that allowed me to strike pure gold personally and change my life forever. I got introduced to a senior stewardess for Pan American World Airways (Pan Am), which was arguably America's flagship airline in those days. We became friends and decided jointly to plan parties between single FBI SAs and some of the Pan Am stewardesses based in NYC. I would invite the SAs, and she would invite the stewardesses (properly called flight attendants today), or sometimes give me a list to help make calls. One stewardess on the list named Irmgard, from Germany, declined my first invitation. She was on my list for the next get-together and once again turned me down. I guess I was intrigued by the challenge here and before hanging up the phone, asked her if she did not want to attend the party whether she would consider having dinner with me. She reluctantly agreed, and we met after her next return flight to New York. After a few more dates, I was convinced she was the woman I wanted and needed permanently in my life. We were married in September 1965, after flying back to the Monterey Peninsula at Carmel, California, where my friends there could participate in the wedding and meet my new wife. After a trip to spend time with her parents and family in Dusseldorf, Germany, we returned to settle in our new apartment in Elmhurst, Queens. Irmgard continued to fly for Pan Am for a couple more years until the arrival of

our first child, Eric, and a move to our first house in Nassau County, Long Island. I admit to lots of mistakes in my life, but marrying my wife was certainly not one of them. On the contrary, having her as a life partner has been my greatest single achievement. In fact, thinking of Irmgard and her career with Pan Am, I often reflect on my days in the military at Fort Dix, New Jersey, and my frequent visits to McGuire Air Force Base nearby. Pan Am had a contract

Irmgard in her Pan Am uniform. Photo courtesy of Pan American World Airways.

with the air force as a Military Air Transport Service carrier to fly civilians and dependents around the world. Many times I was fascinated when I saw one of the Pan Am flights land at McGuire and the crew of beautiful powder blue–outfitted stewardesses get off the plane. I remember thinking to myself, it would be a dream to someday have a relationship with one of them. Now I smile and think to myself that I'm still living that dream.

Work in the NYO

It didn't take much time on the streets of New York to understand why some SAs in other smaller FOs might believe New York SAs have a "New York attitude." For example, a routine lead furnished with a photo and advising that the subject of the photo is known to frequent 7-Eleven stores, and asking the NYO to canvass all 7-Elevens to attempt to locate him, would probably be rejected as unreasonable, without providing heavy justification. It would take an army to contact the volume of 7-Elevens in the territory covered by the NYO.

As for me, as expected, much of my time was spent working with individuals in the Chinatown area of NYC, and having the opportunity to use my Chinese Cantonese language. The majority of the overseas Chinese in NYC were from either the Canton Province of China or Hong Kong, and spoke Cantonese. They were very impressed that an American took the time and effort to learn their language and were mostly friendly and cooperative with me.

As I mentioned earlier, specific cases and details were classified, but I can offer some general comments. As one can imagine, counterespionage or counterintelligence activities normally concern possible penetration of our borders and activities against us by foreign spies. In the NYO, our efforts depended heavily on close cooperation with other US agencies such as the INS and the Central Intelligence Agency, or CIA, and foreign intelligence agencies such as the Royal Hong Kong Police, as well as agencies covering New York's airports and ports. For example, one of my assignments was liaison with the US Coast Guard, and, on occasion, I spent time aboard one of their forty-foot patrol boats checking out the extensive port activity around New York and New Jersey harbors, especially in regard to possible Chinese ship jumpers when foreign vessels were visiting NYC.

When visiting Chinatown, my base for restroom breaks and office space was the Fifth Precinct Headquarters for the NYPD, where they treated me as one of their own. In fact, on one occasion and with FBI approval, I assisted the NYPD in an internal corruption investigation by listening and reviewing court-authorized wiretap recordings of conversations in the Chinese Cantonese language.

A number of investigations by our squad involved some level of physical surveillance and usually involved some mix of vehicles, augmented by a number of SAs on foot. In the super-dense traffic in downtown Manhattan, it was sometimes easier to keep up with subjects by running through traffic or in between stopped vehicles, and even occasionally sliding over a car's hood or trunk. Actually, most surveillance activity in NYC eventually ended up on one or more of the subway lines, where it became a cat-and-mouse game with the subject getting in and out of a subway car before the train departed. Sometimes, one of the SAs got left on the platform, while, hopefully, at least one other was in the train as the doors finally closed. Having been involved in the past surveillance of American criminal subjects, suffice to say that foreign intelligence subjects practiced a tremendously superior and sophisticated level of countersurveillance techniques. Whether stopping to gaze into shop windows to use them as mirrors, turning abruptly and walking back in your direction, entering one door of a subway car or a building and quickly leaving through another, they were always intensely aware of their surroundings and always looking for us.

Although my regularly assigned cases and activities were always interesting, the value of working in the NYO was really experiencing the amazing and unexpected happenings that seemed to occur frequently and materially impacted the FBI in America's greatest city. Often, major events for one squad necessitated detailing SAs from other squads to assist for short periods of time.

In 1966, NYC was honored by a visit from the Prime Minister of India, Madam Indira Gandhi. Unexpectedly, I was assigned to represent the FBI as part of her security detail in the event of any attempt to attack or assault this visiting head of state. Joining the large convoy and escort detail, along with US Secret Service and the US State Department security agents, I was able to remain with her during her entire visit. I would hasten to add how impressed I was during that experience, as well as others to follow, to observe the effective work of the NYPD in traffic control. It was amazing how a convoy of several vehicles could leave Kennedy Airport and move easily through the traffic of New York into Manhattan and its surroundings and never have to stop or slow down, while moving at speeds reaching fifty miles per hour. The NYPD is exceptional at handling traffic situations and security details of this type, and I really learned to respect them immensely.

On another occasion in late November 1968, I was among a number of NYO SAs who were invited to attend a show at a specific Broadway theater, without any details provided for the invitation. Upon arrival we were surprised to learn that the new President-Elect of the United States, Richard Nixon, was there, and we were to provide augmented security along with the US Secret Service Agents. We actually had an opportunity to meet President Nixon and found him quite friendly and engaging.

On another major criminal investigation, I recall being temporarily assigned to assist in trying to identify all the main suspects in a major robbery in the New York-New Jersey area. One of the principal suspects was a resident of the Bronx. SAs had obtained a federal warrant to employ sophisticated monitoring equipment on the suspect's vehicle. In order to do that, we had to have custody of the vehicle at an off-site location, since the work couldn't be completed where the vehicle was parked. One night the vehicle was located in a parking space along a public street in the Bronx, and it was temporarily "borrowed" and taken to the off-site location to have the authorized work done. The plan was to place an FBI vehicle in the parking spot while the other vehicle was gone. Unfortunately, before the FBI vehicle could be moved into place, some aggressive neighborhood resident, frantically looking for very scarce parking spots, made his move into the space. By the time the suspect's vehicle was returned with the required work completed, there was no possibility of returning it to the original spot. Fortunately, after waiting halfway through the night, another spot came open when somebody left in the nearby vicinity of the original space, and the suspect's vehicle was placed into that spot. As surveillance of the suspect continued on the following day, there was no indication that he had detected the movement of his vehicle.

However, this demonstrates well the old adage that the best laid plans on occasion do go awry, but all seemed to have ended well.

Despite all the exciting and challenging investigations in the NYO, strange as it may seem, my most memorable time spent there was a two-week period that occurred at the beginning of 1966, and did not even involve an investigation. It was the time of "the great transit strike of 1966," which shut down the New York transit system for twelve days, halting millions of daily commuters and costing the city an estimated $1.2 billion in lost revenue.

Even though all public transportation, including subways and buses, stopped, the FBI had made plans and was determined to carry on. Lucky me – I was selected to take a brand-new 1966 black Ford Crown Victoria home with me to Queens. In the morning, I was to pick up and deliver a number of clerical employees, who lived in Brooklyn, to the NYO and return them home at the end of the day. So for two weeks straight, starting at about four a.m., I left my residence in Queens and made my way very, very slowly through Brooklyn, picking up five clerical support employees who lived around that borough. We then painstakingly and extremely slowly "crawled" our way to downtown Manhattan, which allowed us to arrive, after starting at four a.m., sometime just before noon. Of course, the traffic was nearly at a standstill everywhere throughout the day, and in order to get them home at a reasonable hour, I had to leave the office around two p.m., which got my last passenger home sometime after seven p.m. This was two weeks when no investigation, whether criminal or security, got accomplished, but I was able to get the clerical employees to the office for a very brief, limited period of time in order to demonstrate that the FBI indeed stayed in business during the great transit strike.

At the end of the two weeks, the brand new Crown Victoria was in need of a major overhaul after driving from zero to two miles per hour for hours on end. Frankly, I'm not sure what happened to the car after that period, and I certainly had no desire to see it again! However, I do remember that I was given a gift by my FBI support passengers, which was a bottle of Seagram's VO Canadian Whisky. That bottle has never been opened, nor the seal broken, and it probably never will be while I am alive, because I want to keep it to remind me of the worst two weeks that I spent in the NYO.

Then, on a day in mid-1969, my supervisor called me into his office and delivered a letter with the news that I was being promoted and transferred to FBI Headquarters, or Seat of Government as it was then called. I was to be assigned to the Domestic Intelligence Division in a supervisory capacity. As we prepared for the move in the following days, I recalled all of my benchmark achievements since arriving at the NYO in 1964 – the incredible investigative experience in our largest FO, fascinating celebrities and other persons met, relationships with some of the FBI's finest personnel, a new wife and first child, and moving into our first house.

As a footnote to the size of the NYO and timeless nature of personal relationships, I recall visiting the NYO again five years later in 1974, as part of the FBI Inspection Staff. I was on the elevator one day, when the door opened and a couple of old friends assigned to one of the Soviet squads got aboard.

"Hi, Bob, haven't seen you around for a while, how's it going?"

"Right" I answered, "guess it's because I got transferred to Washington five years ago."

We all smiled and agreed, "That's life in the NYO for you."

Looking back, I cherished and thoroughly enjoyed all my adventures in the Big Apple.

CHAPTER 6

From Espionage to Vietnam War

First Assignment at FBI Headquarters

FBI AGENTS ARE AWARE that advancement in the Bureau will always involve at least one, and sometimes more, assignments at FBI Headquarters (FBIHQ), or Seat of Government (SOG) as it was called during my first tour of duty there. Located at the intersection of Pennsylvania Avenue and Ninth Street Northwest in Washington, D.C., SOG was, when I arrived there in 1969, in the block-long building housing the US Department of Justice (DOJ). However, since I had been working counterespionage investigations in New York City, I was to be assigned to the Domestic Intelligence Division (DID, also known to us as Division 5) upon arrival in Washington. Division 5 was located outside of the DOJ building in an off-site high-rise building diagonally across Pennsylvania Avenue from the DOJ.

Personally, I had been interested in advancing in the FBI, and was surprised and delighted with the transfer to become a supervisor at SOG, despite the fact we were still settling into our new home in Baldwin, Long Island, New York, with our under-two-year-old son, Eric. I had to leave my family in New York initially for the first several weeks while I reported in for my new assignment, and located our next house in a neighborhood near Rockville, Maryland, in Montgomery County, north of Washington, D.C. It is always easy to frame the time when the family joined me, and the moving van with our furniture arrived. Vividly, I recall opening boxes in our new family room and watching TV, as Astronaut Neil Armstrong, out of Apollo 11, stepped down from the lunar module Eagle making "one small step for man, one giant leap for mankind" as he set the first human foot on the moon – it was July 20, 1969.

Unlike the hectic hours in the NYO, my first couple of years at SOG were relatively stable and hours regular and predictable. It was not difficult to find a carpool, which would arrive at the office around seven thirty a.m. and leave for home fairly regularly at about five thirty p.m. I was working with many of the supervisors whom I had known previously, since they had been supervising my New York People's Republic of China (PRC) investigations. In fact, now I was supervising some of the very cases I had been personally working in the NYO. Of course, the difference was that I was now getting the broader picture by also supervising different investigations being handled by offices all over the world. Since we were operating in the universe of international PRC espionage, one of our key functions was to leverage contacts with FBI Legal Attaché (Legat) offices, whose Special Agents (SAs) were assigned to US embassies or consulates in key locations such as Hong Kong, Mexico City, and Ottawa, and had vital liaison relationships with criminal and intelligence agencies of the host countries. I recall, on one occasion, I was able to visit Hong Kong and through the efforts of the FBI Legat and the Royal Hong Kong Police, made it to the border of Hong Kong and the PRC Province of Canton, and actually looked into Communist China from one of the border observation posts. During my entire FBI career, that was the closest I ever came to entering Mainland China. However, being assigned in Washington, D.C., I did have the honor of being the FBI's personal liaison with the ambassador of the Republic of China (Taiwan), since the United States did not recognize the communist-controlled PRC in those years and had no diplomatic relations.

A New and Demanding Assignment: The Vietnam War

So while our efforts to counter PRC espionage activities against the United States continued at a regular, steady, and unabated pace, things were happening in a faraway nation called Vietnam, which were about to change my assignment, activities, and working hours – very drastically. The Vietnam War, which started as early as 1954, found the United States dipping our figurative toes in it in 1965, with the commitment of a limited number of military advisors. However, from 1965 to 1975, American soldiers continued fighting in Vietnam in what has to be one of the most unpopular wars in which our country has ever been engaged. Later statements by America's military and political leaders spoke volumes as to the probable error of our involvement. Actions of Americans across the country during the conflict gave vivid testimony to the unrest. By 1969, American bombs were dropping, more Americans were dying, and the fires of full warfare were glowing brighter. US incursions and bombing into Cambodia and Laos, against the North Vietnamese incursions, brought widespread protests, violence, and riots to our home front. Americans were showing their extreme displeasure with our country's involvement in what many considered a needless, useless, and unjustified war. Then, eventually, to exacerbate a delicate situation even further, the scope of turbulence widened as President Richard Nixon and his administration became embroiled in the infamous Watergate scandal, and he ended up resigning his presidency in 1974.

Many readers will remember the radio and TV accounts of what was happening in the war, as well as some of the incidents at home that were generated by the growing disgust for it, including demonstrations and protests that grew increasingly violent. For some readers, the only experience as to what occurred in the United States between 1965 and 1975, when the last Americans were rescued from the US Embassy in Saigon, South Vietnam, in July 1975, is contained in the dispassionate pages of the history books. So let me set the stage a bit with some of the real experiences during those years, faced and dealt with by the FBI and America's law enforcement agencies.

- Shortly after the first American advisors were committed to the area in 1965, and certainly by 1967, numerous Americans individually and in groups believed the involvement of the United States in the war was a mistake. Legitimate protests and demonstrations sprang up and involved every kind of organization – labor groups, women's liberation groups, African American civil rights groups, musicians' groups, to name just a few – whose members took to the streets to demand US withdrawal from Vietnam. A draft was in place, and some draftees protested with burning of their draft cards, while some draft dodgers fled to Canada.

- In August 1968, protests increased and became violent during the Democratic National Convention in Chicago. Contacts between antiwar demonstrators and the Chicago Police became bloody, resulting in mass arrests and several injuries. Eventually, the national election brought President Richard Nixon into office. To add to the confusion and instability in the country that same year, two national leaders were killed at the hands of assassins. Civil rights leader Martin Luther King, Jr. was shot by a sniper, later identified as James Earl Ray, on April 4, 1968, while in Memphis, Tennessee. US Senator Robert Kennedy, former attorney general and candidate for president, was shot during an appearance in Los Angeles, California, on June 5, 1968.

- By 1969, and with some troops actually being withdrawn from South Vietnam, the war suddenly escalated with a massive US bombing incursion into Cambodia and then into Laos. The situation was intensified when the draft changed to a lottery-draft style, which did not allow deferrals for college students and professors. This caused a corresponding violent reaction on college campuses all around the United States.
- On May 4, 1970, Ohio National Guard troops called to duty to handle student protests at Kent State University in Kent, Ohio, opened fire on unarmed students, killing four and injuring nine others.
- On August 24, 1970, violent antiwar activists parked a bomb-laden vehicle outside Sterling Hall at the University of Wisconsin in Madison, hoping to bomb the Army Math Research Center located in the building. The bomb missed the intended target but destroyed a different department, killing one person and injuring another.
- On March 1, 1971, members of the revolutionary and violence-prone antiwar organization called the "Weathermen" were responsible for bombing the US Capitol, causing about $300,000 in damages but no casualties.
- During massive May Day demonstrations in Washington, D.C., from May 3 to 5, 1971, designed to shut down the US government, violent encounters led to the arrests of nearly thirteen thousand protesters by the Washington Metropolitan Police Department.
- On May 21, 1972, demonstrations in Washington, D.C., sponsored by a variety of antiwar organizations, were again determined to shut down the city of Washington and the federal government. Intelligence reports advised of efforts to roll boulders down hills onto highways and spread thousands of nails on access roads in order to disrupt commuters. During the day, violent incidents abounded in downtown Washington, as squads of police on scooters moved continuously from fires set, cars and

buses attacked, and building windows shattered, as well as other widespread violent incidents.

- In July 1972, popular screen actress and national celebrity Jane Fonda suddenly appeared in Hanoi, North Vietnam, and propagandized against the US government and the war, while posed sitting atop a North Vietnamese anti-aircraft gun. She incurred the wrath of our troops and many Americans, but especially the troops in South Vietnam who gave her the nick-name of "Hanoi Jane."

- In another bizarre situation on February 4, 1974, while a student at the University of California in Berkeley, Patricia "Patty" Hearst, nineteen-year-old daughter of the newspaper publisher Randolph Hearst, was kidnapped from her apartment by members of the revolutionary Symbionese Liberation Army (SLA), a leftist group, who were conducting a so-called guerilla war against the US government. Unfortunately, Ms. Hearst showed up later in 1974, engaged with the SLA in a bank robbery in San Francisco. It was popularly believed that she had been brainwashed by SLA members. Nevertheless, she was apprehended by the FBI in 1975, and stood trial for bank robbery. She was convicted and spent time in prison, but was released early and later pardoned by President Bill Clinton.

It would have been enough of a challenge if law enforcement were facing just the violence and conspiratorial acts of the revolutionary student groups such as Students for a Democratic Society and the Weathermen, or other legitimate protest organizations, but it wasn't that simple. The intense unpopularity of that war brought with it a plethora of activities by known subversive organizations vying for the opportunity to infiltrate the antiwar movement for a piece of the action to bring down the US government. We saw activities by the Communist Party USA, the Socialist Workers Party, the Progressive Labor Party, and a raft of others. Similarly, interwoven into the complex national crisis were the violence-prone revolutionary efforts of black nationalist organizations, such as the Black Liberation Army and the Black Panther Party.

The difficulty of prosecuting violations in those troubled years was clearly demonstrated in the case of several members of an organization called the Vietnam Veterans Against the War. They were legitimate veterans and were indicted and charged with violation of America's antiriot laws in connection with a plot to disrupt the 1972 Republican National Convention in Miami Beach. The heart of the plot was a plan to use potentially lethal metal slingshots, called wrist rockets, to fire metal ball bearings to kill or disable mainly police officers. The lengthy trial was held in Gainesville, Florida, in 1973, and was filled with disruptions. For example, at one point a request was made for an FBI countermeasure team to conduct a sweep of the rooms during the trial to ensure there were no bugs or any illegal overhearing or audio surveillance occurring. In sweeping one room, which was apparently adjacent to a room occupied by defense counsel, some unrelated discussion by the FBI team, who were unaware of the occupants next door, led to an allegation that the FBI was monitoring the defense attorneys. It was totally untrue and baseless but caused a court hearing to clarify the situation. Unfortunately, since the trial was being covered by the national media, the situation was portrayed as an incident, which probably left unwarranted questions about government actions and illegal surveillance. In any event, despite the evidence and testimony during trial, the defendants were acquitted of all charges. Typical of feelings during that time, and probably not too surprising was the reported comment from one of the jurors to the effect that "no way could we convict Vietnam veterans after what Nixon was doing." Richard Nixon was nominated at the Miami Beach convention and won his reelection as president by a landslide.

While the situation was deteriorating badly on the home front, the situation with troops on the war front was equally depressing. This was partially buttressed by the ugly news from home, but the troops obviously were feeling firsthand the hopelessness of a pointless war. Reportedly, the ready availability and low cost of illegal drugs in Southeast Asia also made the depressed troops heavy users. Other reports had the mostly young and unwilling draftees refusing to go out on missions, and even, on occasion, resorting to "fragging" or killing officers who were deemed incompetent or disliked. However, regardless of the horrendous situation faced by the troops, and the flag burnings and flagrant disregard for the law by protests at home, the ultimate disrespect, I believe, was the reception of our returning soldiers by the

American public. No parades, no welcoming ceremonies to speak of, no memorial until much later after the war, those troops went into an almost impossible situation, and nearly fifty thousand never came home alive. For those who did make it back, we refused largely to welcome them or express our appreciation for their sacrifice.

With that as some background information, early in 1971, some of the supervisors (including me) in the DID were reassigned within the division to assist with the flood of investigative activity arising from the increasing lawlessness and violence generated by antiwar activists. Urgent information was reported by teletype, and teletypes from nearly every FBI Field Office (FO) were bombarding FBIHQ, twenty-four hours per day, every day. Our working hours were incredibly long, extending to many nights and weekends. Teletypes with significant and urgent information had to be summarized into a three-by-five-inch note, attached to the first page of the teletype, and routed up through the chain of command, usually directly to Director Hoover. A summary of the night traffic had to be crafted into a memorandum that would be on Mr. Hoover's desk when he arrived in the morning.

The Director had a keen and personal interest in all facets of antiwar activities and monitored the FBI actions continuously during the war years. His time was valuable, and he had an unwritten rule that all memoranda coming to his attention should be limited to one page, to include the summary or synopsis, the details, and the recommended action. Unfortunately, it was frequently difficult to squeeze everything that Mr. Hoover should know into a one-page document. On one legendary occasion, a supervisor tried to include all the details he needed onto one page by spreading the margins on the paper nearly to the top and bottom and on the left and right side nearly to the very edge. Now, in all of Headquarters, only Mr. Hoover used a pen, with rich blue ink (everyone else used only a pencil), and all we really wanted to see, when a memorandum came back out of his office, was the notation "OK. H", signifying his approval of the memorandum context. If there was a lot of blue ink on the memo, somebody was probably in trouble. In the case of the memo in question, Mr. Hoover squeezed his blue ink in the narrow space left all around the page, in all four directions. In addition to his specific instructions, three other words were visible on the page – "watch the borders." It was always risky to question the Director's instructions, so the story goes that Special Agents (SAs) were sent to the Mexican and Canadian borders just in case. I have no idea whether that actually occurred, but I did see a file copy of that very memo.

In those years, the antiwar situation in the United States was not just a "ticking bomb" for the FBI and nationwide law enforcement but also a hot button of interest to the highest levels of government. In addition to sharing information of planned bombings and other violent acts back and forth among law enforcement, the FBI prepared countless thick packages of what we called "letterhead memoranda," normally highly classified due to the sources involved, and always with a cover letter over Director Hoover's name and signature. Due to the intense interest, recipients would include the Attorney General, highest command levels of the military services, leaders of other US intelligence agencies, and specific representatives at the White House.

I had my share of experiences hand-carrying these White House packages up through the Bureau's chain of command, usually ending with Miss Helen Gandy, who was Director Hoover's gatekeeper and executive secretary. However, before arriving at the Director's Office, the most important stop was the feared Reading Room, staffed by women with expertise in all facets of the English language. As they pored over all pages of the Director's outgoing communications, the slightest error in grammar, spelling, or punctuation could result in a letter of censure for the writer. Showing utmost respect for these ladies, I developed a good relationship with them, which on a couple of occasions allowed me the opportunity to expedite a minor correction and get the documents back to them within a very narrow time period, without any further repercussions. With this dispensation, I had to run wing-footed back to the steno pool and appeal for immediate assistance to retype the offensive page(s). There was no quick correction fluid allowed, and no computer to quickly correct the error and reprint the page – the entire page needed to be retyped. Then, with the final "perfect" product in hand, and with the blessing of the Reading Room, I entered the Director's Office. "You wait right here, Mr. Pence," was the usual greeting from Miss Gandy, as she disappeared into Mr. Hoover's office. Within a short time, she would reappear and hand me the file copies. "Thank you, the Director will sign the letters," she would say. Then, thankfully, I would see the much-desired blue-ink "OK. H" on the package cover memorandum. Mr. Hoover seemed to always be accessible and available and never made you wait long.

The hectic days of Vietnam spawned hundreds of preliminary inquiries for the FBI to run down widespread allegations of subversive activity aimed against the US government. Many, and, frankly, most, were determined to have no merit and were based on fear, hatred, revenge, or a frenetic instability and uncertainty caused, or, at least, occasioned by the war. Of course, there were also genuine efforts by a number of groups to use the occasion to further undermine or commit deliberate acts to bring down America. Altogether, the events of those days, months, and years stretched the resources of the FBI, as well as law enforcement across the nation, as close to the breaking point as I had ever seen. During a couple of the Washington demonstrations, I watched from windows up in our Headquarters as mobs, right below on Pennsylvania Avenue, started fires, attacked buildings and vehicles, and caused mobile groups of police officers to dart from one violent incident to the next. There is a national Posse Comitatus law that prevents our US military (not our state national guard organizations) from engagement in domestic law enforcement activities. There were times in those days when some of us felt that the US was close to anarchy, and help from our military might actually need to be requested. That said, the dam held, and our law enforcement held the line. Many times I reflect on how many potentially explosive incidents were quietly thwarted in those days, through sharing intelligence information back and forth among law enforcement at every level – federal, state, county, and local – as well as their cooperating sources of information.

Although most workdays during the war years were more than hectic, there were occasional breaks to give us a welcome change of pace. For example, in the late 1960s and early 1970s, public tours of the FBI Headquarters were wildly popular with the American people; in fact, the FBI tour was widely advertised as one of the best in Washington, D.C., and not to be missed if visiting the nation's capital. A number of young tour guides were FBI support employees or clerks, whose only assignment was to conduct the tours daily for the hundreds lined up around FBIHQ. For certain dignitaries and celebrities, based on specific requests, a number of "special tours" were available and were conducted by Supervisory SAs assigned to Headquarters.

The special tours gave guests a few additional liberties such as walking "behind the glass" with an SA, into the active FBI Laboratory to view actual examinations being conducted by technicians, or even firing the famous Thompson submachine gun, or Tommy Gun, of the gangster era in the FBI's indoor firing range.

I was trained to conduct these special tours, and recall one day getting a call from the tour office asking if my schedule would permit a tour for some very special celebrity entertainers. Accepting the assignment, I had the pleasure of spending a good part of the afternoon with the famous Bee Gees and some of their family members. I think many readers will remember brothers Robin, Barry, and Maurice Gibb as the red-hot pop and disco musical singing group and songwriters of the 1960s and 1970s, and some of the best-selling musical artists in history. They were very polite, inquisitive, and exhibited very warm, friendly personalities. A couple of them thoroughly enjoyed the opportunity to fire the machine gun. All in all, it was a real pleasure spending my afternoon with the Bee Gees.

Worthy of mention on a lighter note and even a possible smile and chuckle, would be an informal event that some of us in DID witnessed at around five p.m. on most workdays. Simultaneous with the drama raging on the streets of Washington, D.C., during the early 1970s, the brand new FBIHQ, to be aptly named the J. Edgar Hoover Building, was being built directly across Pennsylvania Avenue from the DOJ building, between Ninth and Tenth Streets. From DID in our off-site building, we could look directly down across Ninth Street at the construction site. We watched from the time ground was broken and a huge hole was excavated allowing construction of the building from a third basement level up. We would watch for a few minutes at a time as work progressed. It became almost a ritual to gather at the windows for a short time when the construction workers quit for the day. Until construction reached ground level and higher, and as dusk arrived every day, a literal army of Washington's subterranean rat population arrived to devour what remained of the workers' uneaten lunches and just about anything else their appetites could handle. I don't know how much of this show, if any, might have been visible to viewers outside the windows of the DOJ building across Pennsylvania Avenue, but we in the DID could certainly attest to the number and size (we first thought they were cats) of Washington's underground rats. Ironically, after watching it being built floor by floor, slab by slab, and wall by wall, I did not realize I would eventually leave Washington, D.C., but later be reassigned back to FBIHQ in 1978, to a position that would involve responsibility for all the physical, as well as the internal, security of the very same J. Edgar Hoover building.

Unfortunately, Mr. Hoover did not live to see the completion of his building, which was not completed until 1975 (although some FBI employees occupied the building as early as 1974). He passed away at home peacefully during the night on May 2, 1972. He left us after nearly fifty years as Director, still in service "with his boots on," and probably would have wanted it no other way. I will never forget the shudder of disbelief and quiet numbness that seemed to prevail throughout Head-quarters the next day.

A few days later we were all at the windows of the DOJ building as his funeral procession moved slowly down Pennsylvania Avenue. We watched with a smile and nod as it turned right at the Justice Department Building and made one last pass around the building, before proceeding on down Pennsylvania Avenue where he would lie in state at the US Capitol, an honor given to precious few Americans. In reflecting on my Hoover years, mostly very positive thoughts come to mind. His policy of having field SAs stop wherever they were, every two hours, and call in to the office might have seemed unwieldy and unnecessary at the time, but it demonstrated the safety concern the FBI had for its SAs under Mr. Hoover, when easier and quicker forms of communication were not yet available. His insistence on recruiting SAs and support personnel of integrity, establishing the FBI Identi-fication Division for maintenance of fingerprints, creating the FBI Laboratory, establishing the FBI National Academy for training local law enforcement, and so many other innovations, clearly put him in a league of his own.

It was probably true that SAs at SOG did not relish waiting at the fifth floor elevator, stressed that the door might open with Mr. Hoover aboard. They would be concerned that the Director might believe the SA needed a haircut, might notice that the shirt worn was not a clean white one, or that his shoes were not shined, or that his necktie and suit were not tastefully conservative. True, a derogatory comment from the

Director to his staff could have led to some form of discipline or action against the SA.

Rumors also flew that Mr. Hoover kept secret files on his enemies as leverage to keep them in check. There certainly was a special file room requiring special access. It was always my understanding that these files contained information on celebrities, politicians, or controversial personalities and subject matter that had been reported to the FBI in the due course of business, but might not have any factual basis or corroboration and should be protected from perusal by FBI employees merely out of curiosity. On occasion, I had legitimate investigative reason to check these files and had no difficulty accessing them whatsoever.

Whether he ever leveraged file information to influence decisions, I personally doubt, but have no real knowledge one way or the other. However, Mr. Hoover was, without question, a power broker who regularly and routinely convinced Congress that the budgets he requested for the FBI were merited, warranted, and justified. They were nearly always granted. Inside the Bureau his power was absolute, and only in his last few years was there any attempt by insiders to weaken his rule. Throughout the field, the rumor was that no Special Agent in Charge would leave his office until word from Washington came that the Director had left the building for the day. The inside word was that managers at both FBIHQ and the Washington FO stayed well aware of Mr. Hoover's movements and activities, both for his personal safety and their self-preservation. The FBI had, and probably still has, a rumor grapevine second to no other agency. The staff talked a lot about many issues, including Mr. Hoover. However, in spite of some unsavory allegations regarding his personal life coming in the years following his death (when he had no way to confront or refute them), I can say with utmost sincerity that such possibilities were never part of our discussions as SAs. In other words, out of all the other information we had about the Director, if any of it had indicated an alternative lifestyle or improper relationships and activities, it would have been a hot issue for the grapevine, and it never was, at least not in my social circles.

Tough and strict yes, but we were also aware of certain circumstances when Mr. Hoover could be extremely compassionate and generous toward his employees. If I had to agree with any criticism, it would probably be the thought that perhaps he stayed in his position too long. The world had changed, and crime had changed. He did not want his FBI SAs involved in drug investigations, since he feared it could lead to bribery and corruption involving them. Similarly, he did not favor undercover operations, which he believed might tempt the undercover SA to the dark side by associating too closely with criminals involved in the operation. Both of these types of investigative activity have become essential in fighting modern crime; and yes, unfortunately, they have yielded some of the results directly feared by Mr. Hoover.

Without a doubt Mr. Hoover cared seriously about his personnel. Not only could you expect to hear from him if you did something wrong, but he wanted to reach out to you personally when he learned you did something well. There follow below examples of personal letters received from him in 1966 not long after I arrived in the New York office, and the last just a few weeks before his death in 1972.

OFFICE OF THE DIRECTOR

UNITED STATES DEPARTMENT OF JUSTICE

FEDERAL BUREAU OF INVESTIGATION

WASHINGTON, D.C. 20535

July 21, 1966

PERSONAL

Mr. Robert L. Pence
Federal Bureau of Investigation
New York, New York

Dear Mr. Pence:

The work you have done in the developing and handling of a confidential source of information of interest to the Bureau in the security field is commendable and I want to express my appreciation.

Utilizing much resourcefulness and diligence in developing this source, you have achieved desirable results in that he has been placed in a position through which he may obtain important data. Your assiduous efforts are of a high caliber and a credit to you, as well as to the FBI.

Sincerely yours,

J. Edgar Hoover

I think it appropriate to conclude comments about my Hoover years by stating adamantly that I was never asked, or instructed, to conduct or participate in any investigative activity during those years for which I was not properly convinced it was under existing legal guidelines, was approved personally by the Attorney General, or was based on a warrant issued by a US court judge or magistrate. Certainly, I could extend that statement to specifically include any other investigative activity that I knew, or suspected, to be of a political nature or bias.

Finally, it was not always stress free, fun, or a pleasure to work for J. Edgar Hoover, but I truly considered it an honor and a privilege. Apparently and fortunately, the stress that we felt did not extend to Miss Helen Gandy, the Director's loyal, dedicated, and efficient Executive Secretary, who retired when he passed away in 1972, but lived on until July 7, 1988, in her ninety-first year.

OFFICE OF THE DIRECTOR

UNITED STATES DEPARTMENT OF JUSTICE

FEDERAL BUREAU OF INVESTIGATION

WASHINGTON, D.C. 20535

March 14, 1972

PERSONAL

Mr. Robert L. Pence
Federal Bureau of Investigation
Washington, D. C.

Dear Mr. Pence:

It is with considerable pleasure that I commend you for the high quality of your services from the Seat of Government in connection with a matter of vital interest to the Bureau in the field of security.

The success realized in this endeavor can be attributed in no small measure to the ingenious and adroit fashion in which you coordinated all facets of it. I am appreciative.

Sincerely yours,

J. Edgar Hoover

CHAPTER 7

Onward and Upward at
FBI Headquarters

WITH GRADUAL REMOVAL of our troops from Vietnam, the massive protests waned along with the numerous conspiratorial plans for violence as well as the violence itself. Consequently, the hectic pace at FBI Headquarters (FBIHQ) eased, and our investigative activity tempered to a more reasonable level. I began to harbor thoughts of my next assignment, and the answer came near the end of 1973. I would remain in Washington, D.C., at FBIHQ but would be assigned to the Inspection Division (ID) as an Inspector's Aide (IA).

The FBI ID served essentially as an independent body charged with responding directly to the FBI Director regarding the state of affairs in the entire FBI worldwide. It was headed by an Assistant Director, with staff made up of full Inspectors and a number of IAs. It was definitely the next step in administrative advancement within the FBI. The next desired step for the Inspectors was the position of Special Agent in Charge (SAC) to command one of our FOs, and the IAs hoped to land one of the Assistant Special Agent in Charge (ASAC) positions in a FO. The tours of duty on the "Staff," as we called it, were flexible but usually ended up being at least a full year.

The ID was utilized in two major areas of normally internal FBI matters. Specific problems in a FO or Headquarters Division (HD), such as allegations of wrongdoing on the part of FBI personnel, would normally be referred to the ID. Depending on the size, scope, and nature of the problem, one or more Inspectors, along with an appropriate number of IAs, would be dispatched for as long as it took to resolve the matter.

The other major function, and actually the main mission of the ID, was to provide a regular and intensive examination of every FO and separate HD. The keywords were to ensure that each was operating "effectively and efficiently." Recipients were normally notified in advance by the ID, with a starting date accompanied by a nearly foot-deep stack of interrogatories requiring responses or write-ups to describe the current status of every squad, operation, and management function of the office or division. At FBIHQ, Inspectors assigned to a particular inspection would be receiving any input or additional feedback involving matters of concern to Headquarters supervisors that should be considered and dealt with during the forthcoming inspection. Armed with the responses from the FO or HD interrogatories and Headquarters requests, the inspection staff would arrive at a very nervous and uptight office, particularly on the part of office management.

Inspections were normally scheduled every couple of years on a rotating basis and usually carried out by two full Inspectors and ten or more IAs. The exception was the New York Office, our largest, which required a larger number of Inspectors and virtually all the IAs. The inspection usually lasted two full weeks, with double that time for New York. My entire tour on the Staff involved a nonstop string of regular inspections, with only a week or so between to complete paperwork and assist with the voluminous inspection report, which contained the overall results of our findings.

While on the inspection itself, the IAs would be variously assigned to specific squads and programs as well as all individual functions of the office, such as clerical support, radio and communications, and automotive operations. SAs and support personnel would be interviewed regarding their performance as well as office morale and management. Nearly every case was reviewed for possible suggestions to assist solutions or to take other recommended actions to achieve the desired "effective and efficient" handling. Frequently, minor errors were detected with corrective action required and directed. Unfortunately, on occasion, more substantive errors were detected that dictated immediate corrective action, and sometimes led to censure or administrative action against the offending SA.

With every interview and every case file and program review, a careful picture or flavor was being developed as to whether the FO or HD was practicing and following correct FBI policies and procedures. We were also determining whether they were in harmony with, and supportive of, the FBI's program priorities in general. And for a FO specifically, whether their priorities were appropriate for the territory and population involved. For example, the violent crime program in a major office like Chicago would probably have a higher priority than it would in Kansas, or the counterespionage program might be more important in Washington, D.C., than it would be in South Dakota.

All the days during the inspection were long and busy for the inspection staff, especially in the FO inspections. In addition to all the steps followed internally, during an FO inspection a number of additional bases had to be covered. FOs operate a number of auxiliary offices in their territory, called Resident Agencies (RAs), housing a number of SAs, from perhaps only one to dozens, depending on the size and activities in the RA territory. For example, the Denver FO covers the states of Colorado and Wyoming, with RAs in both states that respond ultimately to the SAC in Denver. While the Jackson, Wyoming, RA might have one or two SAs assigned, the Colorado Springs RA might have in excess of a dozen. During the inspection, each and every RA had to be visited, inspected, and SAs interviewed. Further, in the case of the RAs, as well as FO headquarters, the inspection staff needed to gauge the level of respect for, and effectiveness of, the FO's outreach to the other members of the law enforcement and criminal justice communities, as well as the community at large. This required a number of personal visits by our team to the various office contacts.

Of course, as you might expect, one of the main thrusts of the inspection was to determine if the FO or HD was being managed effectively and efficiently, and this directly affected the SAC, ASAC, and supervisory staff in the FO, and the Assistant Director, Section Chiefs, and Unit Chiefs in the HD. Clearly, based on the Chief Inspector's findings, SACs could be promoted or demoted, staffing levels changed with FOs receiving more SAs or losing them, or recommendations and instructions given to realign SA assignments to better address the correct priorities. Suffice to say, the inspection process played a major and important role in accountability and operations in my FBI days, and probably still does. Hopefully, this account offers some explanation and justification for the increased nervousness and elevated blood pressure attached to a visit from the Staff.

On balance, despite the incredible disruption to a FO or HD during the document preparation prior to an ID visit, and then during the multiple-week visit and exhaustive audit of virtually all operations, it gives the FBI leadership some distinct reassurance of productivity and accountability. Actually, for those of us who participated on the ID staff, participation really gave us even more.

Personally, for a group of SAs who desired to advance to senior FBI management, I could envision no better crucible to forge the ability and knowledge leading to an SAC position than to inspect FOs run by different SACs for an entire year. Yes, the days and hours were long, and paperwork seemed endless, but the experience was incredible. Excellent models of operations were observed and could be patterned, while less successful examples could be avoided. Further, the ability to work on different inspection teams with other Inspectors and IAs for sustained periods of time, through sometimes stressful situations and discussions, and also during bonding dinner conversations, gave many of us friendships and camaraderie that would last for years. The fact that several of us would probably end up in different FOs in the future would also lead to closer relationships, liaisons, and cooperation among our FBI FOs.

It is easy for me to recall vividly my first several weeks on the Staff due to a historic period of difficulty in the United States. Many readers will recall the late months of 1973 and early months of 1974 well, because they were probably in long lines – blocks long – to get to a gas pump and then be eligible for gas only because their license plates ended in a certain odd number or even number on that particular day. To refresh some memories, in October 1973, the Organization of Petroleum Exporting Countries (OPEC), started an embargo to halt oil to the United States and other nations that had supported Israel in the Yom Kippur War of 1973. This lasted into the early months of 1974, and created chaos for American drivers. It occurred at the beginning of my inspection tour, and fortunately, did not affect supplying gas to FBI vehicles in my various trips around the country. Unfortunately, it directly affected my wife, who kept reminding me, when I called home, how many hours it took her that day to find a gas station that had any gas, and then line up for blocks to get some.

Undoubtedly, all the long hours and stress, along with the volume of paperwork during my year on the Staff, brought unquestioned benefit to my better understanding of how an FBI FO operates. The experience also provided me with a more comprehensive, universal picture of overall FBI operations. It certainly exceeded my hopes and expectations in those respects. However, what I never expected was how much it would broaden my horizons in what you might call an extracurricular cultural sense. I wrote earlier about how important it was for a FO, and its SAC, to have contacts that would help gain and preserve respect for the FBI, and the ability to accomplish our mission throughout our communities. During that year, I learned firsthand just how effective some of these contacts were, as the SACs made them known to us. Certainly, some of the contacts resulted in memorable experiences that I will treasure for my lifetime.

Alabama

During the inspection of our Mobile, Alabama, FO, I had the opportunity to travel to the capital city of Montgomery and meet briefly with Governor George Wallace. I recalled some of his comments and actions in earlier years when he was a confirmed supporter of segregation in his state and while I was working for equal civil rights

I and two other inspectors meet with Governor Wallace.

in nearby Louisiana and Mississippi. Frankly, I really didn't know what to expect when I met him. Unfortunately, by the time of our meeting, he was permanently confined to a wheelchair due to a spinal cord injury he received in 1972. Governor Wallace had been campaigning for the Democratic nomination for president of the United States in that year, when on May 15, 1972, he was shot by an individual named Arthur Bremer, while campaigning in Maryland. He had previously renounced segregation, and was a true gentleman during our very pleasant meeting. That particular inspection also left me with a very expensive and valuable reminder. During an inspection-related trip to Point Clear, Alabama, I couldn't resist stopping in Fairhope, the home of the iconic Emperor Clock Company. Once there, I couldn't stop from purchasing a beautiful grandfather clock, which still sits and works well in my home. It reminds me of Fairhope, Alabama, every time I see it (although I understand the Emperor Clock Company has since moved to a new home in the Blue Ridge Mountain town of Amherst, Virginia).

California

During the Sacramento, California, FO inspection, our entire team called at the Capitol to meet and socialize with then Governor Ronald Reagan. That was my first meeting with Mr. Reagan, and little did I know then that I would be meeting him a few more times in future years, with both of us wearing a different hat and under some very interesting circumstances. However, it seemed crystal clear during our first meeting, that from his cordiality and overall personality, the people of California had elected a very special person to be their governor.

Tennessee

The Memphis FO covers the western portion of Tennessee. During that inspection, I was assigned to travel to Nashville and inspect the RA there, which was under the supervision of the Memphis FO. As I made the rounds visiting contacts of the RA, I found myself at the Grand Ole Opry location, interviewing one of the security guards at the performers' entrance. Suddenly, a late-model vehicle approached with a fairly elderly looking gentleman driving. As he stopped at the checkpoint, the guard motioned me over and said, "I want you to meet Roy Acuff." We had a brief discussion, during which Mr. Acuff expressed his admiration and respect for the FBI, and then proceeded into the lot. The guard smiled and said, "You just met the King of Country Music." Not being that familiar with country music stars, I checked later and learned that indeed he was as big as they came in country music, and in 1962, was the first living inductee into the Country Music Hall of Fame.

Oregon

During the weekend break midway through the Portland, Oregon, inspection, interested members of the team took advantage of an offer from an office corporate contact to enjoy what turned out to be a wild ride, but a wonderful Saturday experience. We left late Friday evening to drive and spend the night in Astoria, Oregon. Very early Saturday morning, we boarded one of the corporate commercial fishing boats and headed out for a deep-sea fishing expedition on the Pacific Ocean. Unfortunately for us, we needed to first navigate the several-

mile notorious body of water aptly known as the Bar, which defines where the Columbia River meets the Pacific Ocean. As any person who has experienced it can attest, it was a wild ride that even had the large fishing boat rocking and rolling like nothing most of our group had ever experienced. In fact, the Bar is so hazardous and has caused so many shipwrecks, that it has earned a worldwide reputation and nickname as the "Graveyard of the Pacific."

Some of the team got seasick and went below to lie down. In fact, I recall that at least one of our team didn't come back up on deck until the end of the trip. For those who fished, once we reached the much calmer ocean water, the results were outstanding. Shortly after my line hit the water, a several-pound salmon tugged on it, and the struggle began. After several long minutes, with the fish maneuvering in all directions, including under the boat to escape, I landed him with the help of a crew member. After we all were successful in landing fish, we made it back through the Bar, and into port. We weighed the fish, and the crew delivered them to a cannery for processing and eventual shipment to our homes. That represents my one and only deep-sea fishing adventure, and it turned out to be a very, very adventurous day.

As a sort of postscript, I wondered afterward why no one ever warned us of the turbulent ride through the Bar, but kiddingly passed it off as probably the revenge of the Portland FBI against the Inspectors' presence!

Minnesota

During the Minneapolis, Minnesota, FO inspection, in addition to my assignments in the FO, I was assigned to inspect the RA in Rapid City, South Dakota, a state also covered by the Minneapolis FO, along with the RAs in North Dakota. One of the important contacts of the Rapid City SAs was the National Park Service, responsible for the nearby Mount Rushmore National Memorial. A complete briefing was provided to me by the Park Service officials regarding this magnificent memorial, which is a sculpture carved into Mount Rushmore's granite face depicting the faces of Presidents George Washington, Thomas Jefferson, Theodore Roosevelt, and Abraham Lincoln. After completing inspection interviews and before returning to Minneapolis, one of the Rapid City SAs suggested a stop in Deadwood, South Dakota, to check out an outlet for the popular Black Hills Gold jewelry, with its trademark leaves, grape clusters, and different-colored designs in pink and green gold. Before I left Deadwood, I surrendered my recently earned gold anniversary medal for FBI service of ten years to be set into a Black Hills Gold ring. I wear it now every day, and frequently remember my visit to Rapid City and Deadwood, South Dakota.

Texas

In the San Antonio, Texas, FO inspection, my cultural treasure lay virtually directly across the street. In those days, the FBI FO was in the main post office building, which is located immediately across the street from the famous Alamo. This landmark and site of the 1836 battle in which the Mexican Army overran the small number of heroic

At one time the San Antonio Field Office was located across the street from the famed Alamo.

American defenders, was always of interest to me. This was my first visit to the actual site, and I spent lunch hours there several days studying all its features and history.

Mexico

During my tour, the only inspection of one of our foreign or Legal Attaché (Legat) offices took place in Mexico City. On the recommendation of the SAs assigned there, we took a break on the weekend and made it to Acapulco on the Pacific Coast for a rest on the beach. On the scary side, one evening an earthquake hit, and the rooms in our high-rise hotel started swaying back and forth with fortunately no apparent damage. On the beach next day, events got potentially even scarier, when my associates successfully coaxed me into my first-ever parasailing ride. It started while standing on the beach rigged to a parachute lying behind me and holding a rope rigged to a speedboat waiting just off the beach. When told to run, I had to run straight along the beach, while the speedboat started rapidly and pulled me up with the parachute rising behind and then over me. If it all worked well (and it did), I was suddenly flying for several minutes over the Pacific Ocean. The next tricky part is landing back on the beach, which works when the boat slows and runs parallel to the beach, while you descend and hit the beach running, until the rope and parachute are disconnected.

Fortunately, it all worked well for an extremely exhilarating ride and memorable experience. The final highlight of that trip was my assignment to inspect the Guadalajara Office, which reports to Legat, Mexico City. The SA assigned there was none other than Joe Sparks, who was my partner several years earlier, struggling to learn Chinese Cantonese in Monterey, California. It was a great reunion, and he greeted me in the few Chinese words he remembered, since he had long since been using only his Spanish-language ability.

Florida

Considering my entire tour on the Staff, if I had to evaluate an FO or its SAC on contacts with the outside world, I would probably give the nod to the Miami FO. During our weekend break, the team was invited to have lunch and relax on a Saturday, courtesy of the Ryder Corporation, on its corporate yacht docked in Miami. On our afternoon cruise, we were delighted to have fellow guests aboard in the persons of Billy Davis, Jr., Florence LaRue, Marilyn McCoo, Lamonte McLemore, and Ronald Townson. If these names are not familiar to readers, together they were known as The Fifth Dimension, one of the most popular musical groups of the day. They were not there to sing and entertain us but rather for a relaxing afternoon that allowed us some stimulating and great networking and conversation.

The team was further surprised by an invitation one weekday evening, after work, to travel up to Fort Lauderdale to enjoy dinner at the residence of entertainer Jackie Gleason, star of movies and his TV shows *The Honeymooners* and *The Jackie Gleason Show*. Unfortunately, his schedule had Mr. Gleason on the road the night of our visit, but his gracious staff was primed to make our stay truly memorable. His spacious, single-story rambling ranch-style residence was located right on a golf course, with a large garage replete with numerous golf carts, suitably decorated to fit the comic style of Jackie Gleason. After a delicious meal, the team was afforded a tour of his beautiful home and allowed to play on some of his state-of-the-art electronic video game machines. It was my first opportunity to play the popular Pong video game. Many will remember that this was the first sports video arcade game to gain nationwide popularity, with its simple table-tennis game model. Jackie had considerable prowess as a pool player and had an incredibly fashionable pool table, situated into a sunken pool room section of his family room. We had an opportunity to take a few cue shots, as we stopped to admire his setup.

Finally, it was during this inspection that some Miami SAs introduced us to the very exciting game of Jai alai. Imported from the Basque area of Spain and played mainly now only in Florida, it is similar to handball or racquetball with the ball (called a pelota) bounced off a wall space called a fronton. The difference is that the player wears on one arm a wooden device called a cesta, which catches the ball and releases it back toward the wall at an extremely high rate of speed. I found it to be a thrilling and interesting game to watch one evening. The sport was very popular at the time, but has since lost its interest in many parts of our country, and has almost disappeared, except in Florida.

To be sure, there were other adventures in other states during that year, but to summarize, there were three main points to be made concerning my year on the inspection staff. First, it gave me the best possible opportunity to learn overall and firsthand how the FBI works, both from an FO perspective and involving field relationships with FBIHQ. Second, the group got to know each other better as, hopefully, future FBI executives, with much promise and hope that it would lead to an era of closer coordination and teamwork in the years ahead. Finally, in regards to networking with outside businesses and cultural contacts, the group broadened our knowledge of, and appreciation for, the importance of these contacts for accomplishing the FBI's mission throughout the country.

CHAPTER 8

First Taste of Command and Nonstop Action

AFTER COMPLETION OF MY TOUR in the Inspection Division, I was transferred to the FBI Administrative Services Division and spent a short time in the Commendation Unit. Here we were responsible for reviewing and approving recommendations from all the FBI Field Offices (FOs) and Headquarters Divisions to commend FBI employees, both Special Agent (SA) and support. We recognized them for superior efforts that went above and beyond those normally required for their various assignments. It was really inspiring for me to read, and initiate approval, for appropriately rewarding some of the finest, often dangerous and heroic, efforts of my fellow employees.

Then, when an opening occurred, I was promoted and transferred to my first FO command position as Assistant Special Agent in Charge (ASAC) – second in command – of our Louisville, Kentucky, FO, which is responsible for FBI activities in the state of Kentucky. I had never visited Kentucky but had heard that the FBI office there was an excellent mid-sized FO with a heavy workload, and in a beautiful state.

FBI Director Clarence Kelley sends me to Louisville as ASAC.

In addition to headquarters for the FO being in Louisville, there were a number of smaller FBI Resident Agencies (RAs) located in other key Kentucky cities, with a varying number of SAs, the largest being Lexington. SAs in the RAs all reported to SA supervisors in Louisville, and ultimately to the ASAC and SAC.

Further to my good fortune in being assigned to the Louisville FO, I learned that the SAC was Stanley Czarnecki, a former associate of mine in the Domestic Intelligence Division. He couldn't have been more helpful in making me feel welcome and getting me paired with an excellent realtor to find my new home.

My family quickly got settled in the beautiful Thornhill section of metropolitan Louisville, located in suburban Jefferson County. Thus commenced nearly three years of what I would describe as some of the most varied, interesting, instructive, and valuable experiences in my FBI career. My secretary, Martha Medley, was like my right arm, briefing me on the various personalities among the FO SAs and support personnel, as well as some of the important cultural priorities for successfully living in and enjoying the state of Kentucky.

One of the more frequent questions asked of me later in my FBI career, and even more frequently into retirement, is, "Which assignment was your favorite?" To be honest, I decided right at the beginning to do my best in whatever investigative or administrative position I was assigned, no matter where, and enjoy the benefits and advantages offered there. With that perspective as my guide, I would rank the Louisville FO right near the top, for two reasons: one, warm, friendly people in an incredibly beautiful state, hosting a state park system and other scenic landscapes second to none, and two, criminal investigations spanning almost the entire spectrum of the FBI's jurisdiction, from corruption to violent crime and white collar crime, which provided invaluable experience to a first-time ASAC. The second point was especially important, since my investigative experience up until that point was more heavily devoted to national security and intelligence matters.

It should be noted that in the FBI there is a firm policy and understanding that the SAC of a FO is not only in charge of the office but is also expected to be on the scene, if at all possible, during each and every operation that involves significant risk to FBI personnel. Further, in those instances in which the SAC is not in the FO territory, or is otherwise unavailable, the ASAC is expected to take the SAC's place. For me, the action came almost immediately. In the first week, I responded to an "all available agents" radio call for a bank robbery in downtown Louisville. It was reassuring to see our SA Bank Robbery Coordinator take charge and deploy the responding SAs effectively, and in coordination with, the responding Louisville police officers.

The following week, I found myself expediting, with lights and siren, the approximate seventy-five miles to Lexington, Kentucky, in response to an armed robbery of a business involved in interstate commerce (a violation of the federal Hobbs Act). Unfortunately, this was also the scene of my first embarrassing incident as an ASAC. In my haste to get details and the location of the incident, and without the benefit of a mobile phone (which we did not have in those days), I barreled into the parking lot of a diner upon arrival, and jumped out of the vehicle to use a pay phone in the restaurant. Running back to my vehicle with the information, I found the car locked and much to my dismay, could see the keys still in the ignition. Well, so much for the emergency response!

After a responding police officer used a jimmy tool to unlock my vehicle, I was finally able to join the Lexington SAs in the search for the suspect. Fortunately, through excellent police work, jointly between our SAs and the Lexington Police, late into the night led us to the location of our robber in a rundown motel in the suburbs of Lexington. With the occupants in nearby rooms evacuated, the sleeping bad guy's locked door was forced open, and he was arrested without incident and no chance to get to his loaded shotgun. Although it was the middle of the night, the Lexington media responded to the incident, and the resulting impromptu press conference held jointly with the police commander, was my first media briefing as an FBI official.

The action continued, and within a few weeks, in the SAC's absence, I was requested by the Jefferson County Police Department (a separate police department then, but merged with the Louisville Police Department in 1989, to make it now the Louisville Metro Police Department), to proceed to a trailer park in the county just outside the Louisville city limits. There I found that the police had surrounded a trailer, with officers armed with rifles on top of other trailers, and other officers maintaining a tight perimeter around the suspect trailer. The police commander informed me that a white male in the trailer was armed with a large Bowie knife and perhaps a handgun, and was threatening to kill himself. The commander then smiled and said, "We found out that the subject is an escaped federal prisoner and that would be the FBI's jurisdiction. So Bob," he said, "we'll back you up, and it's all yours."

FBI hostage negotiators dealt with the man from early evening into late night without any resolution. Then one of the neighbors came forward with what turned out to be a vital piece of information. She told us that the subject had a German Shepherd in the trailer, and we needed to be careful. That bit of intelligence was forwarded to the negotiators, and they put it to good use. "What will happen to your dog if we have to shoot you, or if you kill yourself?" (or words to that effect). That found and struck a nerve that we had been looking for all evening, and he changed his threatening tone and asked for a cigarette. Several minutes later, he put down his weapon and surrendered peacefully, in exchange for our promise that his dog would be cared for and placed in a loving home. This promise was kept, and fortunately, my first hostage situation had ended without any further incident.

At this point I think it important for me to insert a few more parenthetical thoughts about hostage situations. True, my first such situation was resolved peacefully, as were others in which I would become involved in my career. They involved criminals who took hostages because they wanted something of value, or got caught in an unexpected situation and wanted to negotiate a way out. With those criminals, it always seemed that the key involved finding some rational bargaining chip (like the dog in this case) that mattered to them, which gave our hostage negotiator leverage to bring the crisis to a peaceful resolution. We needed to get it done without violence or loss of life, even if it took hours or days to wear down the hostage taker. Unfortunately, in today's world, law enforcement is not just dealing with ordinary desperate criminals. The stresses and strains, not just in the United States, but especially in the United States, have produced some large numbers among our population of not only severely mentally ill and suicidal individuals but also determined, fanatical international and domestic terrorists. These individuals are particularly dangerous, and with them the best of hostage negotiating will many times, possibly or probably, just not work. These are individuals who will instigate hostage situations with a determined and unshakable purpose to kill others or to die themselves. I personally would be much more concerned, and a lot less confident, in dealing with such hostage situations in today's current settings.

One of the high priority investigative areas for every FBI FO has always been public corruption, whether it involves illegal activities such as theft, extortion, or bribery of government officials at any level, including local, county, state or federal. Unfortunately, Kentucky was not immune to such activities, and a case in and around the Bell County and city of Middlesboro areas was wrapping up shortly after my arrival in the state. That matter involved the arrests and prosecution of members of the county sheriff's office for illegal protection given to some local moonshiners, producing bootleg liquor and spirits. In today's world, the protected activity would probably involve illegal drugs, perhaps marijuana growing. Based on some research, barring changes in that part of the state, it's probable FBI SAs and other law enforcement officers remain busy with criminal investigations in southeast Kentucky.

During my time in Kentucky, another hotbed of corruption involved gambling, extortion, and prostitution, with public official participation, in the northern area of the state around Covington and Newport. We made it a priority project to clean up the area, and challenged the SAs of our Covington RA to make it happen. They initiated intensive surveillance activities and developed key informants and sources, which led to gambling raids, searches, and other evidence. This eventually culminated in a number of arrests and prosecutions. The area is located immediately across the Ohio River from Cincinnati, Ohio, and apparently existed in large part as a playground for sex, gambling, and other illegal activities for large numbers of Cincinnati patrons. Due to the proximity of Cincinnati and identities of some of the Ohio players, we had the participation and support of the Cincinnati FBI FO, as needed.

Eventually, the media in Cincinnati became aware of the campaign to restore honor and decency to Newport, and they began to cover our activities at every opportunity. One particular TV reporter and anchorman for a Cincinnati TV station was a regular responder when our actions and raids went public, and he became a familiar face. He seemed to know when I was in the area, and apparently suspected that something was about to happen. Nick Clooney was always the first on the scene after our actions. Today, Nick is a very popular figure in the Cincinnati area and northern Kentucky, and hosts his own cable TV show. After my FBI retirement, consulting engagements have taken me back to Kentucky on a number of occasions. A few years after retirement, I attended the annual conference of the Kentucky Police Chiefs Association, held in northern Kentucky near the Covington area. The banquet speaker was none other than Nick Clooney, and we had an opportunity to recall our prior meetings. He kiddingly commented that nobody cares about him, but everyone remembers his sister and son. They happen to be the 1960s hit singing star Rosemary Clooney, and current world-famous actor George Clooney. By the way, anyone visiting the Covington and Newport area today would enjoy it immensely as a greatly changed and modern, beautiful cultural and commercial center.

The Kentucky experience also allowed me exposure to its own style of organized crime, albeit not the traditional mafia-type operations found in cities like New York or Chicago. A family in south-central Kentucky, near Lake Cumberland, came to the attention of our SAs after allegations of widespread illegal activities, including burglaries, robberies, and extortion, to name a few. We were able to develop a close associate of the principal subject as a cooperating source, who attended late night meetings with the subject. Over the course of several weeks, we waited on numerous occasions in vehicles at night, concealed in the rural neighborhood, and recorded the warrant-approved conversations in the meetings, courtesy of our source who was wearing a wire (transmitting device). Ultimately, a conversation was heard that involved a plan to rob an elderly lady who operated a country store in the area, and possibly take her life to eliminate a witness. This information dictated immediate and decisive action to prevent the robbery. In so doing, we needed to culminate the ongoing investigation and arrest the subject.

The staging site for the arrest plan was the lodge at Lake Cumberland State Park, where several FBI SAs met the night before with officers of the Kentucky State Police (KSP). The plan was to surround the subject's house at dawn the following day and effect his arrest. We knew he had at least one German Shepherd that could be a problem, so we brought resources with us to control or tranquilize the dog.

At daybreak next morning, we moved to execute the arrest. We had no problem with the dog, but quickly made contact with the suspect's wife, who claimed he was not home and stayed the night before with a relative. While SAs and KSP troopers began to search the house, one young KSP trooper grabbed me and yelled, "I know where he is, jump in my car." The two of us took off at a high rate of speed without turning on any emergency equipment that might alert our quarry. About five miles later, we saw a cloud of dust and a vehicle up ahead racing down a dirt road, heading for the intersection that we were fast approaching. The trooper confirmed, "There he is, that's him." Both vehicles made it to the intersection at about the same time, and our vehicle, now with lights and siren activated, cut him off just as he tried to access the main road.

I had not been paying close attention to anything behind us, but assumed that the "cavalry" with the other SAs and KSP cars were on our heels. Speaking excitedly into the radio, I said, "That's him, let's get him." Then looking behind us, I suddenly realized there was no cavalry and that we were alone, while the others were still apparently a few miles away. My KSP partner and I jumped out of the car with guns drawn, and I ordered the suspect to shut off the engine and get out of the car. I placed him under arrest, and then realized I had no handcuffs with me and had to borrow a pair from the KSP trooper. The arrest party arrived soon after that and took custody of our prisoner.

A successful prosecution followed, but the case had one sad post mortem result. Due to the exposure of our cooperating source and the dangerousness of the group the perpetrator testified against, we offered him the opportunity to enter the Witness Protection Program and be relocated with a new identity. Unfortunately, he refused the offer, and not long afterward, was found dead near a riverbank with barbed wire strung around his neck. Thus, the struggle against the Kentucky brand of organized crime marched on.

Indeed, if I thought that my days of working civil rights cases and violations had ended earlier in Louisiana and Mississippi, I learned the error of my thinking during my time in Kentucky. In September 1975, the Louisville and Jefferson County school systems began to be desegregated, and the FBI braced for possible problems. During the initial days, our SAs and a heavy police presence were on duty every school day in the morning and afternoon to ensure that the desegregation efforts progressed peacefully. To the credit of the Louisville citizens, with the exception of some loud protests and some brick- and rock-throwing incidents, the process was essentially smooth and successful.

I was asked a question once about what type of incident or investigation to which the FBI responds causes the most personal trauma for SAs to handle. For me, it was a mass disaster with horrific injuries and multiple deaths, such as an airplane crash, explosion, or fire. The reasons for an FBI response in those cases are twofold: first, to determine if there was criminal activity such as sabotage or terrorism, and second, to offer the services of FBI experts in taking fingerprints from badly damaged human bodies and providing other resources to aid in making positive identifications.

One of these horrible disasters occurred in Southgate, Kentucky, in 1977 while I was assigned to the state. At the large and very popular Beverly Hills Supper Club, an enormous fire broke out, causing the death of 165 victims and serious injuries to more than two hundred additional occupants. In viewing the bodies of the victims in this particular case, it was difficult to observe the bloated faces and looks of stark fear and panic when they weren't able to evacuate the building. Most of the deaths occurred not from burning but rather from suffocation, and the bodies were stacked up at the too-few exits. There were hundreds of people in the building at the time, and obviously, the entrances and exits were not sufficient to allow fast evacuation from the building. There was no criminal motive determined in the tragedy, and FBI services were offered. However, the graphic sights are lasting and really never forgotten.

To add to the diversity of criminal activity handled while in Kentucky, I could add a serious situation in the environmental crime area. During my early months in Louisville, a troubling crisis situation occurred when workers at the Louisville Water Treatment Facility were falling ill from an unknown but potentially lethal substance in the sewage water. The FBI was notified, and initiated an investigation to identify and locate the source of the poisonous liquid being deposited into the city sewer system. Working with agents of the Environmental Protection Agency, Louisville SAs expedited a full-scale investigation. Through citizen tips and painstaking inquiries, we determined the exact location in the city where a truck had been observed dumping a large amount of liquid material into a neighborhood sewer. Ultimately, the urgent investigation led across the Ohio River to a hazardous waste disposal company in New Albany, Indiana. With participation and support from FBI SAs in our New Albany RA, evidence was developed that the waste disposal facility was apparently backed up due to machinery failure or material overload. Management then opted to solve their storage and processing problem by dispatching tanker trucks to dump the deadly waste into the Louisville sewer system. The individuals responsible were arrested and prosecuted for violation of federal environmental laws. This case was worked as a particularly urgent matter due to the recklessness of the illegal activity and the extreme health risk to so many citizens of Louisville. I give a lot of credit to Louisville SAs who worked on it, and especially the case agent responsible, SA Eugene Thomeczek.

Unfortunately a number of kidnappings also occurred during my years in Kentucky. One with the most satisfying result, for me, is detailed in chapter 16, and involved the successful and safe recovery of a young female victim taken from her home in Virginia and transported across the state line into Kentucky, bringing it under the FBI's jurisdiction. It was particularly memorable to me, not only because of the rescue of the victim unhurt, but also because of the heroic actions of our SAs, particularly one of our early recruited female SAs. It was a bit unusual that we were also faced with a few phony kidnappings in which young teens would fake being grabbed for ransom, and demand payment from parents or relatives. These ended up being worked as extortion cases rather than kidnappings.

Speaking of kidnapping, by far the most noteworthy and publicized one we worked while I was in Kentucky did not even involve a human being. At the time, probably the most cherished and celebrated horse in the world was Secretariat, the 1973 winner of the Triple Crown in horse racing, and the first such winner in twenty-five years. He happened to be retired, residing at Claiborne Farms in Lexington, Kentucky, and available for stud purposes at an incredibly high price. The Horse of the Year in Canada was a mare named Fanfreluche. She had recently been successfully mated with Secretariat, and was waiting at Claiborne Farms for a short rest period prior to her return to Canada.

One night during that time, while exercising outside her stable, someone carefully spread a path of hay toward a back fence, lured Fanfreluce to the fence and kidnapped her. Because of the horses involved, this criminal act took on the nature of an international incident and triggered a worldwide investigation by the KSP and the FBI. Stops were placed at airports, ports, and everywhere else that might be a possible point for shipping a horse out of the country. Media calls were coming from all over the world wanting information about the incident.

Finally, after several weeks of intensive investigation and covering hundreds of leads, the widespread publicity brought us a valuable tip. A caller reported that a strange horse was seen in a partially hidden and remote area, just across the southern Kentucky border in Tennessee. With directions provided, we responded immediately to the area and quickly identified Fanfreluce from her markings. She was still pregnant and shaggy in appearance, but otherwise healthy. The subsequent investigation identified the perpetrator, and determined that the immediate alerts by the KSP and FBI made it too difficult to move her any farther than across the border into Tennessee.

The joint investigation, which the FBI worked as a major theft under the Interstate Transportation of Stolen Property statute, ended quite well and also had some interesting aftereffects. First, and personally for me, I was honored and pleased to be invited back to Claiborne Farms to have a little private time with the famous Secretariat. He was truly a magnificent horse, and I enjoyed a photo opportunity and sort of a one-sided conversation, while walking around with him. I whispered to him that we were able to locate his girlfriend, that she was fine, and that their baby was healthy. He raised his head up and down vigorously and made some happy horse sounds, so I think he was very pleased. Secretariat remained at Claiborne Farms, and was euthanized at age nineteen on October 4, 1989, after developing an incurable and very painful hoof condition. Interestingly, a necropsy performed by a veterinarian found that he had one of the largest

With Secretariat, one of the greatest racehorses.

and most perfect hearts that they had ever seen in a racehorse. His body was buried, out of honor, in its entirety, and not in the usual practice for racehorses of just interring the head, heart, and hooves.

Another separate turn of events, as a result of this investigation, actually involved the US Congress, and evolved into an example of the so-called comparison of apples and oranges. It so happened that this well-publicized investigation and recovery of an important international horse was in progress during a special time in the United States. In the late 1970s and early 1980s, our country was obsessed with the notion that we had thousands of kids who were being snatched off of our streets by child predators. Pictures of missing kids were on milk cartons, billboards, candy wrappers, and just about everywhere else. It took time, and a lot of effort, for the American people to understand that the vast majority of these kids were either runaways or were taken by one of their parents in violation of court orders. Factually, the number of actual child victims of stranger abductions was comparatively small and not historically unusual. Nevertheless, for a period of time, a few members of Congress, particularly on the Senate side, were critical of the FBI for conducting a massive investigation, using lots of resources, to locate a horse instead of the thousands of missing and kidnapped children.

Aside from the FBI's role in conducting federal investigations, I recalled from my days in the Inspection Division how important it was for executives in our FOs to engage in community outreach and become familiar with the people and the cultural opportunities in the territories we covered. It was in that spirit that I accepted speaking engagement requests from civic organizations throughout the state, and visited historical sites, such as the tomb of frontiersman Daniel Boone in Frankfort, and the birthplace of President Abraham Lincoln in Hodgenville. During Derby Week in May, I never missed attending the famed Kentucky Derby. I even had my very own mint julep cup for partaking of the traditional brew. During that week, I always enjoyed being invited to ride on the iconic *Belle of Louisville*, the paddle-wheel steamboat, in the traditional annual race on the Ohio River against the visiting *Delta Queen* steamboat. I also enjoyed the honor of being commissioned "Kentucky Colonel" by the governor of Kentucky, and have continued to support the Honorable Order of Kentucky Colonels, which is a nonprofit charitable organization.

On one occasion, I recall meeting a fellow Kentucky Colonel, who is probably the most famous "Colonel" of all. His name was Colonel Harland Sanders, and most readers should recognize him as the original founder of the Kentucky Fried Chicken chain. True to his image on the company logo of today, he was dressed in his white suit, black string tie, and white goatee. At the time, he was running a restaurant with his wife, Claudia, near Shelbyville, Kentucky, east of Louisville, named Claudia Sanders, the Colonel's Lady. He had been commissioned a Kentucky Colonel by the state's governor in 1935, and he continued to use the title for the rest of his life. Colonel Sanders passed away in 1980, at the age of ninety years, and is buried in Louisville.

Speaking of restaurants and food, it was in Kentucky that I first met and fell in love with the "Hot Brown" sandwich. It is an open-face, calorie- and cholesterol-laden concoction, lying atop a piece of toast or baked bread and layered thick with turkey, bacon and tomato slices, covered by a rich cheese sauce. I believe it once also contained a layer of ham, but current versions have no ham. The story goes that it was first developed at the historic and iconic Brown Hotel in downtown Louisville, but various versions have since spread to restaurants throughout Kentucky. In fact, I recently encountered and enjoyed a Hot Brown in Florida. In several postretirement consulting trips to Kentucky, I never miss feasting at least once (sometimes more) on the Hot Brown at the Galt House Hotel in Louisville, where I first experienced it, and still consider it the best in all of Kentucky.

Finally, as a recap of my thoughts concerning Kentucky, I will always remember and appreciate the tremendous support I received from my SACs, Stan Czarnecki and later Benjamin Cooke, as well as the professional men and women of the Louisville FO. I recall the evening in 1978, when my family and I made our final departure from Kentucky for my next assignment back at FBI Headquarters in Washington, D.C. The moving company had our household goods spread all over the front lawn, and they were in the process of loading their van. That night, SAC Cooke stood watch over our possessions until it was finally loaded. I learned later that this took nearly the entire night,. Mr. Cooke waited with the property until the moving van finally departed. My thanks will also always be there for the Kentucky law enforcement officials and officers who assisted the FBI so much during my assignment there, with particular appreciation going to the KSP troopers who were outstanding. Now back to Washington, D.C., again, and a promotion to a very different but interesting assignment.

CHAPTER 9

Taking Charge of Security at
FBI Headquarters

WOW, TALK ABOUT FLEXIBILITY and diversity of assignments for an FBI Agent, and I could surely add a firsthand experience. As my time as Assistant Special Agent in Charge (ASAC) of the FBI in Kentucky was completed, I was transferred to a position back at FBI Headquarters (FBIHQ), which included none of the investigative responsibilities I had been accustomed to in a field office command position.

FBI Headquarters in Washington, D.C. Photo by I, Aude, CC BY-SA 3.0, Wikimedia Commons

Promoted to Section Chief, I was up to the next rung of the FBI advancement ladder, and even more important, I was back in the Administrative Services Division (ASD), my previous assignment before being transferred to Kentucky. Now, at that time, the ASD was probably one of the most, if not the most, powerful and influential divisions at FBIHQ, since it housed the Transfer Unit and the officials who had a lot of influence regarding who goes where and when. I was to be in charge of managing all space and property that the FBI occupies around the world, including the massive J. Edgar Hoover FBI Building (FBIHQ), and its security. It seemed somehow ironic that I would now be responsible for the very building that I had watched being constructed just a few years earlier. My responsibilities extended to managing the Headquarters auto fleet and the extensive FBI printing operation. All of this was in stark contrast to supervising investigative operations in an FBI FO, but I was to learn how important a role this assignment would play in my overall management development and future.

As difficult as it was to leave field operations, I quickly began to have an appreciation for the FBI's overall strategy in blending investigative with administrative assignments. It served to provide upcoming executives a comprehensive understanding and appreciation of the management/leadership landscape. To be sure, executive positions in the ASD offered even more benefits in this regard. For example, more than once I received a personal call from the FBI Director complaining that his office temperature was too warm. Bear in mind that when I returned to Washington, the FBIHQ building was only a few years old, and many of the systems were not totally stabilized. An immediate dispatch of one of my staff to the Director's Office with a thermometer could only verify that his office temperature was uncomfortably warm. We would confirm that the temperature reading was excessive, and promise to see what we could do about it. Unfortunately, there was really nothing that could be done, short of major changes in controls that would affect the entire building.

Speaking further of heating, I can recall a few instances when I received emergency calls, on the weekend, to return to the Hoover Building. Upon arrival at the entrance to the massive boiler room, I found ruptures in the steam pipes spewing searing hot steam in every direction. It had the appearance of a war zone, and I had to order all of our personnel out of the room, until the emergency repair technicians could arrive and regain control.

Having access to the entire building and frequent contact with the Director, I occasionally had the opportunity to get invited for lunch in the Director's private dining room. I would have to also admit that an additional benefit of being assigned back at FBIHQ was the return to more normal working hours. During most days I would arrive around 7:30 a.m. and leave around 5:30 p.m. (with exceptions, of course). This would allow carpooling and save expenses in using my personal car, since take-home use of Bureau cars was not permitted. With regard to carpools, probably one of the most valuable benefits of my position was found right in the FBIHQ parking garage, located in the building's basement. Since my Section had control over the Headquarters fleet and all the parking, I had my pick of parking spaces, which was a tremendous benefit. Further, since, as mentioned, Bureau policy in those days did not permit anyone, except the Director (who had his own government car and driver), to regularly commute in a Bureau car, I was left in a very interesting position with regard to our fleet. Situations arose frequently in which high level FBI executives would find themselves in unexpected work-related situations, dictating they remain at Headquarters late into the night and miss their own carpool departures. As policy would have it, those situations would necessitate calls to me for permission to take a Bureau car home for the night. The policy allowed me to get better acquainted with several of the upper-level command structure, and it should be no surprise that I would not find any reason to deny any of those requests.

Physically, my office was located deep in the bowels of the building, in the third basement down. Unfortunately, I had no windows, but the office was very spacious and generously appointed with some of the best furniture in the entire building. I recall working late one evening, when I looked up from my desk and across the office to the open entrance, and then smiled. A mouse came through the door and proceeded around the interior of the room to an exit through a rear door, that he probably knew well from previous excursions. I couldn't help but think, with a broader smile, that he was probably related somehow to the rats that I had watched years earlier, when the building was under construction.

Security for the Hoover Building was made up of two components. Internally, the Security Patrol from my Section had mostly young, unarmed FBI support personnel, who wore blazer jackets. They were supervised by SAs, and some of them had ambitions to someday become SAs themselves. The outside perimeter of the building, including all pedestrian and vehicle entrances, was protected by armed officers of the Federal Protective Service. Our Security Patrol was particularly professional and efficient, frequently documenting minor violations, and sometimes more serious infractions, such as doors left unlocked, documents left out on desks, or even safes open. The next day, I would usually receive a phone call, routing slip, or memo from the offender, praising the work of our security clerks and begging for forgiveness, promising the error would not reoccur. On infrequent occasions, the Security Patrol would aid the overall building security by waking a drowsy Protective Services officer.

In those days (late 1970s), the Hoover Building was relatively open with several employee entrances. In addition, the center of the building on Pennsylvania Avenue Northwest had an entrance, open during the day into a beautiful courtyard, which welcomed public access. Pedestrians could freely visit and enjoy a rest on the benches, which were spread around the courtyard. The Security Patrol was kept busy patrolling the courtyard and checking abandoned bags and packages, considered potentially suspicious, which had been left by casual visitors. The other daily concerns in those days were the hundreds of tourists who virtually wrapped around the Hoover Building in long lines, waiting to join one of the most popular free tours in all of Washington, D.C. I personally made it a point to stroll around the inside and outside of FBIHQ regularly to visit our personnel as well as some of our visitors. I vividly recall an occasion, while out in the courtyard, when I met and chatted with a charming visitor. He had been a lawyer with the Department of Justice, would become a US Court of Appeals judge, and ultimately become an associate justice of the Supreme Court – it was Antonin Scalia.

Fast forward now to more recent days and the advent of serious terrorism concerns, and the appearance of the J. Edgar Hoover Building has changed dramatically. Security is now the responsibility of an armed and uniformed FBI police force, and the building is virtually buttoned up and shut down to anyone, except employees and others visiting the FBI on official business. There are no lines of tourists around the building any longer, since public tours were suspended after the disastrous 9/11 terror attacks.

Although tours remained shut down for several years, there is currently some good news for those who desire to visit FBIHQ. Coordinated through their congressperson, US citizens and green card holders (permanent residents) can request, in advance, a tour of part of the FBI Education Center and a new section of FBIHQ called "The FBI Experience" museum. It is about a two-hour self-guided tour, opened in 2017 with approval after some personal background checks, and with tight security and a number of restrictions. For more information, interested persons should make contact with their congressional representative.

Vehicle barriers are now in place around the FBIHQ building, which occupies the entire block between Ninth and Tenth Streets Northwest, along Pennsylvania Avenue Northwest. Most of the pedestrian entrances have been closed, and heavy security protocols are in place for any persons or vehicles entering the building. As a matter of fact, after retirement and with my current consulting business taking me frequently back to Washington D.C., I try to maintain contact with friends still active at FBIHQ. However, frankly, it seems much easier to meet them for coffee or lunch somewhere outside FBIHQ than to contend with the security procedures to regain access to my old building.

It is now impossible for passersby on Pennsylvania Avenue to even look inside to see the courtyard, let alone enjoy its ambiance. So, for readers who might never have the opportunity for a visit, it might be interesting to offer a brief word-picture of the courtyard, as it appeared in safer times. Entering the courtyard entrance at the center of the Hoover Building off Pennsylvania Avenue Northwest, one would walk directly across the courtyard and across a vehicle driveway to the main visitor entrance to the building. Crossing the courtyard, one would notice, on the long concrete wall on the right, a quote from Director Hoover that read, "The most effective weapon against crime is cooperation ... the effort of all law enforcement agencies with the support and understanding of the American people." – J. Edgar Hoover.

Glancing to the left, one would see a sculpture entitled Fidelity, Bravery, Integrity, the motto of the FBI. The Former Agents Society commissioned the bronze sculpture, which portrays three human figures placed against a large waving US flag

Sculpture for former agents at FBIHQ. Photo courtesy of GSA.

backdrop. A female (Fidelity) is seated on the ground looking up at a standing male (Bravery). To his left is another male (Integrity) kneeling on one knee with his right hand on his heart, and also looking toward Bravery. The sculpture is placed on a rectangular base of marble slabs and surrounded by flowers. Other flowers, shrubs, and benches were placed strategically throughout the courtyard.

Another essential function of my Section involved the FBI Printing Shop. Staffed with career support personnel, this shop ran as a self-contained, full-service print shop independent of, but in coordination with, a similar operation across Pennsylvania Avenue in the FBI's parent Department of Justice. They were responsible for the mass printing of myriad documents, reports, publications, and communications that the FBI prepared for law enforcement and other consumers throughout the country. For example, most readers will be familiar with the Identification Order that pictures FBI wanted fugitives, and used to hang in post offices and other public places. The efficiency of this unit, along with the employees' positive attitude and morale, always amazed me, and I often thought how successful they would be in operating an independent printing business in the private sector.

Of all the tasks and responsibilities assigned to my Section, probably the most challenging involved managing the space occupied by FBI FOs, Resident Agencies, and Legal Attaché Offices scattered throughout the United States and the world. Hundreds of facilities were involved, and there was a constant need to honor requests to modify, enlarge, close, or relocate existing space. Experts in our Section were constantly handling phone calls and written requests, as well as meetings with visiting FBI FO representatives, to discuss needs and desired changes. The changing role of FBI investigative resources, involving multiagency task forces and changing priorities, such as cybercrime and international terrorism, required unending requests for additional or modified physical space.

Probably the most complicated and demanding request that occurred during my tenure in the Section involved our largest office in New York City. The New York Office (NYO), where I had served earlier in an older high-rise building on Manhattan's Upper East Side, was to be moved to new quarters in lower Manhattan, at 26 Federal Plaza, in the area dominated by other US government and local New

York City government offices. This move took months in the planning, with myriad personal meetings and phone conversations with the move coordinators of the NYO and officials of the General Services Administration (GSA).

It needs to be clarified and understood that the final approval for our requests for location, modifications, and purchase of space, rests with the GSA. It was essential that we maintained continuous, excellent relations and liaison with appropriate approving officials there. We worked hard at accomplishing a great working relationship, and in my estimation, were quite successful. Unfortunately, GSA had certain restrictions and formulae that they were required to employ. Oftentimes, these rules and guidelines restricted, or drastically cut, our desired requests. Considering the FBI's rapid increase in personnel to handle changing priorities, I believe the GSA restrictions undoubtedly led to the many extra off-site locations that needed to be acquired and occupied in later years.

To be fair, let me put in perspective that those limitations on the part of GSA were accurate during my years at FBIHQ. However, in recent years since my retirement, I have visited newer FBI FOs and observed others from the outside. Based on my observations and casual conversations with current SACs, I have to believe that current GSA guidelines and formulae have been relaxed and made more realistic. The buildings I've observed certainly appear to have adequate space for current operations, and possibly some extra for needed future expansion. Further, the earlier requirement that any new FBI building be located in or near the central business district appears to have eased. Many new FBI FOs appear to be located in less congested areas, which permits more of a campus atmosphere, secure parking, and better overall security protocols.

In sum, the memories of my time in the Printing and Space Management Section were overwhelmingly positive. The contacts and relationships I made while back in the ASD were invaluable and served me well into my future years.

In addition, in 1979, my Assistant Director of ASD allowed me an opportunity, to attend a course in executive leadership and management at the esteemed Federal Executive Institute in Charlottesville, Virginia. The experience there with other executives from US federal agencies broadened my management capabilities, and also presented opportunities for several future liaison relationships. With my Section Chief position, I also appreciated the community outreach and liaison with the GSA, the Department of Justice, and the Federal Protective Service. Incidentally, there was one other agency, called the Pennsylvania Avenue Development Corporation, with which it was very important for us to maintain a good relationship. It has since been disbanded, but, in those days, had the role of pushing revitalization of Pennsylvania Avenue Northwest and held sway on what buildings and businesses along this key avenue were allowed to sell, display, and otherwise operate.

As an aside, the very location of the Hoover Building provided an outstanding opportunity for me to study, up close and personal, an incident and a person of immense importance in American history. Ford's Theatre sits almost directly across the street from FBIHQ on Tenth Street Northwest. Short periods of many lunch hours were spent visiting the site where President Abraham Lincoln was shot on April 14, 1865. I could review and inspect important relics and memorabilia in the theater's basement museum, or cross the street to the house where President Lincoln passed away the next day. Through these visits, I richly increased my knowledge and appreciation of my favorite historic leader.

Finally, during this entire assignment, I appreciated and respected, most of all, the support I received from my secretary, Pat Chancey, and my own staff. My Assistant Section Chief, Bob Olsen, was truly an expert in every facet of the work required of our various units. He was extremely capable of running the Section, and probably more capable of accomplishing that than myself. I have already written here about the performance of the various units (space, fleet, printing) and applaud the SAs and Support Supervisors who managed them. Although separated from investigations, I fully enjoyed and valued my time in the Section. Ready to return to field operations, my opportunity came early in 1980, when I was ordered to assume command of the highly desired Charlotte, North Carolina, FO as SAC.

CHAPTER 10

First Field Command

Charlotte, North Carolina, Field Office

YES, I WAS FINALLY GOING to be an SAC, but it was the FBI Director himself who braced me with what that truly meant. I would be held to the standard articulated in the age-old saying, "The buck stops here."

In early 1980, the Assistant Director of the Administrative Services Division summoned me to his office and handed me the letter that represents the ultimate achievement goal for the vast majority of FBI Agents seeking advancement in the agency. I was being transferred from FBI Headquarters (FBIHQ) and ordered to Charlotte, North Carolina, as the Special Agent in Charge (SAC) of the Charlotte Field Office (FO), which covers the state of North Carolina. I felt humbled, honored, and delighted all at the same time. I had never visited Charlotte or North Carolina before, but I was well aware that the FO was high on the list of our most desirable assignments for several reasons. Not only was the state reported to be great for its natural beauty and lifestyle, but the FO had an excellent reputation for good work and productivity.

Prior to my departure from Washington, D.C., and FBIHQ, I made the rounds of the various Headquarters Divisions to get briefed on the personnel, investigative priorities, and accomplishments of the FO. From the congratulations and positive reports I was getting from the supervisors at FBIHQ, I was further convinced that I was heading for a very well-run and productive FO.

Just prior to departure, it was a meeting with the FBI Director that allowed me to absorb the full reality of my new position. Yes, I would personally represent the Director, and yes, I would be the face and voice of the FBI, and in many instances get the credit for the good work of the SAs assigned to the FO. However, on the flip side, the buck would stop with me, and I would be held responsible for everything the FO did wrong, or failed to do at all. I must be familiar with, and responsible for, all occurrences and operations of the FO, and if activities or incidents should occur outside of my knowledge, I would be responsible to answer why I was not aware.

FBI Director William Webster sends me to Charlotte, NC as SAC.

I needed to be active in the community, especially with my fellow law enforcement agencies, and encourage full two-way cooperation. I should prepare for speaking engagements and media appearances to explain, in a fair and balanced manner, the work of the FBI. Finally, I should personally be on-site anywhere in my FO territory and at any hour of the day or night, if at all possible, when any action occurred or was anticipated that placed FBI personnel in danger or at personal risk.

Little did I realize at that point how many times during the next twelve years I would worry about FBI SAs going out on the street in certain situations. How could I imagine all the situations, the times I would be concerned about risky operations and suffer sleepless nights, or frequent calls throughout the night, which would interrupt sleep? So, sobered, but still eager and ready to go, I prepared for Charlotte.

After arrival, based on my initial contacts and review of the geography, the beauty of North Carolina was obvious. I would soon begin to experience the highways and byways of my new state, personally and frequently, often describing it as a mini United States, with the Atlantic Ocean on the east, the Great Smoky Mountains on the west, and its lush Piedmont area in the middle. It became my home for the next six years, great years never to be forgotten.

Similarly, the capabilities, activities, and successes of the nearly one hundred FBI SAs assigned to the FO and scattered strategically in Charlotte Headquarters, as well as eight other sub offices or Resident Agencies (RAs), became pleasantly and dramatically apparent. The RAs were located in Asheville, Greensboro, Raleigh, New Bern, Wilmington, Fayetteville, Elizabeth City, and Hickory, with the largest concentration of SAs in Raleigh (the state capital and center of the Research Triangle Park technology area) and Greensboro (center of the beautiful Triad area, which included Winston-Salem and High Point).

Soon after arrival in North Carolina, I experienced what I found to be a somewhat common occurrence for heads of agencies – being sued as a defendant in a frivolous lawsuit. It so happened that on November 3, 1979, a confrontation had occurred in Greensboro resulting in deadly violence, when six National Socialist (Nazi) Party of America and KKK members shot and killed five members of the Communist Workers Party (CWP), during a CWP-sponsored Death to the Klan Rally. The alleged shooters were subsequently charged with murder and tried in a very lengthy state trial. The results were acquittals for all six charged. Later, the US Department of Justice and the FBI conducted a civil rights investigation of the shooting, eventually leading, in April 1983, to indictments of nine current, or former, members of the KKK and the Nazi Party of America, for violating the civil rights of the five slain CWP members.

In the interim, the CWP filed a $1,000,000 lawsuit in federal court, alleging that numerous local, state, and federal government law enforcement figures had conspired to have the CWP members assassinated. Not surprisingly, I guess, I suddenly became a named defendant in the lawsuit. Although distracting and requiring plenty of paperwork, the DOJ was eventually able to have me dropped from the suit, since clearly, at the time of the incident, I had no connection whatsoever with North Carolina matters.

Aside from arriving to become a defendant in the CWP lawsuit, one other situation became at least a temporary and unfortunate distraction. One question that I'm sure is a standard one from the press to any newly arrived SAC, will be something like, "What will be your priorities for investigations here in our state?" My response to that

My first press conference in Charlotte.

question was to recite our national priorities at that time, which included white collar crime (WCC), public corruption, and violent crime. Somehow the message got twisted, and the wire services picked up an assertion, attributed to me, that the state was filled with corruption. This brought a scolding from Governor Jim Hunt to the effect that North Carolina was a clean state, and that I had just arrived there and maligned it, without having any knowledge or basis for my comments. Coming from the Governor, his comments, along with those erroneously attributed to me, got headline coverage. The sum and substance, bottom-line editorial message seemed to be: "Okay, Mr. Pence, put up or shut up!" As upsetting as this situation was for a time, I will say, quite honestly, that this was the first, and only, time in all my future dealings with the press that I felt seriously misquoted or had any of my words taken out of context. Furthermore, as Governor Hunt and I got to know each other, we developed an excellent relationship. I had regular meetings with and opportunities to visit and brief him at his office in Raleigh regarding several later situations. However, more importantly and unexpectedly, that initial media misunderstanding ultimately generated some surprising and unexpected beneficial results.

I began to get a flurry of calls and letters with information and tips that began to lead us in several interesting directions. For example, after I arrived in North Carolina ready for business in March 1980, a solid tip came to us in August of that year from a citizen in Columbus County, in the southeast portion of the state, to the effect that he had been solicited to pay a bribe in order to do business in the county. That was the beginning of an undercover operation (UCO) that the public

Meeting with North Carolina Governor Jim Hunt.

would learn about two years later, and long remember as COLCOR, code named for Columbus County Corruption.

SAs Robert Drdak and Bradley Hoferkamp went undercover, posing as members of organized crime and major drug dealers. They set up at various times in a cottage used as a gambling house, and then in a store used as a business involved in buying gold and silver, which became a front for buying stolen property and drugs. Their center of operations was an apartment in Whiteville, North Carolina. Started for the purpose of investigating corruption, this operation branched out to lead the SAs in many different directions. At its peak, COLCOR was detecting drug trafficking, stolen property, illegal gambling, counterfeiting, arson, bribery, prostitution, and voter fraud.

In July 1982, the initial round of indictments led to twenty-one arrests, including fifteen in southeast North Carolina, two in South Carolina, and four in Tennessee. These included a North Carolina district court judge, a county commissioner, a police chief, and a North Carolina state legislator. Information was later used in March 1983 to charge a state senator, whose federal trial ended in acquittal when the jury did not consider the evidence sufficient to bring forth a conviction. Other information was later furnished to the state of North Carolina, whose authorities, in turn, brought corruption charges against the state's lieutenant governor, who was also acquitted in state court.

Overall, COLCOR led to the recovery of more than $1,000,000 in stolen property. It also effectively put out of business four major drug operations, a pair of major auto and heavy equipment theft rings, an arson ring, and four gambling operations. Items recovered included weapons, marijuana, hashish, counterfeit currency, cars, trucks, jeeps, tractors, and other heavy equipment.

One of the factors leading to the operation's termination came based on SAs' efforts in becoming involved with a referendum and proposal for the voters of Bolton, North Carolina, to vote for and approve liquor-by-the-drink. As the date for the vote approached, the decision was made by the FBI and the US Attorney's Office that we should not be involved in any type of election process. Accordingly, the US Attorney notified Bolton town officials that fraud was believed involved, and the election should not be held. Despite this notification and warning, the referendum was held, and the proposal was passed. Subsequently, the referendum was nullified by the North Carolina Board of Elections, based on a formal notification and request from the US Attorney.

By March 1983, COLCOR had led to twenty-two convictions. In June 1983, a COLCOR spinoff investigation joined another federal and state investigation dubbed Operation Gateway, resulting in charges against a county sheriff, police chief, and thirteen others on drug charges. It also led to the recovery of several tons of marijuana and other illegal drugs, and the seizure of six boats and two airplanes. By July 1983, COLCOR had accounted for nearly forty federal convictions, with the final tally as of January 1985 at nearly fifty convictions, with the single federal acquittal being the North Carolina state senator.

At the time of the primary election in 1984, we were hearing reports of street talk in Columbus County that, because of COLCOR, this was the cleanest and most honest election in the county in years. Frankly, I was feeling quite a bit reassured during COLCOR when I read some of the newspaper articles and editorials. For example, after the first wave of arrests in 1982, an excerpt from the editorial page of the August 1, 1982, issue of the *Raleigh News and Observer* newspaper read, "When challenged to put up or shut up, Pence and his FBI Agents have put up. Their emphasis on white collar crime merits praise!"

To be sure, corruption cases did not end with COLCOR. For example, in December 1981, the former president of the North Carolina AFL-CIO union was convicted of unlawful obtaining and misapplying federal job training funds from the Comprehensive Employment and Training Act program for underprivileged citizens. In another case, a state representative pleaded guilty to bank fraud, involving two banks and thousands of dollars. With WCC and corruption being our top priorities in the 1980–1981 years, the convictions reached eighty-one and involved banks, corporations, unions, and government

With Supervisor Roger Schweickert in a vault surrounded by seized drugs.

agencies. In other examples, the former director of the Burlington, North Carolina, Housing Authority was charged with taking illegal kickbacks, and an Iron Workers Union officer in Durham, North Carolina, was charged with embezzling union funds. Throughout the next few years, more corruption cases continued, including the indictment and conviction of a North Carolina Department of Transportation officer in 1984 for a multimillion dollar highway-bid rigging scheme.

Some of the other cases under the WCC umbrella were quite varied, and some even bizarre. In 1982, SAs in our Greensboro RA worked a case involving an elaborate scheme to embezzle nearly $4 million worth of diamonds from the West African Nation of Guinea. It amounted to more than forty-seven thousand very small stones weighing more than thirty-seven thousand carats. Most of the diamonds were recovered when SAs obtained a search warrant and drilled a safety deposit box in a Greensboro bank. The subject, who initially fled back to Guinea, later returned to Greensboro and was arrested by FBI SAs. For Greensboro SAs, the sight of a large suitcase filled with diamonds was a sight not soon forgotten. The diamonds were ultimately returned to the government of Guinea.

Bank fraud cases appeared to be an ongoing staple for our WCC program, and were frequently very costly to the institutions. One such case involved the criminal activities of the treasurer for a savings and loan in Morganton, North Carolina, who, along with three others, committed an embezzlement involving the loss of nearly $9 million, ending in arrests, convictions, and lengthy prison terms. Another case involved the loss of nearly $150,000 from a federal savings and loan in Rockingham, North Carolina, and likely represented the first computer crime arrest and conviction in the state. A computer repair specialist was hired to repair the bank's computer. He fixed it all right, and then cleverly added a few extra features to make illegal deposits into his business and personal accounts.

Although bank fraud cases were regularly occurring and being worked in several of our RAs, as well as Charlotte Headquarters, I especially remember the efforts of one particular SA in our Greensboro RA. SA Tom Brereton was indeed the worst nightmare for the WCC criminal. He carried a heavy caseload and moved with lightning speed in his investigations. So fast, sometimes, that during file reviews he might have only a few, if any, written results in his file jacket, but was already in negotiations with an Assistant US Attorney to have a subject indicted by a federal grand jury and arrested. Talk about a coincidence, Tom Brereton was the very soldier that I met years earlier at the Defense Language Institute in Monterey, California, while he was in the US Army. I remember at that time he had expressed to me the desire to become an FBI SA someday.

Another interesting WCC case came to our attention in the Elizabeth City RA area in 1985. This one had historic significance and came to us courtesy of a retired Elizabeth City obstetrician, whose hobby was collecting verified historic documents and signatures. The case involved literally thousands of original documents and artifacts stolen from the life and works of the world-famous inventor Thomas Edison. The perpetrator turned out to be a former Stanford University professor who had been doing research regarding Edison in 1976, and had access to the Thomas Edison National Historic Site in New Jersey. While there, he had apparently helped himself to letters, drawings, documents, and other artifacts maintained at the Edison Library. Through his hobby of collecting authentic historic and rare signatures, our cooperating obstetrician became associated with the thief, who was living in Redwood City, California.

Initially, our criminal subject offered an original letter, which had been written to Edison by then Assistant Secretary of the Navy Franklin D. Roosevelt, and had a written notation on the top by Mr. Edison. The obstetrician verified the signature and purchased the letter for $275. He was then offered an early drawing of Edison's tin-foil phonograph, which was signed by Edison and several of his staff, and dated January 8, 1878, shortly after the device was patented. This was also verified as legitimate, and purchased for $600. Thereafter, the cooperating citizen was suspicious, consulted with officials at the Edison Library, and the FBI was notified.

What followed was a personal visit to the subject's residence in California by the cooperating obstetrician, accompanied by an undercover Elizabeth City SA posing as his friend, supposedly for the purpose of viewing other similar items for purchase. What they witnessed upon arrival at the residence was almost unbelievable. There were thousands of original items, including a number of Edison's phonographs and hundreds of old phonograph records, as well as an incredible number of other documents and devices. The two potential "buyers" left after agreeing to consider which items they wished to purchase. Two days later, California FBI SAs, accompanied by officials from the Edison Library, arrived with a search warrant, raided the residence, and recovered what they described as "many thousands" of original Edison artifacts and documents. It was difficult, if not impossible, to accurately estimate the value of stolen property recovered, since many of the documents would certainly be considered priceless. Soon thereafter, the subject was indicted by a federal grand jury and arrested by the FBI in California.

There are also a number of other crime classifications that fall under the WCC umbrella. SAs in North Carolina experienced and worked many of them with the following results.

Gambling and Sports Betting

We found illegal sports betting rampant throughout the state, and conducted a number of large raids throughout North Carolina during my years there. For example, in March 1982, we executed coordinated raids of twenty-eight locations in North and South Carolina, using more than one hundred SAs. Similar but smaller operations seemed to occur nearly every year, and in practically every region of the state. The raids would normally net gambling evidence that was sent to the FBI Laboratory for evaluation. After receipt of the results, which frequently identified operations handling betting of millions of dollars, indictments would be sought and the principal offenders arrested. More often than not, those charged would enter a guilty plea and avoid going to trial. Each year, our FO averaged nearly fifty convictions involving illegal sports gambling rings.

Copyright Violations

For some reason, it happened that large-scale trafficking in bootleg and pirated music and video recordings had also found a home and comfortable operating base in several areas of our state. Working with representatives of the Recording Industry Association of America and the Motion Picture Association of America, our SAs conducted numerous coordinated raids in 1982 and 1983 throughout the state. For example, coordinated raids in Kinston at four locations, which appeared to be the center for manufacturing and distribution for eastern North Carolina, recovered a huge number of fraudulent audiocassette tapes and records. Another raid near Charlotte realized a seizure of fifteen hundred illegal master tapes, from which at least four thousand additional bootleg tapes could be made. The music industry valued this particular seizure as saving the industry about $15 million. A raid in Winston-Salem, in 1983, recovered five thousand bootleg record albums, and that same year a raid in Greensboro netted fourteen hundred pirated videotape movie cassettes that the movie industry valued at saving over $1 million. According to the industry investigators, in the year 1982, more than 40 percent of pirated music and video recordings recovered in the United States were seized in our state of North Carolina.

Of course, what really crippled the bootleg business was the seizure of their audio and video duplication and mastering hardware and equipment, which was always a major part of the search warrants executed by the SAs. Fortunately, in waging our operations against the music and video pirates, as it was with the sports betting rings, there was seldom any violence encountered. Also, similar to court proceedings with the illegal gamblers, there were usually guilty pleas and relatively lighter prison sentences for these offenders.

DIPSCAM

Then there was DIPSCAM, arguably the granddaddy of them all in our WCC program, and certainly the case with the greatest scope and impact. It started a few months after I arrived in North Carolina in August 1980, and landed on the desk of the best possible SA to carry the ball. SA Allen Ezell was certainly among the most detailed, talented, energetic, relentless, and aggressive WCC SAs in the Charlotte FO at the time. One of our informants happened to show SA Ezell a diploma from a Greenville, South Carolina, college, which he claimed was purchased without performing any class work or study of any kind. So, a UCO was initiated that involved SA Ezell, as well as numerous other undercover SAs, working to unearth and identify a far-flung network in the United States and some foreign countries. The case involved illegal diploma mills, with sometimes impressive-sounding names, which were selling graduate degrees and diplomas of all levels and disciplines to hundreds of Americans.

Interestingly, due to the growing size of the investigation, we requested that FBIHQ designate this a major case, allowing it to acquire a code name. We were disappointed that FBIHQ did not consider it sufficiently significant to justify major case status. So we decided to give it our own code name, and this is how "DIPSCAM" was born. For the next nearly three years, undercover agents (UCAs) led by SA Ezell, and mostly with his personal participation, plugged along acquiring degrees from a wider growing assortment of "diploma mills," and with interesting incidents and results.

During the investigation, SAs collected not just diplomas but accompanying grade transcripts, class rings, baseball caps, T-shirts, and other clothing bearing names of the colleges. During one negotiation with a school, SA Ezell was officially appointed as a member of their board. We also discovered, in addition to the colleges and universities, there were phony or illegal alumni associations to which buyers could attain membership. In another case, SA Ezell sent more than $1,600 to the school, but instead of complying with their request for at least a short paper, he explained he was too busy and backlogged from a vacation to write it. By return mail, he received his MBA degree, along with a full transcript showing all B grades in ten courses for thirty credits. For another advanced degree, SA Ezell prepared a couple of pages for a term paper entitled "Psychology of Embezzlement" and received a B grade, with a handwritten note saying "Excellent, very well done," along with his diploma. With some schools, UCAs had to negotiate for the various degrees. For example, one school was charging $2,000 for a BA, $3,000 for an MBA, and $5,000 for a PhD. However, with some skillful negotiation, we bought all three for a combined $7,000.

It all "hit the fan," so to speak, on May 10, 1983, when the covert phase of DIPSCAM ended with a press conference in Charlotte, along with simultaneous raids in Phoenix, Arizona, and Miami, Florida. Raids followed shortly in Arkansas, Ohio, Oklahoma, Maryland, New York, California, and Missouri. Additional raids came later in Georgia, Oregon, Louisiana, Tennessee, and Washington, D.C. Ultimately, fifty large filing cabinets of evidence were seized. Nearly sixty raids were conducted involving more than fifty schools, with their principal operators indicted for federal wire or mail fraud, and arrested. Most of those charged eventually entered guilty pleas. Seized were many reams of documents, as well as similar items to those purchased during the operation. It was also interesting to note that blank diplomas for a number of legitimate and well-known universities and colleges were among the documents, as well as blank forms for a phony Bronze Star medal to be awarded by the US Marine Corps.

Immediately after the press conference on May 10, the media exploded on the story. DIPSCAM was front page the next day in *USA Today*, with featured articles appearing in most of the other major newspapers in the country, and some even coming from the world press, including the *Rheinische Post* in (then) West Germany. There was also a raft of favorable editorials on the FBI action, which appeared later in several newspapers. An appreciative citizen even took the time to clip a feature article from the May 23, 1983, edition of *Newsweek* magazine, mount it on the cover page of the magazine, custom frame it, and mail it to me. With each new raid and seizure revelation, DIPSCAM stayed in the news for months. Requests for speaking engagements and TV appearances were numerous and mostly handled by SA Ezell or me. I recall invitations to appear on talk shows in the studios of KDKA-TV in

Pittsburgh, Pennsylvania, and WBZ-TV in Boston, Massachusetts, and received tremendous audience interest during both of the appearances.

The size and scope of DIPSCAM notwithstanding, the real shocker was the number of diploma buyers in important real-life positions. Except in some later court proceedings, the identities of the buyers were not released by the FBI because they were considered "victims" of the phony college administrators, who were considered the criminal "perpetrators." Yet, the FBI identified nearly seventy-five hundred individual buyers of the bogus diplomas, some who held surprising and significant positions. Some of the government employees holding the degrees had even used government funds to pay for them.

Since buyers were not subjects of the investigation, we furnished their identities to authorities in their states of residence, as well as local, state, or federal agencies, if they were employees. It was left to these authorities to determine whether the bogus degree was used to obtain employment, or to advance in their employment, and if so, what further action was appropriate. Although feedback to us regarding any final dispositions for buyers was not requested or required, we did get some information of firings and other personnel actions. In California, SAs interviewed one of the buyers of a medical degree and determined he was indeed practicing medicine, with his bogus degree hanging in his office. In another situation, we were advised that a degree recipient, working as a court counselor in Virginia, received a jail term after a local conviction for using false credentials.

Without identifying the purchasers of the degrees, the following are some examples of the positions they held.

U.S. Military

US Army chaplain

US Army colonel

Doctor, Office of Undersecretary of the Navy

Instructor, Industrial College of the Armed Forces

Employee, US Military Joint Chiefs of Staff

Seventy-five employees at the Pentagon

Federal Government

Duty officer, White House Situation Room

NASA employees

Member, White House staff

Financial
    Bank supervisor, New York City
    Hospital supervisor, New York City
    Escrow officer, savings and loan at Beverly Hills, California
Education
    Public school teachers
    College administrator, Brooklyn, New York
    Private school principal, Tampa, Florida
    South Florida college professor
Medical
    Psychologists
    Chiropractors
    Psychiatrists
    Chief of medical service at Indiana hospital
    Chief of radiology at Texas hospital
Miscellaneous
    Police officer in Philadelphia, Pennsylvania
    National Football League running back
    Advertising executive, Pittsburgh, Pennsylvania
    Number of officials in law enforcement and corrections
    Minister in a southern church
    US Secret Service technician
    Nuclear power plant engineer

Of the total identified buyers, two hundred were employed by the federal government, and two hundred were employed by state governments.

On the lighter side, during a few of the undercover purchases, SA Ezell used my name as a purchaser. Even now, I occasionally dig out my class rings and diplomas, and fondly remember DIPSCAM, as I review my law degree from Harvard University, various medical degrees from other well-known colleges and universities, and of course, my doctor of divinity degree. I believe it was money well spent! My only regret was that my transcripts had some B grades, while I thought I deserved at least an A in criminal justice.

Certainly, DIPSCAM did not identify all the bogus colleges and universities out there, but, hopefully, did give pause to public agencies, as well as private business employers, to be more careful in reviewing the educational credentials of potential employees. In sum, in looking back at DIPSCAM, one might deduce that if American industry and government want to require advanced degrees from their employees, some of those same enterprising employees will figure out paths of least resistance to acquire them. Similarly, scheming fraudsters will gladly make the acquisition quick and relatively painless for them.

As a bit of a postscript, SA Allen Ezell is now retired from the FBI, but remains passionate in tracking down diploma mills. He is considered an authority and expert on the subject, and the author of books on the problem as it exists today.

Outlaw Motorcycle Gangs and Operation COUNTERVAIL

During my Bureau career, I would get occasional questions about which case, or cases, gave me the most worry or concern about SAs' personal safety. Certainly, over the years a number of situations developed that posed serious or extreme potential for risk of violence and personal injury. Some occurred unexpectedly and were resolved quickly, while others were carefully calculated for risk and subjected to extensive planning and preparation. Fortunately, although these types of situations popped up rather frequently, they were normally of short duration and caused a more temporary worry and stress. A UCO, code-named COUNTERVAIL, intensified the worry and caused some sleepless nights for several months.

During the 1980s, criminal activities of outlaw motorcycle gangs throughout the United States became a serious concern to citizens, and a real problem for law enforcement. Their violations were diverse, frequently violent, and represented their own style of organized crime. The two most prominent gangs in North Carolina were the Outlaws motorcycle gang, and the Hells Angels. In March of 1981, we undertook the challenge to survey the organizational structure and activities of the two gangs in order to develop an investigative strategy to deal with them. The first effort was dubbed Operation SUPERGLIDE, and involved SAs going undercover on motorcycles, and acting as vendors at swap meets offering to sell biker clothing and paraphernalia. They networked well with some of the gang members and won their trust. After a period of months, it became apparent that, for purposes of concentration in the Charlotte area of North Carolina, the Outlaws appeared to be the best organized, largest, and most active gang. Hence, the focus of a more intense UCO would be targeted against the Outlaws, and the code name became COUNTERVAIL.

In February 1982, the lead team was made up of an FBI SA and a local law enforcement officer on loan from a different state. The pair were assigned full-time and traveled together on motorcycles. They became very close to the Outlaws and were welcomed into their midst. Unfortunately, daily life with them usually presented a daily challenge. Members were frequently drunk, or using drugs, and capable of violence at any moment. On one occasion, the UCAs were held at gunpoint, threatened, and accused of being law enforcement officers. Although they were able to talk their way out of that situation, similar incidents and challenges occurred almost daily. Our FBI Supervisory Special Agent Roger Schweickert and other SAs, including nine part-time UCAs at different times, provided as much covert support as possible, and when possible. However, there were obviously many times when the primary UCAs were on their own, with groups of drunken, drugged, and armed gang members. Of course, this was true both in the Outlaws clubhouse and while on motorcycle trips to Tennessee, Florida, Georgia, and South Dakota.

In November 1982, the COUNTERVAIL operation went public with the arrest of fourteen Outlaws members for drug trafficking, prostitution, and various other federal violations. They were arrested without incident, with the timing dictated by the need for the UCAs to provide testimony in a Florida court concerning earlier arrests. However, another reason for surfacing the UCO was, quite frankly, to extricate our UCAs from such a dangerous and deplorable lifestyle. In addition to the COUNTERVAIL arrests, and later convictions, the operation provided information important to solving a recent murder, as well as other information critical to preventing a contract killing set for Charlotte. The UCAs also developed important background details surrounding the July 4, 1979, slaying of five Outlaws members and associates, in addition to a wealth of intelligence for local authorities working various other criminal investigations.

Understandably, the Outlaws members were not happy that their Charlotte chapter had been infiltrated and virtually left in total disarray by COUNTERVAIL. We began to pick up details of calls and threats on the street that the Outlaws were "going to get the snitches." With the crescendo of death threats, we decided to assemble teams of SAs and pay a friendly "courtesy call" to the Outlaws clubhouses in Charlotte and Lexington, North Carolina. It was made abundantly, and rather forcefully, clear to the Outlaws membership, that they

Paying a courtesy visit to the Outlaws clubhouse.

were not penetrated by "snitches" but rather by sworn law enforcement officers, and that any further threats or actions against them would simply not be tolerated. Our visits were apparently well received, since the threatening talk and calls abruptly ended.

In December 1983, our lead FBI UCA, SA Allen Lance Emory and his local law enforcement UCA partner, were recognized for their efforts, with a meritorious award from the Attorney General of the United States.

Having dealt rather decisively with the Outlaws between 1981 and 1982, our opportunity to take on the Hells Angels came a few years later. In 1982, the FBI's Baltimore FO launched a similar UCO, code named ROUGHRIDER, aimed at the violence-prone Hells Angels. Some of their UCA activities developed evidence against the leaders of the Hells Angels in the Durham, North Carolina, chapter. In May 1985, we became part of a fifty-raid day in eleven states, culminating in more than one hundred arrests of Hells Angels members for a wide assortment of criminal activity, including drug trafficking and racketeering. We had warrants to arrest four members, including the president and vice president of the Durham chapter.

This particular clubhouse was heavily fortified, surrounded by a chain-link fence topped with barbed wire, and closed-circuit TV. There were also some Doberman Pinschers roaming the property. After a briefing at 6 a.m. with other city, county, and state law enforcement officers, we surrounded the building with guns drawn. The arrest team unexpectedly made friends with the dogs (maybe they were accustomed to lots of people creeping around with guns), and then used sledge hammers to break the main steel door and two other doors. The arrests went without much resistance, and drugs along with a variety of weapons were recovered, including handguns, machine pistols, sawed-off shotguns, and rifles with scopes.

In reflecting on those days, although it took awhile, we dealt with both of the most dangerous outlaw motorcycle gangs in North Carolina, and did it successfully. And the best part – not a shot had to be fired.

Voter Fraud and Project WESTVOTE

Based on widespread and longtime rumors of voting irregularities in western North Carolina, we teamed with Charles Brewer, US Attorney for the Western District of North Carolina, prior to the general election of November 1982, to encourage the public to report any voter fraud after the election. The ensuing response of more than thirty complaints and tips led to our intensive investigation called Project WESTVOTE. In July 1983, the first results were obtained with twelve indictments in Clay and Alexander Counties, which included the Clay County sheriff and the former sheriff, a magistrate, and a Clay County Board of Elections employee. In Alexander County, a deputy sheriff and a deputy county clerk of court were indicted on numerous vote fraud charges. Those public officials and others were charged with a number of violations, including buying votes for a minimum of $50 in Clay County, and forging names of elderly senior residents, who resided in a rest home in Alexander County, on absentee ballots.

Between 1984 and 1985, the massive investigation had spread to Cherokee County, with indictments and arrests that included the county sheriff, two deputies, and a magistrate. In April 1985, an official of the Public Integrity Section of the US Department of Justice was on-site in North Carolina to assist the US Attorney with prosecutions. While there, he made public statements to the effect that WESTVOTE was the most significant and successful election law enforcement action since his Section in Washington, D.C., was created almost ten years earlier in 1976. He described the voter fraud in the western region of North Carolina as being as well organized, sophisticated, and lucrative as anywhere they had experienced in the country.

This was not an undercover operation but rather a full-scale traditional FBI investigation, involving dozens of SAs from the Charlotte FO, who conducted approximately two thousand citizen interviews. Project WESTVOTE eventually racked up nearly forty convictions for vote buying and/or conspiracy, and reportedly changed, for the better, how elections would be conducted in the future in that region.

Drugs in North Carolina

When I arrived in the state in 1980, illegal drug trafficking investigations were not yet a high priority for the FBI, since at the federal level it was the principal responsibility of the Drug Enforcement Administration. However, as the scope of the problem escalated, as of January 1982 the FBI became committed to assisting with drug investigations. Due to its extensive seacoast on the east and geographic state location in the mid-South, North Carolina was a very important strategic center for drug-related crime. We in the Charlotte FO got our feet wet, so to speak, early in the drug fight.

In February 1982, Charlotte SAs participated with Miami FO SAs in culminating a two-year undercover investigation into a narcotics smuggling ring involving NASCAR stock car drivers, mechanics, and pit crew members. Seventy individuals were indicted in the operation, which involved transportation of narcotics between Florida and North Carolina, frequently in their race cars. Charges included estimates that the ring was responsible for more than one million pounds of marijuana alone every year from at least 1977 to 1980. The ring had been trafficking in drug amounts worth several million dollars annually.

By April 1982, I recall making a statement in a speech that our FBI FO, going forward, would be naming drug trafficking, along with WCC, as our two highest priorities in the state. By December 1982, working with US Customs and the Internal Revenue Service, SAs in Raleigh had a nine-person drug racketeering ring indicted. They were part of an aircraft company that was acquiring small planes by furnishing fraudulent information to banks, and then using the planes for drug transportation between South America and cities in the southeast United States.

In March 1983, a federal/state investigation, code named Operation GATEWAY, secured indictments against the sheriff of Brunswick County, North Carolina, and the police chief of Shallotte, North Carolina, plus twenty others, delivering a severe blow to drug smuggling into Brunswick County along the southeast North Carolina coast.

In March 1984, sixteen individuals from the United States, France, Australia, and the West Indies were indicted in schemes involving forty thousand pounds of hashish, after purchasing a trawler in the Netherlands and transporting the drugs from Tripoli, Libya. This operation was supposedly being provided weapons and alleged protection by the Palestine Liberation Organization terrorist group.

That same month our SAs participated in a mass arrest by drug task force agencies on the east coast of the state. The drug ring in this case was moving about two hundred thousand pounds of marijuana annually, worth approximately $40 million, and operating between Colombia, South America, and some Caribbean islands, with drugs moving into North Carolina, Virginia, Michigan, Maryland, South Carolina, and Florida.

Civil Rights

The final investigative area I will describe was certainly one of the most important in the Charlotte FO, as it is in every FBI FO. Its protection strikes to the heart of the freedom we hold dear in this nation. As it did for me in Louisiana and Mississippi, then in Kentucky, and now in North Carolina, the importance of civil rights investigations once more jumped to the highest possible priority in my field experience. In August 1981, SAs of our Greensboro RA were alerted to a situation in which a number of migrant farm workers were being held against their will in a Caswell County camp in north-central North Carolina. The complaints were that the tobacco laborers were being held at gunpoint, were beaten if they tried to leave the camp, were not being fed properly, and were living in unsanitary conditions. They had originally been recruited from several states through promises of employment, but then were kept in virtual bondage. What little they were paid was kept by the crew boss in exchange for inflated prices for food, liquor, and other supplies, which always exceeded the wages and kept the migrants in continuous debt.

FBI SAs and Caswell County Sheriff's Office deputies visited the camp, assembled the migrant workers, and asked if any desired to leave. There were about twenty-five of them, and at first, a few of them, then eventually all, stepped forward and were liberated. In December 1981, the crew leader and his two sons were indicted, charged, and arrested for Involuntary Servitude and Slavery (ISS). In January 1982, all were found guilty and sentenced to prison.

Hardly one month had passed after the liberation of the Caswell County migrant workers, when FBI SAs assigned to the Raleigh RA were approached by two migrant workers who claimed they had escaped from a similar camp in Nash County east of Raleigh, where thirty laborers were being held against their will. FBI SAs responded immediately to the camp and liberated thirteen workers who claimed they were threatened, witnessed beatings, were kept in debt to the crew leader, and were afraid to leave. The men had been enticed with false promises and transported from various states, including New York City and Atlanta, Georgia. It was determined that one worker had collapsed and died when ordered to keep digging potatoes, even though he was spitting blood. Based on our investigation, the crew leader and three assistants were indicted, arrested, and charged with ISS. Apparently, this was also the first case of ISS ever charged involving a death under the slavery statute. They were all convicted and sentenced to federal prison.

Then in 1983, a series of incidents started in Statesville, North Carolina, with a cross burning and shots fired into the home of a church pastor and local civil rights activist. A two-year probe, code named Operation CROSSFIRE, was then initiated by SAs in the Hickory RA, and focused on Iredell and Alexander Counties in the area north of Hickory in northwest North Carolina. By September 1985, after investigation into more than twelve cross burnings, and additional reports of threatening calls, shooting into or near residences, and other racially motivated incidents, nine leaders and members of the KKK in Iredell and Alexander Counties were indicted and arrested by the FBI. Then followed a number of guilty pleas, and nine more indictments in January 1986. This case was still in the prosecutive stage as I prepared to leave North Carolina for a new assignment.

These narratives, reporting activities of the SAs of the Charlotte FO in our priority investigative areas during my years there, allow me to reflect on why I will always be extremely proud of the men and women of the North Carolina FBI. There will be more activities from my days there in the pages to follow, but I really appreciated and want to mention what FBIHQ reported, in part, about fieldwide year-end results for 1982. I went on to be proud and pleased for every year I was in the state, but, for example, for the year 1982, FBIHQ announced that the Charlotte FO, while thirtieth in size of the fifty-nine FOs we had at that time, ranked fifth in felony arrests, sixth in felony indictments, and seventh in felony convictions. Looking at per capita SA production, Charlotte SAs looked even better, since they ranked first in arrests, third in indictments, and second in convictions.

Considering how important statistics were in determining the success of an FBI FO, it would also be appropriate to mention that the Charlotte FO usually would be included among the top five FOs in the country for recruiting candidates to become new FBI SAs. That achievement, in my mind, could be attributed to two factors. First, North Carolina was blessed with large numbers of men and women of the highest caliber who desired to become an FBI SA. Second, we had an SA recruiter named Chuck Richards who was nearly seven feet tall and a former professional basketball player in the NBA. Chuck traveled the state, visited the colleges and universities, and was a virtual magnet for drawing interest to the FBI from the best and most qualified candidates in North Carolina.

With our recruiter Chuck Richards at the Charlotte office.

CHAPTER 11

Charlotte FBI

The Rest of the Story

AS BUSY AS THE NORTH CAROLINA SAs were in working important cases in the highest priority investigative areas, that was only part of our responsibilities. It became obvious early on, in my role as a Special Agent in Charge (SAC), that my agency would routinely become involved, in one way or another, in nearly every incident occurring in our territory that had a significant bearing on public safety. Initially, our interest would be to determine if the incident (shooting, theft, robbery, kidnapping, arson, explosion, airplane crash, etc.) constituted a crime, out of the more than two hundred federal violations, under our jurisdiction. If so, we would immediately initiate an investigation, but if not, we would normally offer cooperation and support under our provisions for domestic or foreign police cooperation. Frequently, this would involve the offer to cover out-of-state leads, provide laboratory and technological services, or participate in joint task forces with the other agencies involved.

In the realm of personal contacts, the range was vast and extended on the high end to celebrities and corporate executives in most fields, and public officials extending to state governors, and even visits from the President of the United States. We worked well with the US Secret Service, and were close at hand during presidential visits to our territory in the event of an attempted assault on the President, which would trigger an immediate FBI investigation. On the low end, some days we would be dealing with the depth of humanity, including murderers, robbers, drug lords, spies, terrorists, and the like.

As a further illustration of the diversity of interesting cases, as well as situations and personalities encountered during my stay in North Carolina, the following are highlighted.

In the Asheville area of western North Carolina stands one of the greatest American castle-like structures in the United States called the Biltmore House. It was built between 1889 and 1895 by the railroad millionaire George Vanderbilt, and is still among the largest, if not the

The Biltmore House, Asheville, NC.

largest, privately-owned mansions in the country. Rumor was that Mr. Vanderbilt built the structure as an escape from the ordinary. Today, it hosts thousands of visitors annually from all over the world.

In 1980, it served as the location for a feature film called *The Private Eyes*, starring the famous comedy duo, Don Knotts (also known as Barney Fife in the popular *Andy Griffith Show* television series) and his partner, Tim Conway. The two played bumbling Scotland Yard detectives in the movie. Now, the story goes, during the filming it just so happened that one of the two, supposedly Tim Conway, wanted to examine firsthand one of the priceless literary works contained in the amazing library at the Biltmore House. Taking firm hold of the huge dust jacket sleeve, which contained a famous volume such as *The History of Locomotion*, Tim Conway lifted it off the shelf only to find the sleeve empty. Thus commenced an inventory that discovered numerous valuable works missing, and launched a worldwide FBI investigation.

A Biltmore employee had been stealing the volumes and then selling them around the world. He was identified and arrested, and, very fortunately, we ultimately recovered most of the volumes. In January 1981, the former security guard at the Biltmore House was tried, and pleaded guilty to stealing sixty rare books from the approximately twenty-five thousand-volume library at the house. At the conclusion of the case, we took the opportunity to formally recognize the assistance that we received from the two "Scotland Yard detectives." I crafted a letter of commendation and thanks to Messrs. Knotts and Conway, citing the fictional private eyes as real and true detectives, without whose curiosity a massive theft at the Biltmore House might have gone undetected for a long, long time.

The SAs in our Asheville RA would confirm that their territory was one of my favorites to visit. I was fascinated by the Biltmore House, and whenever in the area and time permitted, I would try to stop by there for a brief visit. Not far from Asheville was also the home of a very famous and well-respected American – the Reverend Billy Graham.

During my assignment to the Charlotte FO, I was indeed fortunate to become friends with Reverend Graham's staff. I was invited to his residence atop a mountain near Montreat, North Carolina. At that time, the property was protected by two beautiful German Shepherds, which appeared to take orders and commands only in German from the property caretaker. The property was a simple and humble, yet elegant, log cabin–style structure, surrounded by incredibly lush and beautiful mountain scenery.

Given my first opportunity to sit across from Reverend Graham, with his long legs crossed, and listening to his warm, measured tones, with a tinge of a "North Carolina southern" accent, I somehow developed a mental picture that I was in the presence of, and speaking with, a figure not unlike President Abraham Lincoln. It is hard to explain, but a distinct impression fell over me that I was in the presence of someone very special, very important, and easily blessed by a higher power. I was truly captivated by his intelligence and thoughtful, caring statements.

I often reflect on my association with that unique gentleman and his entire organization, and have traveled back to Charlotte, North Carolina, to visit his museum and continue to enjoy the relationship with his staff. Unfortunately, the world lost the Reverend Billy Graham in February 2018, as he passed away peacefully in his mountain Montreat home, just shy of his one hundredth year of life.

One of the frequent questions I would get from audiences during speeches was whether it was really exciting to be an FBI Agent. I always smile when I recall that very question during a luncheon speech to a civic group in Charlotte in April 1981. The person asking the question went on to ask, "For example, what was your day like yesterday?"

I remember smiling as I told the group that yesterday I started the day in Raleigh, North Carolina, where I briefed the state's governor in the morning regarding some activity in which the FBI would be involved in the near future, and which he should be aware. After the briefing, I drove west on I-40 toward Winston-Salem and joined, for a short time, a moving surveillance of suspected Soviet spies, who were passing through North Carolina. The assistance of the state's FBI SAs was requested by our Washington FO SAs, who were running the surveillance. Then I moved north on US Hwy 52 to the area of Mount Airy, which is the closest real town to the fictional town of Mayberry where Andy Griffith portrayed the sheriff on TV.

Near this area of North Carolina, SAs were staging for an evening raid to recover a tractor trailer loaded with stolen cigarettes from the R.J. Reynolds Tobacco Company in Winston-Salem. Intelligence information had the huge vehicle hidden in a quarry and preparing to leave that night. The quarry was located at the end of a dirt road with a locked gate at the exit, between two large mounds of earth. As darkness fell that night, I joined the group of SAs concealed behind both mounds of earth at the exit gate. After a short wait, an FBI surveillance aircraft reported that the vehicle with the stolen cigarettes, worth more than a half-million dollars, was leaving the quarry and heading toward the exit. When the tractor trailer slowed and stopped at the exit gate to open it, we pounced from both directions, reminiscent of the notorious Jesse James gang of the Old West about to rob an unsuspecting stagecoach. With that action, the expensive load of hijacked R.J. Reynolds cigarettes was successfully recovered without further incident.

Afterward that night, I told my audience, I flew back to Charlotte with the FBI pilot so I could be here today to speak with you folks. The crowd response was "Wow!" Of course, they asked the question on the right day, since every day in the FBI is not going to be that adventurous. However, that said, I went on to explain that almost every day in the Bureau is different and definitely not dull.

On March 30, 1981, President Ronald Reagan was shot along with three others, as they were leaving a speaking engagement at the Washington Hilton Hotel in Washington, D.C. President Reagan nearly died during this attempted assassination. I had met him earlier in 1974, during our FBI inspection visit to Sacramento,

California, while he was governor of California. And I had just met him as President of the United States shortly before this assassination attempt. A young man named John Hinckley was the shooter and was immediately arrested.

Ironically, shortly after the shooting, I received a call from FBIHQ, which relayed a request from the US Bureau of Prisons that the FBI take on a very important mission. The mission was to provide security transport for a very important prisoner at the Butner Correctional Institution in Butner, North Carolina. I mentioned to FBIHQ that this sounded like a mission for the US Marshals or some other federal agency. The FBIHQ caller agreed, but stated in this case the Bureau of Prisons wanted only the FBI to handle it, and that we were requested and permitted to proceed. This transportation was to be to Duke University Hospital, in Durham, North Carolina, for psychiatric testing. Sure enough, it was President Reagan's would-be assassin, John Hinckley. During the next couple of weeks, complete with FBI aircraft cover, we spent a few nights together with John in a very heavily secured escort convoy. John Hinckley was a very quiet and very polite young prisoner. In fact, on one occasion he was sweating profusely and nearly passed out, until we realized he had accidently been outfitted with not one, but two, bulletproof vests, on one of North Carolina's hot and humid summer evenings. We quickly removed one of the vests, and he was profoundly appreciative, returning to normal very quickly.

After President Reagan's complete recovery, a couple of years later in 1983 I had the honor of visiting him again, when he and his wife came to Camp Lejeune, North Carolina. They came to visit the relatives of the nearly two hundred and fifty Marines and other service personnel murdered in October 1983 in the vicious terrorist attack on the Marine barracks in Beirut, Lebanon.

Before the President had private and very emotional meetings with the relatives of the murdered Marines, he spoke at a public gathering on the parade grounds to a very large crowd and in a driving rainstorm. I remember this day very well, since while the President was covered by a number of large umbrellas during his remarks, I was invited to seek refuge from the storm in the President's own limousine, joined by the US Secret Service Agent in Charge at the event.

Remembering other important celebrities I met in North Carolina, Sam Ervin was a colorful and beloved senior US senator from North Carolina, who served from 1954 to 1974, and who will be remembered by many as the chairman, in 1973, of the Senate Select Watergate Committee hearings into the notorious Watergate incident. This involved

A visit with Senator Sam Ervin.

a break-in at the headquarters of the National Democratic Party in Washington, D.C., and a subsequent cover-up, which eventually forced the resignation of President Richard Nixon in 1974. Sam Ervin was a North Carolina native, and in 1974, he resigned from the US Senate and returned to practice law in his hometown of Morganton. Early in my FBI assignment to the Charlotte FO, I traveled to Morganton and paid a courtesy visit to Senator Ervin. I was honored to spend some time with him, and congratulated him on his illustrious career and distinguished service to the citizens of North Carolina and the entire nation. We met one final time, in July 1983, at a memorial service during the International Conference of Police Chaplains at the All Souls Episcopal Church in Asheville, North Carolina. Senator Ervin passed away in 1985.

Since Charlotte was in the southeast region of the United States, I also benefited culturally from being able to attend important law enforcement meetings and conferences in other southern states. The meetings would involve other agencies and FBI FOs and included topics such as illegal drug trafficking, organized crime, and national security matters. Two specific examples, in two different states, jumped immediately to mind and ended with two different outcomes. During a conference at Cape Canaveral, Florida, we were honored to experience the safe return of one of the space shuttle missions and greet the exhausted astronauts. However, on January 28, 1986, during a conference in Charleston, South Carolina, we watched and stood aghast as the space shuttle Challenger exploded in midair just after lifting off from the very same Cape Canaveral, killing all seven crew members aboard.

On the flip side, it was not only visits outside the FO territory that made life interesting, but also certain visits to the FO always got the SAC's full and undivided attention. In the FBI, for an SAC, nothing is usually more nerve-wracking or tensely awaited than; one, a visit from an inspection team, or two, a visit from the FBI Director himself. In the early 1980s, one visit from the FBI Director, Judge William Webster, was unforgettable. He arrived for a speaking engagement and stayed for a few days for meetings and visits around the state. Needless to say, every minute of his time in the FO territory needed to be meticulously planned, from meeting at the airport through delivery back to the airport for the farewell and "wheels up" (when everyone felt relief), as the plane lifted off for Washington, D.C.

During this visit all events went according to plan until the last day. I had a speech scheduled in Raleigh, North Carolina, around the time that Judge Webster was scheduled to head for the Charlotte Airport, and I asked him if he desired me to cancel and remain with him until his flight departed. He was very complimentary as to how well the visit had gone, and assured me the SAs escorting him would get him to his flight without any problem. He insisted I proceed to Raleigh to handle my speaking commitment, which I did. Thereafter, departure plans for the Director began to slip. He decided to make a last-minute visit to a judge at the federal courthouse, leaving precious little time to get him to the airport for his scheduled departure. Unfortunately, due to the short time left and some confusion at the airport, Judge Webster was rushed to the wrong plane, one going to Chicago instead of Washington, D.C. Fortunately, when the error was discovered, due to the immediate and skillful efforts of the attending SAs, both of the planes involved were stopped, and the Director was transferred to the correct one. Needless to say, the incident was not a "fun thing" at the time; however, in subsequent years, it gave a number of us something to reminisce and smile about. I also think (and hope) that Judge Webster later found some humor in the entire situation.

Another one of the questions that I had presented to me frequently in North Carolina centered around which investigation in the Charlotte FO personally gave me the most satisfaction. After a lot of consideration, I decided that, while any investigation with a successful resolution always gave me a great sense of satisfaction, the one that pleased me most involved an SA from a different FBI FO.

In October 1982, in Coffee County, Georgia, an Atlanta FO SA was working undercover against an auto theft ring. Some of the bad guys apparently identified him, beat him badly, dumped him on a rural road from a pickup truck traveling at a high rate of speed, and left him for dead. In August 1983, we received intelligence information that a man and woman responsible for the attempted murder were currently located somewhere in the Atlantic Beach area of North Carolina.

A couple of us flew to the area on FBI aircraft and joined SAs from all eastern North Carolina RAs, as well as a number of Atlanta FO SAs. With a vehicle description, part of a license number, and an assembled team of approximately twenty-five SAs, we searched all night and located the suspect vehicle parked at an upscale condominium building on the beachfront in the Atlantic Beach area. At dawn, we identified the unit occupied by the subjects in the condo building, and after developing an arrest strategy, we moved by late morning to surround the building. Once in place, an Atlanta SA and one of our Charlotte FO supervisors, pretending to be condo maintenance workers, knocked and successfully gained entrance, tackling the resisting male subject. Not long afterward, the female subject approached the building from the beach area, along with a child, and was arrested without incident by SAs outside the building. A search incident to the arrest recovered several handguns, approximately $100,000 in cash, and probably about $250,000 in cocaine.

What made these two arrests not only memorable, but especially satisfying, was the fact that the recovering Atlanta undercover FBI SA, although not involved in the arrest operation, was on the scene (located in a safe position), and personally able to observe the entire operation and the arrests.

But if the Atlantic Beach arrests were my most satisfying while in North Carolina, certainly the most bizarre, unbelievable, unexpected, and potentially dangerous case broke out in the northern part of the state in June 1984.

Actually, the incident started next door in neighboring Virginia at the maximum security Mecklenburg Correctional Center near Boydton, Virginia, and presented the immediate risk of danger and potential violence to the surrounding community. It happened that a group of inmates, all on death row, had, for some time, been hatching a plan to take over their cellblock and escape. One evening during their return to cells after an outside rest period, the group overpowered their guards and executed their plan. They took the guards' uniforms and produced a fake bomb, fashioned somehow out of a TV monitor and a fire extinguisher. They then used the "bomb" to take the guards hostage and bluff their way out of the prison.

There were six of them, and they were all convicted murderers. In fact, two of them, the Briley brothers (Linwood and James), working together, were linked to nearly a dozen homicides in Virginia. The prison was located very close to the Virginia–North Carolina border. An attempted carjacking in Warren County, North Carolina, near the border after midnight, indicated the escape route was into North Carolina. We were immediately alerted, and by the next day, dozens of FBI SAs from North Carolina and Virginia joined scores of other law enforcement officers from every state, county, and local agency in southern Virginia and northern North Carolina. Every stop was pulled and every resource applied, including tracking dogs and multiple aircraft. The community of Warrenton, North Carolina, was virtually an armed camp, and even the residents, who were not buttoned down in their homes, were out with their weapons searching for the killers.

Apparently two of the escapees were just trying to get out of prison for a while, since they were captured the next day without incident as they sat in a local laundromat sipping cheap wine. Two more were desperately attempting to reach Canada and nearly succeeded. They were apprehended just south of the border by alert Vermont State Troopers, who were responding to a robbery report. As expected, the notorious Briley Brothers presented the greatest challenge. After an intense investigation covering a couple of days, information was developed that they were hiding out at a certain location in Philadelphia, Pennsylvania. FBI SAs and Philadelphia police, working together, zeroed in on their location and arrested both of them, without further incident. A search of the nearby area located the guards' uniforms and a badge, hidden in a tree in the neighborhood. All of the escapees were returned to Virginia under heavy guard. The final chapter of the story was written in the death chamber. Below are the identities of the six escapees and their execution dates:

Linwood Briley – October 12, 1984
James Briley – April 18, 1985
Earl Clanton – April 14, 1988
Derick Peterson – August 22, 1991
Willie Leroy Jones – September 11, 1992
Lem Tuggle – December 12, 1996

The good news for the public was that this escape did not lead to any serious injury, or worse, serious injury for any citizens. The bad news for Virginia was that this was considered one of the most serious escapes ever in the history of the state's prison system. It resulted in a number of changes and personnel actions for the system. It is understandable that an incident of this magnitude would spark and foster a spate of articles, books, videos, and even a motion picture; and it certainly did just that.

In April 1985, an interesting and very high profile case developed in the Winston-Salem area, which had a direct connection to a major case in an area that would mean a lot more to me personally, about a year later – Denver, Colorado.

On June 18, 1984, a controversial talk show radio host for radio station KOA in Denver, named Alan Berg, was assassinated by machine gun outside his residence. He had been particularly critical of the KKK and Nazi extremists. The assassination was determined to be a hate crime, resulting in an intensive FBI investigation. Eventually, the killers were identified as part of the extremely violent section of the Aryan Nations group, called The Order, which was also an extreme antigovernment organization. The shooter was identified as neo-Nazi Bruce Pierce, and he was apprehended by the FBI, tried, convicted, and died in prison in 2010. The driver of the getaway car was identified as David Lane, and he became a badly wanted fugitive. FBI efforts eventually determined Lane was being hidden by white hate group supporters, probably KKK members, in an area of Virginia just north of North Carolina. Intelligence information developed by the Richmond, Virginia, FBI FO, indicated the possibility that Lane would be getting a phone call on March 30, 1985, a Saturday morning, somewhere in the greater Winston-Salem, North Carolina, area. We deployed a large contingent of SAs from our offices in Charlotte and Greensboro, as well as a heavily armed arrest team concealed in a van.

SAs were in small teams, on roving patrol, saturating the area where the phone call was expected. We also had FBI aircraft covering the operation. Around mid-morning, SAs in Virginia alerted the Charlotte FBI FO that Lane was active at that time talking on a telephone in the Winston-Salem area. The number was traced to a pay phone located just outside a Winn Dixie supermarket in a Winston-Salem mall. As it turned out, I was driving in the closest vicinity to the fugitive's location. With guidance and direction assistance from our FBI aircraft, I was led through alleys and other shortcuts (even over a few lawns) to arrive at the entrance to the mall parking lot, just in time to observe Lane dangle the phone handset, but not hang up, from an outdoor pay phone, and head back toward a vehicle in the parking lot.

The arrest team van arrived very shortly thereafter, and were alerted to his location. The van pulled up adjacent to his vehicle, and to the surprise and astonishment of several onlooking shoppers, David Lane was apprehended at gunpoint, without incident, immediately outside the vehicle of his Klan supporters. I ran to the outside of the supermarket, and picked up the dangling receiver from his unfinished conversation. After a few exchanges of "Who is this?" between us, someone on the other end said, "This is FBI Virginia," and I answered "This is FBI North Carolina, we got him."

After the arrest, a search of the vehicle recovered a .45 caliber pistol and a knife. The subsequent location and search of the rural Virginia farm where he had been hiding located pistols, an automatic weapon, ammunition, binoculars, radio scanner, valuable documents, and considerable cash. David Lane was subsequently tried, convicted, and died in prison in 2007.

Finally, to give a "flavor" to the widely diverse types of cases we handled, let me mention one last North Carolina case. In late 1983, a father and his two sons in Carroll County, Maryland, stole four liquid nitrogen tanks containing enough bull semen to impregnate thousands of heifers, and worth more than $250,000. The semen was produced by a dairy bull named Round Oak Rag Apple Elevation, ranked in dairy circles as one of the "greatest Holstein studs of all time." The semen was recovered, and two of the subjects arrested in

Delaware and New Jersey. In June 1984, the third subject was traced to a dairy farm near Granite Falls, North Carolina, working as a herd manager. SAs from our Asheville RA had the unfortunate experience of locating the fugitive in the pasture, in the middle of the cattle herd, and stomping through a lot of "droppings" to make the arrest. They complained of a very "smelly" trip with the prisoner in the car en route back to Asheville, and the Buncombe County Jail.

Well, as the year 1985 ended, and we entered the early months of 1986, consistent with FBI policy, I knew that my assignment in North Carolina would be coming to an end soon. As expected, I got a call from the Director's Office in the spring, and got the word that I would need to move to a new assignment. I explained that I was quite happy with the Charlotte FO and would gladly stay on for a while if FBIHQ desired but, personally, really knew I would need to go. The response came back, "No, we need to move you, but the Denver Field Office is open, so how does that sound?" Frankly, it sounded like music to my ears, since it was another highly desired assignment, and another area I had never visited. However, not wanting to sound too delighted, I answered along the lines of, "Well, if I have to leave North Carolina, I'll gladly move to Denver and do my best." And so I began to make the preparations necessary to transition, once again, to a new home and assignment in the West, as SAC of the Denver FO.

CHAPTER 12

Denver

"Pikes Peak or Bust"

"PIKES PEAK OR BUST," of course, was the famous slogan and goal of early Americans seeking their fortune in the gold-rich hills of Colorado during the gold rush of the late 1800s. It also could have been mine as the family packed up into our two cars, with two cats and two dogs, and headed west from North Carolina. As allowed by FBI policy, I had already been house hunting and had a new home waiting for us. At the time, I honestly harbored no thoughts that this would be our "forever" home, but now it certainly appears to be a reality.

My new territory consisted of the two states of Colorado and Wyoming, officially referred to as the Denver Division or the Denver Field Office (FO). I frequently called it the Rocky Mountain Division, because of the sheer beauty and magnificence of its central feature. Driving across the wide and mostly flat state of Kansas en route, we expected to see mountains when we crossed into Colorado. Alas, it was several more miles of flatland before the front range of the Rockies started to appear in the distance, with a tinge of white leftover snow, and then the skyline of Denver appeared. What a beautiful sight it was, with the skyline perfectly laid out in front of the magnificent Rockies as its backdrop.

I felt very humble and happy to claim residence in the great state of Colorado, where, as this is written, I still reside. Upon arrival, I joined a FO staff of more than one hundred Special Agents (SAs), and a support complement of nearly an additional one hundred, in the two-state FO territory, with Headquarters located downtown in Denver's Federal Building. We also had Resident Agencies (RAs), in a number of Colorado and Wyoming cities. Scattered strategically in Colorado were six RAs, including Boulder, Colorado Springs, Durango, Fort Collins, Grand Junction, and Glenwood Springs. Part of the Denver FO in Wyoming included the RAs in Casper, Cheyenne, Rock Springs, and Riverton.

Outside of Denver Headquarters, the largest contingent of SAs were assigned in Colorado Springs, due to the heavy population and number of military bases in that territory. As with any FBI FO, the Division was responsible for the more than two hundred federal violations occurring within our jurisdiction in both the states. The office in Riverton, Wyoming, had a heavy caseload, with FBI violations occurring on the Wind River Indian Reservation in Wyoming, while the Durango RA in southwestern Colorado was almost fully occupied with violent crimes occurring on the Ute Mountain Ute and Southern Ute Indian Reservations in Colorado.

I arrived in Colorado in the late summer of 1986, and recall it was literally just in time to join a visit to Colorado Springs by the Attorney General of the United States, Ed Meese. As it was, my timing was perfect since I was able to share, with Attorney General Meese, probably the most comprehensive and security-sen-

A casual meeting with US Attorney General Edwin Meese.

sitive tour possible of Cheyenne Mountain, the fortress-like headquarters of the North American Aerospace Defense Command (NORAD), built directly into the mountain. Staying overnight on the campus of the US Air Force Academy, I experienced my first detailed tour of the academy, and my first academy football game (Air Force vs. Wyoming), with an impressive air force jet flyover and the flight of the huge falcon mascot. With that rather exciting and spectacular introduction to my new home state, the "work" end of my new assignment got started.

For such an expansive geographic territory, I realized travel time to visit and perform all the necessary functions throughout would be excessive (for example, a drive from Denver to Jackson, Wyoming, could easily consume more than eight hours). Fortunately, I had based in my territory a number of fixed-wing single- and multiengine aircraft, which assisted Denver and other western FOs with both tactical and transport capabilities. Better yet, I had a team of several FBI SA pilots, who were absolutely outstanding, and to whom I entrusted my life on many occasions. Anyone familiar with flying small planes over the spectacular, but windswept, Rockies, and particularly the always-windy Wyoming topography, could really appreciate the skill and expertise of the FBI pilots assigned to the Denver FO.

Just as in the Charlotte FO, the action came quick and often, and I determined early on that the SAs of the Denver FO were going to be very much up to the challenge.

I will discuss the problem of bank robbery in some detail in a later chapter, but want to deal right up-front with one particular bank robber who, in my early days and months in Denver, led me to characterize him as "my greatest nemesis." He challenged us to the max, caused us an incredible amount of work and frustration, and worried us more and more as he continued to rob banks. We had no idea of his real name, but knew him well only as the "Gentleman Bandit".

The Gentleman Bandit

When I arrived in my new assignment, the supervisory staff alerted me to the fact that Colorado was being plagued by an unknown, lone, white male bank robber, referred to as the "Gentleman Bandit." He was also suspected of robberies in several other states, including Washington, Pennsylvania, New York, Minnesota, Maryland, and Indiana. We weren't exactly sure of the total number at the time of my arrival, but in

retrospect, the number was around thirty-five, with at least half of them in Colorado. With each succeeding robbery, I would respond to the media that we were doing our best to identify and capture the Gentleman Bandit, about whose identity we frankly had no clue. Our leads were few and always went nowhere. Once outside the bank, the bandit seemed to be a vanishing phantom, and his capture became a frustrating personal challenge.

Gentleman Bandit in action.

The Gentleman Bandit's Description

The Gentleman Bandit first appeared at a bank robbery in Tipton, Pennsylvania, in May 1983. His first bank robbery in Colorado occurred at a Silverado Banking branch, in suburban Littleton, on April 9, 1984. He was described as a white male; about five foot eight inches tall; in his mid-thirties; with a moustache; wearing a wig, baseball cap, and dark glasses; carrying a shoulder bag; and wielding a large silver handgun. Some witnesses and victims described him as looking a bit like Tom Selleck, the TV and movie actor. He normally approached the bank and left on a stolen bicycle.

Method of Operation

He never robbed a bank with a guard inside. In his early robberies, he would get away taking car keys from a bank employee and using their car for his escape, that is until he ended up in a car with a dog at a bank robbery in Colorado Springs. Thereafter, he began using a bicycle. He got his nickname after a robbery in which one of the bank customers offered him money, and he politely refused, claiming he only wanted money from the bank. He was polite to bank employees, normally announcing, "Ladies, this is a robbery, put your money on the counter," and leaving with the wish that "everyone please have a nice day." He never spent more than a couple of minutes in the bank.

The Capture Plan

As time passed and the bank robberies continued, the Gentleman Bandit seemed to become more nervous, not as friendly, and during one robbery blurted out, when the employees were moving too slowly, "What do I have to do, shoot somebody to get action in here?" as he cocked his pistol. Frustrated, concerned, and determined, we decided essentially that enough was enough, since it was becoming obvious to us that more proactive action was needed to get the bandit off the streets. In addition to ordering an all-available SA response to every Gentleman Bandit–suspected robbery, around March of 1987 Supervisory Special Agent (SSA) Chuck Evans was selected to lead a group of SAs from Denver and our surrounding RAs in crafting a plan to capture him. They researched and studied the pattern for all the previous robberies, and ultimately identified thirty banks in Colorado as possible targets. They noted common factors; for example, the Gentleman Bandit normally hit during mid-afternoon between Wednesday and Friday. He hit small, one-story banks with no security guards, located close to malls with restaurants, from which he probably could observe the bank beforehand. He approached and left by bicycle.

SSA Evans and his group worked with dozens of law enforcement agencies and the banks identified as vulnerable. They recommended that the target banks hire off-duty police officers in plainclothes to act undercover as bank employees on certain days for certain hours Yes, this plan was costly for the cooperating banks, but they realized that the Gentleman Bandit had to be stopped before he caused any harm to their employees.

A Successful Plan

It took several weeks using the plan, although some Colorado banks, not participating, continued to get a costly visit from the robber. Ironically, the Silverado Banking branch on Coal Mine Road in Littleton (unincorporated Jefferson County) was part of the capture plan. In a weird, almost bizarre sense, it had been the very first Colorado bank to fall victim to him back on April 9, 1984. This was now October 7, 1987, and an off-duty Denver police officer named Edwin Morales was on duty, in plainclothes, inside the bank. It was late afternoon, and one of the bank employees observed a man on a bicycle approaching the branch, and warned the others that it looked like the Gentleman Bandit. Sure enough, after parking the bicycle against the building wall, the bandit entered with the greeting, "Ladies, this is a robbery, put the money on the counter." With that, Officer Morales announced "Police," the tellers all hit the floor, and the Gentleman Bandit turned his shiny silver pistol from the tellers location toward the officer. Before he could fire, two bullets took him down. He was airlifted to the closest hospital, and reportedly confessed to a nurse, while being wheeled into surgery, that he was Mel Dellinger, and he had robbed fifty banks. Melvin Dellinger passed away the following day without regaining consciousness.

Unmasking the Gentleman Bandit

Recovered at the crime scene were the blue bicycle, probably stolen, along with the silver handgun, which turned out to be a Smith and Wesson, model 39, 9mm pistol with a wooden grip. The weapon was fully loaded, cocked with a round in the chamber. He also had a note in his pocket with his name, telephone number, location of his red Toyota parked nearby, and a request to tell his wife he was sorry, claiming she knew nothing of his activities and thought

Unmasked as Mel Dellinger

he was a traveling carpet salesman. We also recovered his brown wig, his blue baseball cap, a Seiko quartz watch, and his gray Oleg Cassini shoulder bag. The watch aided in implicating him in several previous bank robberies, since it matched perfectly with the watch in earlier surveillance photographs of the Gentleman Bandit.

Subsequent to his death, both background investigations by the FBI and the media produced a volume of information and newspaper articles, portraying Melvin Dellinger as a very complicated individual, who, for all intents and purposes, had indeed lived two separate lives.

Dellinger was born June 6, 1953, in Mechanicsburg, Pennsylvania, to a carpet-layer father and a hotel-maid mother. Growing up, he was variously described as being very kind and polite when necessary, but also capable of living on the edge with others, able to drink, smoke, and engage in illegal activities. His teachers described him as everything from smart to brilliant, and a dedicated follower of the famous writer Ernest Hemingway, whom he wanted to model.

He made his way into the US Army, and was in a program at Fort Rucker, Alabama, to become a helicopter pilot. While there he was apparently failing exams and was jilted by a girlfriend, so he decided to rob a movie theater of $552 with a toy gun. He was caught, placed on probation, and kicked out of the US Army. A few days later, he showed up in St. Louis, Missouri, and attempted to rob a bank, pretending to be part of a terrorist group who had the bank surrounded, with him in the bank carrying a briefcase loaded with explosives. He was captured leaving the bank, sentenced in 1975 to ten years in prison, but he was paroled in 1979, described as a model prisoner. However, while in prison, Dellinger apparently learned about his mistakes from other prisoners, and reportedly made statements that bank robbery was the "ultimate crime," and that he could be perfectly successful, if he followed his new policy and two rules: one, tell absolutely nobody and two, don't get caught in the bank.

After his parole in 1979, he met and married a woman named Lucy Jordan, who made good money selling medical equipment. Living off of her income, the couple moved to State College, Pennsylvania, and Mel enrolled at Penn State University. He apparently developed a reasonably expensive taste in clothing and jewelry, and made occasional trips to New York City, courtesy of Lucy's income. One of his professors at Penn

State described Mel as a very interesting guy "who knew what he was doing and what he wanted in life." He was credited with a thesis, while in college, entitled "White Trash in the Promised Land," about a poor teenager in search of himself. It won a university award. Others at Penn State described him as streetwise with lots of life experience. He also apparently developed a taste for other women. After obtaining his college degree in advertising from the Penn State School of Journalism in August 1983, he told his wife he needed freedom and was moving to Denver. They then got divorced.

Although some information indicated a move to Denver sometime in 1983, after his graduation from Penn State, records tend to show he might have lingered in Pennsylvania a bit longer. In fact, he probably initiated his new notorious career there, even before his graduation in the summer of 1983. For example, as early as May 26, 1983, an armed robber with dark glasses, baseball cap, and a shiny silver pistol entered the First Blair County Bank in Tipton, Pennsylvania, and "politely" asked the tellers for all their small bills. He touched nothing except the money, and hurriedly left after a couple of minutes. It was probably then that the adventures of the Gentleman Bandit had begun. Other bank robberies continued in Pennsylvania through the end of 1983 and early 1984, while the first bandit robbery in Colorado didn't occur until April 1984.

After arrival in Colorado, Dellinger met and eventually married a new wife, Elizabeth Zwinak, and settled into a $550-per-month rental home in a quiet Denver neighborhood. They were a quiet, gentle couple, highly liked and trusted by their neighbors. In fact, they were the go-to people whom neighbors asked to watch their houses when they planned to leave for periods of time. Dellinger was gone frequently, but left neighbors and his own wife thinking he was a traveling carpet salesman. He apparently also told some neighbors that he was a writer and consultant, to explain his travels. When home in Denver, he carefully tended his neat yard and maintained an orderly, uncluttered household. Neighbors mentioned that a few weeks before what was to become his final bank robbery, on October 7, he had some pumpkins for Halloween placed around his house, and made the effort of delivering a few to some of the neighbors.

In furnishing some of the Gentleman Bandit details to the public after his death, many questions were asked about the nearly half-million dollars in loot he had accumulated. Unfortunately, no sizable amount of cash was ever located. We found some expensive clothing, computers, camera equipment, and ski equipment in the rented house. We also determined he had developed an expensive taste in dining and gambling, with frequent travels to Las Vegas and New Jersey, where he rented cars and stayed in upscale hotels. He was even a preferred customer at Caesar's Palace Casino in Las Vegas. We basically concluded that he had spent nearly all his stolen loot, while enjoying "the good life."

Of his fifty robberies, twenty-seven of them occurred in Colorado, and the total number placed him third for bank robberies by a single perpetrator at that time. Edward Dodson, known as the "Yankee Bandit" with his New York Yankees baseball cap, committed more at sixty-four between 1983 and 1984. Also, a gentleman named Gilbert James Everett committed fifty-three robberies between 1980 and 1985. As Dellinger continued to increase his robbery number, I often wondered, as he began to appear more nervous and more threatening, yet refused to change his methods and even removed his dark glasses in the last few robberies – was he taunting us to catch him, did he want to get caught, or did he just want to score the record number of bank robberies? We will never know, but one thing we do know, he violated one of his two basic rules – he got caught in the bank! He had been careful, but also very lucky. On that day his luck ran out.

In retrospect, I give a huge amount of the credit for the Gentleman Bandit's downfall to SSA Evans and his team, who put together the successful capture plan. Looking back at this case, an interesting quote came to mind again, as it had earlier in North Carolina, when we took down the Lumbee Indian bank robbery gang. Recalling the words and comment attributed to General George Patton in WWII as he lay in wait for German General Erwin Rommel, the Desert Fox, in a decisive trap, and uttered the famous words, "Rommel, you magnificent bastard, I read your book." In this case, we could certainly make the assertion to the Gentleman Bandit, "Mel Dellinger – we read your book!" I just wish that he wouldn't have made it end so tragically.

The fateful Silverado Banking branch in Littleton is no longer there. Neither is a McDonald's Restaurant, directly across the parking lot, which might have been the observation point for Dellinger, as he prepared to conduct his last robbery. They were both quite close to my residence in Littleton, and I frequently pass the location, thinking each time about the life and death of the Gentleman Bandit.

Like every FBI FO, in addition to bank robberies we would always need to be in a posture to respond immediately to any and all violent crimes occurring within the dozens of classifications under our statutory responsibility. We handled these instances as "reactive" crimes on one side of the house, and these included such crimes as kidnapping, bombings, hostage situations, and dangerous fugitives, which always occur without warning and are unpredictable. On the other side of the house, we can be more "proactive" in addressing criminal and security areas, based on the analysis of trends and problems, weighed against the realistic allocation of our existing resources. Shortly after arrival, based on case reviews and staff meetings, I determined that white collar crime (WCC), with its fraud, corruption, and environmental crime connections, along with the burgeoning and massive drug trafficking activities, would be our two highest priorities.

White Collar Crime

In February 1987, one of our corruption investigations bore fruit when the former vice president of Colorado's Public Service Company, the state's largest utility, which provided power to Colorado and parts of Wyoming, was indicted. He and three others were charged with defrauding Public Service out of more than $1 million in contract kickbacks over a period of more than seventeen years. This was worked with Internal Revenue Service investigators, and included charges of racketeering, conspiracy, mail fraud, and income tax violations. It involved activities at the Fort St. Vrain Nuclear Power Plant, near Platteville, Colorado, which was shut down in 1989.

In April 1987, a west Denver chemical company called Protex Industries and its executive officers were indicted on charges of illegal dumping of hazardous materials and causing knowing endangerment to their employees. This culminated a yearlong investigation, worked with agents of the US Environmental Protection Agency (EPA). The resulting conviction brought a fine in excess of $6 million, and we were advised that it was the first federal conviction in the United States that also charged causing knowing endangerment to employees.

By December 1988, based on the Protex case and others, the Denver FO was recognized by FBI Headquarters (FBIHQ) for taking a leading role in attacking the illegal toxic waste dumping problem in the country. We were advised that in 1987 there were 130 probes nationwide, with a sizable percentage initiated by our FO. That year we had forty-one indictments, possibly attributed to the fact that folks in the western United States have a great interest in protecting the environment, and were forthcoming with solid public support and many tips. I'm sure our success also had much to do with the collaboration approach and expertise we received from the EPA investigators. Since 1982, the FBI had received authority to assist the EPA with criminal investigations, and we also found this relationship exceptional, and a real winner for the general public.

In November 1987, SAs in Wyoming, working with the US Attorney's Office in Cheyenne, were responsible for the indictment of four prominent Wyoming banking executives and lawyers for defrauding several banks in Wyoming and Nebraska out of approximately $20 million. The federal charges in this case included wire fraud, misapplication of savings and loan funds, and false statements to federal and state banking authorities.

In December 1988, Denver SAs took down arguably the largest Ponzi scheme in Colorado history up to that time. A gentleman named Marvin Morrison had been promising returns over 200 percent to more than one hundred investors in twenty-one states, over a period from 1982 to 1988. He was operating a commodities trading scam, and collected reportedly $6 million for commodity trades, which never happened. It becomes a Ponzi operation when the scammer uses money from later investors to pay off earlier ones, if requested. Apparently, in this scheme, few, if any, investors asked to cash out, while the scammer diverted millions of dollars to his personal purchase of real estate, expensive jewelry, and a stable of expensive, upscale cars. Sadly, I'm sure other WCC-minded scammers would argue that twelve years in prison, with probability of early parole for good behavior, is not so bad for all that wealth and easy living.

In August 1989, a government accountant for the US Department of Housing and Urban Development (HUD) in Colorado was indicted for a $1-million embezzlement from his agency, which was diverted to his personal account for the purchase of a luxury home, real estate, and stocks. Unfortunately, cases such as this were merely the prelude to what hit the national financial markets at the end of 1989, and hit them hard!

By the end of 1989, we were experiencing the perfect storm of financial crimes committed by insiders and outsiders against financial institutions, leading to what was commonly referred to as the "S&L (Savings and Loan) Crisis." Illegal activity and apparent mismanagement allowing bad loans were leading to widespread failure of numerous financial institutions. Suddenly, the SAs of the Denver FO were faced with one hundred and twenty major criminal financial investigations. We had twenty failed banks and savings and loan institutions, and about one hundred cases involving bank fraud and embezzlement over $100,000, in the two states of Colorado and Wyoming. For some reason, we seemed to be squarely in the epicenter of the problem, sharing the high number of bank failures with Oklahoma, Texas, and California. Needless to say, these investigations were extremely complex, some requiring months and even years to complete, usually by multiple SAs.

We needed and asked for help, and Congress and FBIHQ responded with increased resources. The Denver FO received eight additional SAs and four accounting specialists to beef up our financial fraud investigative teams. For a sustained period of time, I would estimate that 35 to 40 percent of our SAs were working financial fraud against failed banking institutions.

Our first results in this initiative came in December 1989, with the indictment of the former president of the failed Buena Vista Bank and Trust. In May 1990, he was convicted of misapplication of funds and false statements, and received a seven-year prison term. However, to provide some idea of the effort required, that case involved fifteen SAs and a review of an entire room full of documents and records.

Interestingly, in 1989, the Failed Thrift Bailout Program, which we called the "S&L Bailout Act," was successfully passed in Congress and did provide us some useful tools in working these cases. In 1990, we successfully used the new law to seize two vehicles in a failed bank case. In 1991, we utilized the law to seize three mortgage companies that were involved in illegally diverting nearly $18 million from a failed Colorado thrift in 1988.

One of the huge losses for a Wyoming institution involved the United Savings Bank of Wyoming in Cheyenne. In September 1991, three former officers were indicted for fraud and losses costing taxpayers approximately $90 million. The bank became insolvent and closed in December 1988. This investigation was worked jointly by the FBI, IRS, and the Office of Thrift Supervision, which had been created by the savings and loan debacle.

In October 1990, we participated in an interstate financial fraud investigation involving three financial institutions in Florida. Twenty-three Coloradans, out of more than thirty individuals in California, Arizona, and New York, were indicted in a massive real estate kickback scheme, with losses exceeding $5 million. Those indicted were charged with racketeering and bank fraud, as they received kickbacks as phony buyers in the purchase of forty-four condominium units in Florida, of which forty eventually went into default. US Attorney General Dick Thornburgh appeared personally at a press conference in Tallahassee, Florida, and announced the indictments and arrests, calling this case one of the broadest financial institution fraud schemes ever prosecuted up to that time.

Despite the full-time dedication of the large contingent of SAs working financial institution fraud and failures in those years, other Denver FO SAs were kept busy working a wide variety of other major WCC cases.

In June 1990, Wyoming SAs, working with agents of the EPA, turned up their own version of an important case involving illegal dumping of hazardous waste. UNICHEM International Inc. made and supplied chemical products for the oil industry. For the previous two years, they had apparently been storing, treating, and disposing of hazardous waste in the Casper, Wyoming, area, without any required permit. The result was a fine exceeding $1 million, the largest for such a violation in Wyoming up to that time.

In April 1990, also on the Wyoming front, and in the corruption area, SAs participated, along with the Wyoming Attorney General, the Division of Criminal Investigation, the Wyoming Secretary of State, and US Postal Inspectors, in what was described by the Wyoming US Attorney Richard Stacy as an investigation involving the first high ranking public official in Wyoming to be accused of corruption. The former Wyoming insurance commissioner, Gordon Taylor, was arrested for receiving bribes in exchange for doing official favors for two insurance companies.

In November 1990, back in Colorado, four real estate brokers in Denver were arrested for conspiring to defraud the US Department of Housing and Urban Development (HUD), by falsely obtaining $2.91 million in government-insured loans for thirty-nine homes in the Colorado Springs area. They were charged with false employer verifications, false deposit verifications, and other false documentation.

HUD, obviously a favorite target of fraudsters, was victimized again in 1991, resulting in thirteen persons indicted in April 1991 from Colorado, California, New Mexico, and Texas (nine of them from Colorado), for crimes involving wire and mail fraud. This was a joint investigation with the IRS, HUD investigators, and US Postal Inspectors into a criminal activity that caused foreclosure of loans on sixty condominiums, and loss of about $4 million to HUD.

In April 1991, we also surfaced a two-year undercover operation dubbed PENNYCON, involving fraud in the penny stock trading area. It involved primarily brokers and traders manipulating trades to artificially inflate the value of penny stocks. Activities involved trading in Colorado, New York, Florida, and California, and resulted in eighteen persons indicted for conspiracy, securities fraud, and wire and mail fraud.

The last case I will mention in the WCC area involved, arguably, one of the largest investor frauds in history. A Denver area money manager named James Donahue operated a Ponzi scheme over a twelve-year period in Englewood, Colorado, which netted about $316 million from about twelve hundred investors. He promised returns of 15 to 20 percent, never had to produce a financial statement, and lost millions in risky trades on hedged investments and stock options. In August 1991, after more than a one-year joint investigation by Denver SAs, the US Attorney in Denver, the IRS, US Postal Inspectors, the Securities and Exchange Commission, and the Colorado Division of Securities, he was arrested and later entered a guilty plea.

Drugs

While Denver FO SAs assigned to WCC matters found themselves up to their eyeballs, immersed in bank failures, scams, and frauds of all types, other squads, both in Colorado and Wyoming, found the pursuit of illegal drug trafficking groups fertile, daunting, and often dangerous. Some organizations were delivering to final destinations and end users in our two states, while others were using cities in the Rockies as cross-shipment points for distribution to the East Coast and other US destinations. Some drugs were "homegrown," or made in the states, but most were being smuggled in from countries south of the United States by air, land, and sea. As with the large and complex WCC cases, nearly every drug investigation was worked jointly with federal agencies, such as the DEA, or local police and sheriffs' offices. After "incubation" periods of several months, as SAs began to focus on drug trafficking as a high priority, results, using both undercover techniques and hard-pressed traditional investigations, started to come.

In March 1988, after an eighteen-month joint federal and local Denver area investigation involving Colorado and six other states and the country of Panama, ten individuals were indicted for a cocaine operation, and approximately $1.1 million worth of cocaine, cash, gold and silver coins, along with four cars, were recovered. This case took down a nearly $3.5-million cocaine network.

A few months later, in July 1988, the arrest of two men from Aspen, Colorado, resulted from a massive illegal marijuana operation, involving boatloads of marijuana containing thousands of pounds from at least 1977 to 1984 in Florida, New England, California, and Colorado. This was part of a ring of more than fifty individuals, distributing marijuana with an estimated combined street value of more than $90 million.

A few months after that, in October 1988, SAs, working with Adams County Sheriff's Office, Colorado, detectives, took down five principals and recovered three hundred pounds of marijuana, after a one-year investigation involving a ten-year active Mexican drug ring. The following month, November 1988, another Denver investigation scored a number of arrests and recovery of a large amount of Mexican black tar heroin, a very expensive and powerful drug in those days.

Press conference with Sheriff Ed Camp, Adams County, Colorado, to announce a major drug arrest.

In August 1989, a two-year undercover operation, worked jointly with the Denver Police Department (DPD), surfaced with fifteen arrests. We referred to this thirty-to-forty-kilo-per-month cocaine ring as the "Yuppie Drug Ring," which operated out of a health club and catered to the upper-middle class physical fitness buffs. The take-down also netted more than $1.3 million in property seized, including two motorhomes, fifteen vehicles, four houses, a speedboat, $50,000 worth of health exercise equipment, and nearly a quarter million dollars in cash.

To finish out the 1980s, in December 1989, a federal, state, and local task force, run by the US Attorney's office in Denver, successfully indicted and arrested thirty-one different suspects from Colombia, South America; California; and Colorado. This was a major blow against a trafficking organization dealing in more than five hundred kilos of cocaine.

Success came again quickly in the 1990s, when in February 1990, a joint undercover effort with the Denver Police Department, Thornton Police Department, and the Colorado Bureau of Investigation resulted in five arrests involving members of a Mexican organization moving forty kilos of cocaine and a volume of marijuana into Colorado each month. It was also very costly to the bad guys, since, in addition to a large amount of cash, investigators seized four houses, gold and silver coins, five race horses, and eleven vehicles.

Later that same month, it was the Boulder Police Department's turn to uncover a major Mexican marijuana operation, at that time described as one of the largest such operations in the United States. Worked ultimately by a large federal, state, and local task force, this case determined that the group had been saturating the country with thousands of pounds of marijuana, by truck and plane, for more than a decade. To give some significance to how successful they had been in accumulating and investing their wealth, I think it would be instructive to list just some of the items seized from a parade of searches in storage lockers in Boulder, Aurora, and Englewood, Colorado, and safety deposit boxes in Denver and Englewood, Colorado. You might call this the granddaddy of them all or a king's ransom, or perhaps a pirate's treasure. Here are some of the items:

- Sacks of rare gold coins and nuggets
- Buckets of silver dollars
- Sapphires, rubies, and diamonds
- Persian rugs and antique furniture
- A Grover Cleveland $1,000 dollar bill, as well as thousands of dollars of cash
- Rare collector stamps
- Dozens of guns of all types – including a pearl-handled and gold-plated revolver, an antique Winchester rifle, automatic and semiautomatic long guns, and assorted handguns
- Original Indian art and antiques
- Expensive jewelry and silverware
- Hundreds of pounds of marijuana and hashish

There were other major drug cases worked successfully during my time in the Denver FO, mainly involving cocaine, crack cocaine, black tar heroin, or marijuana (the most popular drugs in those days), but those highlighted here should give a sense of the problem and how Colorado law enforcement joined together to meet the challenge.

Although not major cases, I will also mention two other drug-related and very interesting situations that our SAs encountered.

In July 1990, a gentleman contacted our Durango, Colorado, RA, and admitted being a middleman in a twenty-five-kilo cocaine transaction involving the Hells Angels motorcycle gang in southern California. He had delivered the cocaine to the gang in exchange for $168,000, which was delivered to the supplier. Soon, he received a death threat from the gang, demanding their money back claiming the "cocaine" was actually pancake mix. He contended that he tried in vain to convince the Hells Angels it was not a rip-off, but now believed there was a contract out to have him killed. Our SAs were able to set up an undercover sting operation, which resolved the drug case, and arrested a Hells Angels associate as the intended hitman for the contract killing.

In January 1991, one of our Cheyenne, Wyoming, SAs was off-duty, returning to Cheyenne from a trip out of state. He was negotiating an icy strip of I-80, located near the Utah border in Rock Springs, Wyoming, when a Ford Ranger pickup truck slid into his vehicle, causing minor damage. During the exchange of driver and vehicle information, The SA became suspicious of the other driver, followed him into a nearby rest area, and radioed the Wyoming Highway Patrol. The responding trooper was able to determine that the driver had a suspended driver's license, and the vehicle contained a sizable amount of cocaine and a semiautomatic handgun. Of course, this led to a much broader investigation. The takeaway for us, and also probably the bad guy – "Be careful whose car you slide into on an icy roadway!"

A Few Other Cases from the "Not So Ordinary" Group

In December 1986, a robber appeared at the apartment of the vault supervisor for the United Bank of Denver, strapped a "bomb" on him, ordered him to go to the bank and pick up more than $2 million in negotiable bonds, and then drop them at a certain location. The bank officer did comply, but while in the bank notified a bank employee exactly what was happening. After dropping the bonds off as ordered, he returned to his apartment to waiting FBI SAs and Denver police, who dismantled the fake bomb, which was really a walkie talkie–type device with some wires. A rather speedy investigation identified the robber and traced him to Panama, where he was arrested trying to sell the stolen bonds to a broker. Within a few months, a secretary at the Colorado Division of Banking was arrested for aiding and abetting the robber by counseling him about how to commit the robbery and convert the bonds to cash. Certainly, not your usual method to rob a bank, but that was what authorities then claimed as the largest bank robbery in Colorado history.

In August 1987, a situation occurred in an important case, which highlights the absolute importance of timing when exposing the results of an investigation to the media. For a full three years, we had been conducting an undercover operation with the US Customs Service out of a cover business in the Golden, Colorado, area. It was called Operation Aspen Leaf, and its purpose was to stop the flow of sensitive US technology to communist countries. The cover company was well organized and run. It actually made about $250,000 in legitimate business, shipping military and high-tech goods to other countries. In doing business, they would always warn foreign importers about US export laws prohibiting shipping to Soviet bloc countries. As anticipated, eventually they would be asked to alter shipping orders to facilitate shipping goods to prohibited nations. For example, in one case a request was made to ship prohibited items to North Korea via Singapore. Ultimately, cases were built on various "trading with the enemy" laws involving shipments to Bulgaria, North Korea, and Cuba. Five Europeans, including four from West Germany and one from Austria, were charged, but arrests in the continental United States were thought to be too difficult to arrange. Instead, the subjects were invited to a Caribbean vacation and meeting in Puerto Rico, which was successful in drawing them to Puerto Rico for arrests.

We notified the media of a press conference on August 10, 1987, and indicated it would be of important national significance. We intended to announce the operations and arrests but, more importantly, to send a message that such trading with the enemy is a serious crime, and being carefully monitored by federal law enforcement. The electronic and print media showed up en masse for the press conference.

With all the cameras and equipment in place and set up, the press conference commenced. Unfortunately, after a few minutes, there was noticeable rustling among the press, all cameras came down, all equipment was packed, and all but a few hurriedly left. "Unfortunate" was indeed the right word, because all attendees had just been alerted by their stations and assignment desks to a massive tragedy. A sightseeing bus, traveling through Berthoud Pass on US Route 40, about sixty miles northwest of Denver, had been literally pulverized by a falling several-ton boulder. One entire side of the bus had been sliced open, leaving seven dead and fifteen seriously injured. There could be no blame for the press action; it was a terrible accident, and the timing literally neutralized any impact to the message we had hoped to impart. There were a few news articles written, but obviously nothing like the coverage we expected.

Then again, if you happened to be around Colorado Springs, Colorado, about 1 a.m. on November 11, 1987, you might have seen an army tank slowly motoring north on I-25 toward Denver. Well, it looked like a tank, but it was really a twenty-six-ton, self-propelled 155 mm M-109 Howitzer Cannon tracked vehicle, valued at $258,000. It slowly motored the eighty miles to Denver at about fifteen to twenty miles per hour, and ended up on a city street, when it ran out of fuel. Officers in the law enforcement convoy or parade of vehicles following the Howitzer then took the two drivers (one army and one civilian) peacefully into custody. The Howitzer had been stolen from a motor pool in Fort Carson, south of Colorado Springs and driven over a field and through a barbed wire fence surrounding Fort Carson. We got involved because of the civilian driver, who was charged with theft of government property.

In April 1990, a bizarre case unfolded, involving a self-described photographer named Gordon Larry Hood from Atlanta, Georgia. Hood arrived in Denver, hired a local pilot, and chartered a twin-engine plane, allegedly to do some mountain photography around the beautiful Longs Peak area near Boulder, Colorado. The plane crashed in Boulder, killing both Hood and pilot Bill Layne, of Aurora, Colorado. The FBI got involved to determine if any federal crime was committed. Extensive background information was developed, including various stories that Hood had told to others in the Atlanta area before traveling to Colorado. However, the bottom line, after all inquiries, indicated that the motive for Hood's actions was simply a sad and misguided plan orchestrated to commit suicide, and the homicide of the pilot was just collateral damage to him.

In December 1990, and again in June 1991, in two separate cases, I was proud and privileged to have my office adorned, albeit briefly, with two different valuable pieces of art. In the first case, we recovered a painting by the nineteenth- and twentieth-century artist William Robinson Leigh, entitled *Rainbow Bridge by Moonlight*. It was valued at $125,000, and it had been stolen in a burglary at an auction house. We got involved since it was federal property, belonging to the Federal Deposit Insurance Corporation, which was auctioning it as property recovered and then being liquidated from one of the failed Littleton, Colorado, banks. The other case involved a painting by the famous nineteenth-century naturalist painter John James Audubon. It was entitled *Head of a Buffalo Calf* and was painted in 1843. It belonged to a very elderly gentleman in Cincinnati, Ohio, whose housekeeper falsely reported to the owner that it had been accidentally destroyed in a minor fire in the house. The housekeeper then posed as the owner's niece and offered it for sale. It was purchased by a legitimate Denver art dealer for $80,000. The FBI received a tip about its true circumstances, arrested the housekeeper and recovered the painting.

Finally, I want to finish this first part of my FBI experiences in the Denver FO with a Wyoming case that illustrates the wide diversity of our jurisdiction. Seldom would an FBI SA find himself or herself called to investigate a car accident. However, crimes of a felony nature on an Indian Reservation fall under the FBI's jurisdiction, and such an investigation could, and did, happen on the Wind River Indian Reservation in July 1991. A twenty-seven-year-old male from the reservation, operating a 1971 Ford pickup, rolled the vehicle, ejecting himself and his nine-year-old stepson, who was killed. We investigated the crash, along with the Wyoming Highway Patrol and the Bureau of Indian Affairs. The driver was charged with involuntary manslaughter, operating his vehicle under the influence of intoxicants, and wanton disregard for human life.

And now on to the rest of the Denver story.

CHAPTER 13

Denver

The Good, the Sad, and Moving On

IT SEEMED THAT IF A SERIOUS public safety matter was involved, we would be there. Looking back at my career, and especially my career as an FBI Special Agent in Charge (SAC), it would be correct to observe that the role and jurisdiction of the FBI extended, in one respect or another, into nearly every major public safety initiative. Whether in an active investigation mode, or in support of other local, county, state, or federal agencies, we would usually be involved.

Back in Washington, D.C., at FBI Headquarters (FBIHQ) in 1986, getting briefed by the various Division officials as to current activities and priorities in the Denver FO, it became clear that I could expect similar higher profile events and occurrences than I had experienced in North Carolina. As it turned out, many of the predicted events were indeed encountered and worked as investigations discussed in Chapter 12. However, other types of challenges were also to be faced and tackled by SAs in Colorado and Wyoming, and always in a most capable and professional manner. Unfortunately, some of these other unexpected and unforeseen events ended in tragic circumstances.

One of my new roles became clear during one of my last meetings at FBIHQ – a meeting with Director William Webster, who preferred to be called Judge William Webster. Judge Webster asked me a question, which I thought was partly in jest: "Bob, do you know how to ski?" "No," I responded. "Growing up in rural western Pennsylvania, I never had an opportunity to ski in my life." Then I knew he was not joking when he explained how important skiing is in my new territory, and how the FBI will be responsible for counterterrorism deployments at many high profile ski competitions. He reminded me of the many world-class ski areas in the Rocky Mountains, particularly those that traditionally host international ski events. As I left that meeting, I looked ahead, with no small amount of trepidation, knowing that one of my unexpected, but urgent, priorities after arrival in Colorado would be to learn to ski at the first snow. As a matter of fact, shortly after I arrived in Denver, Judge Webster called and asked if I had learned to ski yet. I wanted to say, "Are you kidding, it's still August," but recall responding that it hadn't snowed yet, but that I would tackle the mission as soon as the mountains turned white.

As fate would have it, in the late fall or early winter, and after a couple early snows, Judge Webster was a featured speaker at a national conference of the prestigious Young Presidents Organization, held in Vail, Colorado. A security team and I met Judge Webster at the Denver airport and transported him to Vail. Our team included SA Mike Stuart, a qualified ski instructor. After his presentation, Judge Webster stayed for a few days to network with other VIPs, including actor Robert Redford (whom I also had the honor to meet), and enjoy some personal skiing.

As I had feared, the Director then personally decided to stand by while I suited up with my newly purchased ski outfit, rented ski boots, and rented skis. SA Stuart was to be my instructor, and I vividly recall simply trying to stand upright on the sliding skis, and this was on level ground, at a spot directly under the gondola ski lift at Vail Mountain. Looking up the steep mountain, where the gondola rose at least a mile to the top, I was told there was a reasonably flat area at the top, hosting some gentle children's bunny slopes for learning. Mike promised if I gave him two or three days at the top, he would then have me skiing all the way down to the base. I think I uttered something like, "That will be the day! No way!" Judge Webster concurred with Mike and left us to ski for a while on his own, as Mike and I climbed into one of the gondola cars and made it to the top of the mountain. Staggering out of the gondola, I immediately encountered the short green (elementary) runs near the flat gentle slopes, where beginners get their first taste of downhill skiing.

To say that the next three days were fun and exhilarating would be far from the truth. Navigating even the slightest downhill angles was scary, frustrating, and painful. Long story short, after more falls than I could count and clumsy attempts to get back up on those two slippery sliding slabs, I began to get it. Then, true as Mike had predicted, on the afternoon of the third day, I assumed the extreme "snowplow" mode, by keeping my ski tips pointed closely together, and approached the edge of the long green run, which ran down the mountain all the way to the base. With Mike at my side, I actually snowplowed, with a few falls and very slowly, all the way to the base of the gondola run. With that bit of experience and confidence behind me, I never really looked back. In retrospect, I should look back with pride and satisfaction that I am probably the only FBI SA who ever learned to ski under the caring and watchful eye of the Director of the FBI!

For the rest of my time in the Denver FO, I probably skied more than twenty-five days per season as part of our security coverage of major national and international ski events in Colorado. In addition to covering the actual events, it was essential that our tactical and support personnel became familiar with the layout of all the major ski areas, tested our radio coverage, and developed the ability to operate snowmobiles and other critical equipment. Judge Webster was right on target with his comments about how important skiing was to the operations of the Denver FO, and I credit him profusely for launching my "skiing career."

Although I reported to the Denver FO in 1986, I learned on arrival that planning was already well underway for security coverage of the 1989 World Alpine Ski Championships, to be hosted in Vail and Beaver Creek ski areas in Colorado from February 2–12, 1989. Meetings were frequent, and operations would ultimately involve not only the FBI but also police departments and sheriffs' offices in the Rocky Mountain area, as well as the Colorado State Patrol, US State Department Security, and some military units. Thousands of participants and visitors from dozens of countries would ultimately arrive for the events, and hundreds of law enforcement personnel would be deployed to handle crowd control, heavy traffic, and especially to protect everyone from violence and possible terrorism.

In addition to tactical and special support SAs from our

With Vail Police and FBI Agents during the 1989 World Alpine ski events.

FO, FBIHQ supported us as a "special event" and sent the personnel and technological assistance that we requested. In the end, the countless hours of careful preparation, massive deployment of critical manpower, and whole-hearted cooperation of the many agencies, coordinated by the host Vail Police Department, paid off with no major security problems.

However, sadly and unfortunately, the event was not to be without deadly tragedy. On the second day of competition, a visiting member of the International Ski Federation, Duke Alfonso de Borbon y de Dampierre from Spain decided to ski the downhill course at Beaver Creek as darkness fell and the day's races were completed. He apparently could not see the cable stretched across the ski run at the closed finished line, and died instantly when his head hit the cable.

As predicted, ski areas and attendance at related events would continue to involve occasional contact with leading government officials and other celebrities. I had a number of opportunities to meet briefly with former President Gerald Ford and his security detail, since he was almost a regular at major ski championships and maintained a residence near one of the ski lifts at Beaver Creek. Interestingly, I can't ever remember meeting President Ford when he wasn't attired in a ski outfit.

Meeting with President Ford during a ski event.

There happened to be one incident that involved President Ford during which he was not at his home in Beaver Creek; in fact, he was not even in Colorado. We were covering an important ski championship at the Beaver Creek ski area, and I was sitting on the mountain, having a discussion with Eagle County Sheriff A. J. Johnson, whose department has jurisdiction for Beaver Creek. Suddenly, he got an urgent call that a burglar alarm had been activated at President Ford's residence. Unfortunately, he realized that all his deputies were currently handling traffic and other responsibilities at the base of the mountain and on the highway. Seeing that Sheriff Johnson was in a bind to get a rapid response to the alarm, I offered to send a couple of SAs who were with me on the mountain. Not your everyday occurrence for FBI SAs to respond to a burglar alarm, but Sheriff Johnson appreciated the assistance. When we got to the residence, the butler, who answered the door, was more than shocked. As we all suspected, it was a false alarm, set off mistakenly by the butler who apologized profusely. He explained that President Ford was at his California residence, and offered us a quick tour of the Beaver Creek residence and a nice cup of tea.

Incidentally, the leader of the US Secret Service security detail for President Ford during our meetings at ski championships was Larry Buendorf, who later became the chief security officer for the US Olympic Committee in Colorado Springs. He served there for many years after President Ford passed away in December 2006 at his Rancho Mirage, California, home.

In connection with a social affair during another ski championship in Vail, I was invited to a banquet by John Denver, the iconic singer who loved Colorado. The requested attire for the evening was unique – tuxedo shirt, tie, and jacket, over blue jeans and cowboy boots. Of course, John was the headline entertainer and host for the event. John was the face of Colorado in the world of rock and country singing and songwriting. He had a very clean, wholesome image, and a personal love for airplanes. On October 12, 1997, he was practicing takeoffs and landings in a newly purchased experimental-type airplane, maintained at the Monterey Peninsula Airport in Monterey, California. While flying at only about five hundred feet over nearby Monterey Bay, the plane suddenly nose-dived and broke up hitting the water in a tragic accident, killing John. His home was Aspen, Colorado, and his final resting place is in his beloved Rocky Mountains, over which his ashes were scattered. Coincidently, years later in 2014, after my retirement, I was on the Monterey Peninsula in connection with a consulting project and riding with the gentleman who had been the police chief in Pacific Grove, California, at the time of the accident. He was kind enough to point out for me the exact spot just off the Monterey Bay coast where the plane went down. Ironically, it was almost walking distance from the location along the coast where I had lived years earlier when I attended the Defense Language Institute, learning the Chinese Cantonese language for the FBI.

Speaking of the popular mountain city of Aspen, Colorado, the Aspen Security Forum draws a collection of world leaders from government, the security industry, and journalism annually to discuss major world security problems of the current day. At the 1990 summer gathering, I happened to be speaking briefly with visiting US President George H. W. Bush, when the British Prime Minister Margaret Thatcher, passed by, and I was able to be quickly introduced to her. I felt quite honored to be introduced by one head of state to another.

Certainly, the beautiful Rocky Mountains and especially, the upscale resorts and ski areas have their allure for celebrities and political leaders, but so does the mile-high city of Denver, as I quickly found out. Shortly after I arrived, President Ronald Reagan and his wife, Nancy, made a visit in September 1986. I was among the party meeting them at the Denver airport. Not having seen them since their emotional visit to Camp Lejeune, North Carolina, in November 1983, when they arrived to meet with the families of the

Welcoming President and Nancy Reagan to Denver along with Colorado US Attorney Robert Miller.

Marines killed in Beirut, Lebanon, it was good to greet them briefly in a more pleasant atmosphere.

The next year, in July 1987, the Reverend Billy Graham brought a major crusade to Denver for ten days. It was an immense honor and pleasure for my family and me to be invited to spend some private time with him to discuss personal matters. We were invited to his quarters on one of the evenings, prior to his message to a mass audience in the Denver Mile High Stadium. As I've expressed, while speaking to many audiences in later years, conversing with Reverend Graham was always an incredibly motivating experience. As he sat calmly in a straight-backed folding chair, with his long, lanky legs crossed and a caring smile, his confidence and positive thinking comments inspired us with every word. As I've written earlier, being with him always left me with a glowing feeling that I was in the presence of someone very special.

Around that same time period, I had my first opportunity to meet President George H. W. Bush, who was vice president of the United States at the time, and was on an official visit to Denver and was staying (as most high level government officials usually did) at the venerable Brown Palace Hotel. I was in a group escorting Vice President Bush back to his room in the hotel, when a situation occurred that demonstrated to me just how much of a sensitive and first-class gentleman he was. An official photographer was with us, and as we approached his suite in the relatively dark hallway corridor, Vice President Bush asked if I would like a photo with him. Eagerly responding in the positive, he signaled to the photographer, and we posed together. It then quickly became apparent that the photographer was having some type of difficulty with his camera or, at least, the flash capability. Without any question or embar-

rassment to the photographer, Vice President Bush invited us into his suite by making a comment along the lines, "You know, it's really dark out here in the hallway, let's go into the suite for the photograph." We did and struck our pose near a sunshine-providing window, much to the relief of all concerned, especially the photographer.

With Vice Ptesident Bush at the Brown Palace Hotel.

To be sure, the more enjoyable experiences of my time as SAC of the Denver FO were not limited to those in Colorado. Frequent visits to Wyoming, the other half of my territory, held some precious memorable moments. Growing up as a young kid in Pennsylvania, I still remember times trying to decide if I wanted to be a Royal Canadian Mounted Policeman, an FBI Agent, or a cowboy. I recall stories of the Frontier Days Celebration with cowboys, rodeos, and parades held annually in Cheyenne, Wyoming. During my cowboy fantasy phase, certainly one of my wishes, desires, or dreams was to be there in Cheyenne, on my horse, wearing my two toy cap pistols with their holsters.

Honestly, it was hard to believe that the dream would actually come true as an FBI SAC in Wyoming. My thanks will be there for a lifetime to Senior Resident Agent Dave Boyer and the other SAs of the Cheyenne RA for making it happen. For my FBI years in Wyoming,

A dream come true, riding in the Cheyenne Frontier Days Parade.

they arranged for me to have my own horse, a saddle blanket with my name, and the opportunity to ride every year in the Cheyenne Frontier Days parade through downtown Cheyenne. They made it possible for me not just to ride, but to ride with the Wyoming governor and other VIPs, usually including the visiting pilots of the famous US Air Force Thunderbirds. The Thunderbird Precision Flying Team honors an annual custom of performing flyovers at the Cheyenne Frontier Days celebration in July. Later, the pilots were able to ride in the parade, after they had dressed down into cowboy hats and blue jeans. I was also able to join them after the parade, usually to enjoy a celebration Bloody Mary drink together, on the street in downtown Cheyenne.

Sharing a celebration drink with the Thunderbird Precision Flying Team after their flyover and the Cheyenne Frontier Days Parade.

Another pleasant Wyoming experience comes to mind, even though it involved a visit from the FBI Director, which can be stressful and challenging. Director William Sessions and his wife, Alice, traveled to Jackson Hole, Wyoming, in order for the Director to make a presentation to federal judges at a judicial conference at Jackson Lake Lodge Resort, located in the Grand Teton Mountains. After his presentation and a couple of extra days to network with some of his former associates among the judges, he made a request of me. He mentioned that he and Alice had never seen the legendary Old Faithful geyser, located inside Yellowstone National Park, and wondered if we might make a side trip to the park for a look. In checking with the SRA, Gary Adams, from our Riverton RA, who handled investigations in the park and was familiar with the geysers and their location, I determined that we could make the trip from the Tetons over to Yellowstone easily. The only problem, according to Gary, was that Old Faithful was not as faithful and reliable to perform as it used to be.

Apparently, visitors who formerly could rely on it to spout hourly were now waiting for lengthy periods for the explosive performance of Old Faithful. With Director Sessions understanding the situation, he decided we should go ahead and visit, and take our chances. Guided by SRA Adams, we traveled the route to Yellowstone, enjoying sightings of deer, moose, and other species of mammals and birds along the way. After about an hour, as we were closing in on Old Faithful's location, I reminded the Director again of the geyser's uncertain schedule and a possible long wait. On the final approach to the paved viewing platform, we noticed dozens of tourists lined up on all sides with visible signs of impatience and frustration, probably from an extended wait.

We were able to pull the car right up to the platform to drop off Director Sessions and his wife. Then, like magic, just as the car door was closing, Old Faithful exploded into a majestic tower of steaming hot water. As the Director returned to the car, I'll always remember our exchange of comments – "I guess that was the SAC's responsibility to make it blow," said the Director. "No," I answered, "it was actually the SRA's responsibility." Director Sessions and Alice were still speaking of the amazing display and its incredible timing as we stopped at the famous Old Faithful Inn nearby for ice-cream cones.

While indeed there were many highlights and enjoyable events and experiences attendant to my time in the Denver FO, there was also a smattering of those tragic incidents that I regretted most having to experience. I recall the fall of 1987, when, on November 15 at the old Stapleton Airport in Denver, Continental Flight 1713 crashed right after takeoff, killing twenty-five passengers and three members of the crew. I remember it was a very snowy day, and it took me considerable time and effort to shovel the heavy snow out of my driveway in order to be able to respond to that particular crash. However, one of our SA pilots, who lived closer to Stapleton, was able to make it to the airport and initiate our necessary inquiry to determine if there was any criminal or terrorist activity involved in the crash.

By the time I arrived at the airport, the dead bodies, covered with white sheets, were lined up on the floor of one of the airport fire stations, and efforts had begun to identify the victims. What breaks one's heart is to notice that some of the sheet-covered bodies are much smaller and shorter than the others, and you know a child or an infant lies underneath. It became obvious early on that sabotage was not involved in this crash, and it only remained for me to offer the services of our FBI Disaster Squad from Washington, D.C., to assist in identifying the victims through fingerprints, if desired and needed.

Sadly, a few years later on March 3, 1991, on a warm and clear Sunday afternoon, United Airlines 585 crashed upon approach to the Colorado Springs Airport. This was a Boeing 727 aircraft with twenty passengers and five crew members aboard, and all perished. Ultimately, it was determined that the cause in this particular crash was a faulty rudder control system that actually caused the plane to go straight down and enter the ground vertically. It literally appeared that the body of the plane had disappeared into a well. It wedged itself into a very small circular pattern, drilling right into the ground, after shearing off the wings and other parts of the plane, and leaving debris over a wide area in the surrounding terrain. Some parts of bodies were visible, and appeared to be a jumbled mass of partial limbs sticking out the top of the small round opening, caused when the plane's body knifed into the ground. Prior to my arrival from Denver, SAs from our Colorado Springs RA had already responded and were on scene. These scenes from airplane crashes are emotionally very difficult to visit, and the carnage produces horrible memories that one can never, ever really forget.

Merely retelling some of my stories alone, with their vivid and mixed memories, would seem to describe how life in the FBI could play out every day. Frankly, we in the FBI could often and easily relate to the reality of enjoying the "good" and suffering the "bad" developments. However, with the negatives or problems we were constantly trying initiatives that might improve our effectiveness.

In November 1988, we officially teamed up with the DPD to combat juvenile gang crime, mostly caused by the Crips and Bloods gang members out of the Los Angeles, California, area. We were able to deputize police officers as federal officers to allow interstate team travel by SAs and police officers together in order to work federal racketeering investigations, involving primarily cocaine and crack cocaine. The success of that initiative would lead later in March 1991 to another signed agreement with DPD. This time we established a joint team of two senior FBI SAs with two police officers (including one lieutenant) who would be federally deputized to tackle major crimes in Denver. This team was aimed at multiple and repeat offenders committing serious felonies, such as bank robbery, kidnapping, homicide, and drug crimes, as well as armed and dangerous fugitives.

Throughout the majority of my FBI career, the Bureau would have to be classified as a mostly "reactive" agency, whose primary missions were to solve crimes after they were committed, and catch spies who were already spying. Prevention was not in the Bureau's vocabulary, except perhaps as a side effect or deterrent based on investigative successes or the publicity from FBI SAs accomplishing their primary mission. In earlier days, the Bureau was essentially a "bean counter" agency, for which effectiveness was measured by how many cases were solved with arrests, indictments, and convictions. Also important were statistics counting how many fugitives were apprehended, and how much value you could claim in your cases from fines, savings, and recoveries. Numbers were important in nearly every category, and everyone knew that "prevention" almost never allows you to produce numbers that can effectively be measured to claim success.

However, the reality of prevention notwithstanding, FBIHQ correctly evaluated and understood the massive drug problem that seemed to be swamping our country in the 1980s. The problem espe-cially impacted our youth, and FBIHQ took the initiative to announce our first prevention program – the Drug Demand Reduction Program (DDRP). The DDRP provided funding and allowed time, fieldwide, for every FO to develop a program to help prevent our nation's kids from getting hooked on drugs.

I'm sure each FBI FO greeted this opportunity with varying degrees of interest and application. In Denver, it was viewed as pure prevention and a real opportunity to accomplish its stated purpose. We appointed an SA DDRP coordinator and fashioned a circular logo, with a depiction of the Rocky Mountains inside the circle, along with the wording "Rocky Mountain High, FBI – Colorado and Wyoming – Free of Drugs." We had the logo printed on all types of giveaway items, including blue T-shirts, balloons, white sweatshirts, and an ink-pad stamp that would allow the logo to be applied to various communica-tions. We also acquired a supply of comic books featuring FBI Agent heroes fighting drug criminals, and had a supply made of small Junior G-man badges for pinning on the children.

Before personal interaction with any youth, we carefully crafted a comprehensive survey to attempt to ascertain the scope of drug problems involving students in the schools of Colorado and Wyo-ming. With the approval of school administrators, we distributed the survey to 157 schools (112 in Colorado and forty-five in Wyoming). It was left to individual schools to determine how they would distrib-ute the survey to elementary, junior high, and senior high students. Responses were received from more than seventy-four hundred stu-dents in total for both states, and the results were fascinating. Among several valuable findings, we found: (1) major drugs in use were marijuana, cocaine, and alcohol; (2) experimentation with mostly marijuana was going on among youth as young as elementary school; (3) presentations about drug prevention would be most valuable and effective up to grade nine; and (4) most effective presentations would be by parents, FBI SAs, or former drug users.

Based on these results and others, I asked for volunteers to make up small teams to prepare an antidrug message to the students of Colo-rado and Wyoming. Ultimately, these teams were open to FBI SAs, FBI clerical and support personnel, a few former drug users, retired FBI

SAs, and a few sports figures. The targeted students would be in elementary, and, occasionally, in junior high schools. The program would normally involve: first, explaining the danger of drugs with some photos showing dramatically ugly graphic results; second, explaining the role played by the FBI, showing a variety of weapons, including the handgun, the Model 870 Remington shotgun, the old Thompson submachine gun (Tommy gun), and the H & K MP5 9mm submachine gun, as well as bulletproof vests and handcuffs – along with a strong and clear explanation that SAs really hate to use the weapons, but have been forced to adopt heavier and more powerful weapons to defend themselves and others from the more violent drug criminals; and third, giving out a variety of literature and assortment of FBI trinkets, along with some more special prizes for correct answers to questions.

For us, there would be four major goals for our program: (1) Let the students meet real FBI personnel; (2) Aim to have the FBI SAs accepted as role models and "good guys;" (3) Demonstrate some of the weapons and tools needed and used for the drug fight; and (4) Deliver a clear message that using drugs provides no good future for the students.

In December 1989, the program was tested at an elementary school in Pueblo, Colorado, and the results were outstanding. During January 1990, a press conference in Denver launched the two-state program that explained the survey, its results, and the new FBI school program. What followed for the next couple of years were literally dozens of requests from schools in both states requesting

a visit for our program. The word continued to spread, and before long we were contacted by ABC News and requested to allow one of their correspondents and crew to visit one of our programs. The visit came at a school in Castle

Press conference announcing the FBI student anti-drug program

Rock, Colorado, for a story that appeared nationally, during the *Good Morning America* show on ABC. Did the DDRP program accomplish its goals? It's hard to tell, since it involved that unmeasurable "prevention" factor, but I can assure you we gave it our best effort. What it did for me personally was to solidify my dedication to the need for youth crime prevention and Juvenile Justice, which was to play a big part in my life after the FBI.

Now, I think it appropriate to conclude this chapter with the story of my last major case investigation, in what would be my last field assignment tour before retirement from the FBI. This would be a most unusual investigation, with a number of twists and turns, and some firsts for me, if not

An aerial view of Rocky Flats nuclear weapons plant. Photo from Wikimedia Commons.

the entire Bureau. It was code-named Operation Desert Glow, and it involved a location in Colorado called Rocky Flats.

The Rocky Flats plant was located in an isolated location, about sixteen miles northwest of Denver, in neighboring Jefferson County. It was a highly protected federal facility sitting on sixty-five hundred acres, which, from 1952 until 1992, produced an essential component for the reported seventy thousand nuclear weapons in the US arsenal the vital plutonium trigger. It was originally controlled by the US Atomic Energy Commission, but control passed to the Department of Energy (DOE) in 1977. At the time of this investigation, the DOE had contracted Rockwell International to operate the plant. It was reported that, at its prime, the plant was akin to a small city with a multilane highway running through it, and as many as ten thousand employees working throughout eight hundred different structures, twenty-four hours a day, seven days a week.

Starting in 1987, plant insiders began to notice what they considered suspicious and unsafe practices with the handling and destruction of very toxic radioactive substances and waste products at the plant. Eventually, certain employees felt obligated to report the unsafe activities to the FBI and the EPA.

At the Denver FO, the information made its way to SA Jon Lipsky, who had developed valuable experience in working other environmental crimes cases, and would become the FBI Case Agent for Operation Desert Glow. Due to the serious allegations involved, the highly classified and sensitive nature of the facility, and the potentially dire consequences to the employees and the surrounding community, this investigation was worked as a highest priority major case, jointly with EPA agents. As much discreet testing of emissions from incinerator smoke stacks as possible was conducted, using aircraft, as well as other appropriate radioactive testing of ground and runoff water. Testing was supplemented by equally discreet interviews of possible witnesses during the next several months. By the spring of 1989, SA Lipsky had accumulated what prosecutors at the US Attorney's Office in Denver considered sufficient evidence to support, and move forward to secure a federal search warrant for the entire rambling Rocky Flats complex. Planning then began for what would have to be considered a raid like none other that most of us in the Bureau would ever experience.

We did have a listing of the target structures and locations that specifically needed to be searched. However, we also had to employ sufficient personnel to effectively control and protect the entire vast premises of the property subject to our search warrant, and for a period of time necessary to complete the search (which I estimated to be at least a few days). Further, it was essential that the control would be continuous, twenty-four hours per day.

Next, for personal safety of all participants, considering what we expected to find, everyone had to be appropriately outfitted. Large-scale acquisition included steel-toed boots, neck-to-ankle coveralls, hard hats, gloves, protective eye gear, and plenty of dosimeters to detect radiation. A logistical plan also had to be crafted to supply food and other necessities to the "occupying force" for the duration of the search. Finally, an operational plan had to be created to determine assignments and exactly how to proceed once the warrant was served and the search commenced. In this particular case, the first absolutely vital decision focused on how to approach the facility to execute the warrant. A traditional raid in a criminal investigation can usually start by surrounding the target location, and then, with weapons drawn, make a loud announcement of the raid, along with a demand for entrance. At Rocky Flats, however, protected by a well-trained, heavily armed (even with missiles) security force, and with shoot-to-kill authority, the traditional raid was obviously not a good option, Instead, we opted to set up a meeting with Rocky Flats authorities to supposedly discuss a possible future terrorist attack. Once quietly and peacefully past security, SAs could then, in a business-like manner, serve the search warrant.

Once all preparations were complete, the raid to execute the search warrant was launched on June 6, 1989. As planned, SA Lipsky and an initial team peacefully accessed the facility through security and upon entering the meeting area, served our search warrant on the Rockwell International internal plant manager. After careful explana-tion of exactly what was happening, the larger convoy of FBI and EPA vehicles, loaded with SAs and other security experts and waiting at a discreet distance outside of the facility, were able to enter without resistance, and the search began. Incidentally, this was believed to be the first historic incidence of one or more federal US agencies taking possession of the property of another US agency by force.

Nearly simultaneous with the search initiation at Rocky Flats, in Denver, US Attorney Mike Norton and I were meeting with then Governor Roy Romer at the State Capitol. We had hastily scheduled the meeting to coincide with the Rocky Flats raid in order to brief the governor on the events transpiring. His reaction was immediate, as he dropped his head on his conference table, buried his head in his hands, and stated, "Oh, no!" In the meantime, back at the search site, the initial contingent of FBI and EPA agents began a very tedious, and potentially dangerous, search for evidence of illegal dumping and stor-age of toxic substances – a search that would ultimately involve nearly one hundred FBI personnel and a heavy number of EPA specialists.

When I recall the search and my estimate that we would probably be in control of the facility for a few days, I have to smile to myself and shake my head at how far off my estimate was. Faced with the number of structures involved, the water and liquid runoff areas to be tested, the number of earthen areas impacted by discharges, the com-plex measurements needed, and the volume of interviews needed to be done, it was not surprising that the hours and days dragged on and on. At final count, we had custody of Rocky Flats for nearly twenty days, and that might very well be a record for the duration of an FBI search warrant execution. It certainly was the longest in my FBI career!

The evidence obtained resulted in calling what I was told was the first special federal grand jury in Colorado history, which lasted until 1992. In March 1992, the tangible result was a plea agreement, wherein Rockwell International pleaded guilty to ten environmental crimes and received a fine of $18.5 million, which was supposedly the highest fine ever imposed, up to that time, for an environmental crime. With that, the proceedings of the grand jury were sealed as per federal law, and the FBI/EPA investigation was completed. However, to finish the Rocky Flats story, the criminal case was certainly not the end of hot button issues for the troubled plant.

Finally closing in 1992, Rocky Flats was later designated a Super-fund site, and literally more than $7 billion was appropriated to clean it. Buildings were demolished, and radioactive segments of the buildings were buried six feet underground in a central location called the Central Operable Unit. Also, reportedly, several tons of nuclear waste were then transported for proper destruction at nuclear sites in New Mexico, Idaho, and Nevada. Finally, in 2005 the site was declared clean.

Approximately four thousand acres were eventually transferred to the US Fish and Wildlife Service for a future wildlife refuge, and the remaining thirteen hundred-plus acres were retained by the DOE to protect the buried nuclear waste and monitor the contaminated area into the future. However, dating back to the Rockwell pleas, and for years thereafter, there have been tension and disagreement, and even litigation, on the part of activists, including former members of the federal grand jury, as to whether justice was truly served.

Concerns seem to be located in three specific areas: first, whether some specific individuals should have been charged with environmental crimes in addition to the corporation; second, whether a report prepared by the grand jury should have been made public to alert the community to the danger of Rocky Flats illegal discharges; and third, whether the Rocky Flats site and surrounding area are now really and truly clean and safe. Contrary to activists' concerns and protests, several published studies and tests have insisted the land given to the Fish and Wildlife Service is indeed safe, and has been opened for use by the public. It is entirely possible that the final chapter on the fate of the old Rocky Flats site is yet to be written.

Nevertheless, from our perspective, the subsequent controversy notwithstanding, SA Lipsky and his team, along with their EPA counterparts, conducted a thorough investigation. They developed the evidence, along with the US Attorney's Office and the US Department of Justice, and presented it to a special federal grand jury. The offending corporation pleaded guilty and received the heaviest fine for a crime of its kind up to that time. Simply put, we identified and shined the public spotlight on a very dangerous radioactive threat to a community. We then led the efforts to shut down the threat and alert the community to the threat damage, leading to the damage cleanup.

I think the FBI and EPA, working together under difficult and potentially dangerous circumstances, accomplished our mission to the very best of our ability. As an aside, in memory of this unusual investigation and record search, I still retain a few tokens – a pair of almost new, hardly worn steel-toed boots, a hard hat, glasses, and coveralls. By the way, I keep them carefully isolated in a remote home location (just in case!).

Well, as completion of my sixth year in Denver approached, a combined twelfth year as SAC in both Charlotte and Denver, I knew my continued field time was limited. At the beginning of 1992, the Director's Office called and reminded me of my completed tour in two of our favorite FOs. As expected, I needed to be transferred again to receive a promotion and take an assignment back in Washington, D.C., at FBIHQ. As much as I loved the Bureau, I didn't really want to return again to Washington. So, after careful consideration, much discussion with my family, and with my thirty-year Bureau anniversary approaching, I retired and dropped anchor, so to speak, at the foot of the Rocky Mountain Front Range.

My last day as an FBI Agent.

With my decision made, a couple of questions normally came up during exit interviews by the media and from speech audiences well into retirement. Worthy of mention, I was more than willing and happy to address them and repeat the answers here:

1. *Did you ever shoot anyone?*

   Thank goodness, I was able to stay among the vast majority of FBI SAs who never had to fire their weapons in a live combat situation. The Bureau's policy is to use deadly force only in situations in which your life, or the life of another person, is considered at imminent and great risk. I might add, that although I never had to fire a weapon, except in frequent firearms training sessions, it was drawn and ready on a number of occasions. Those incidents, I recall, involved high-risk raids and fugitive apprehensions.

2. *Overall, what was the most satisfying accomplishment of your FBI career?*

   I never had to think long about the true answer to that question. I think back over nearly thirty years of frequently tense, occasionally high risk, personal safety situations, involving dozens of SAs I have worked with around the field. I recall some shootings, some physical combat, some car crashes, and some dog bites, but then I feel truly blessed and forever thankful that none of the SAs lost his or her life, or was seriously injured. That fact will always remain my most satisfying accomplishment.

Thus, my days as an active FBI SA officially ended in early 1992. However, before departing the FBI and changing course to discuss some adventures that followed, I would like to spend some additional time exploring, in greater depth and detail, some important FBI-related group and transitional topics that might be of interest.

CHAPTER 14

A Changing FBI

ONE OF THE MOST FREQUENT speech topics requested of me in recent years has centered on how the FBI has changed from the early days of J. Edgar Hoover. How I will deal with that topic here is not intended to be an intensive or extensive history of the FBI. However, what might be of interest are my personal thoughts and observations, some at the forty-thousand-foot level, concerning the major changes. My comments come as an insider until retirement in 1992, and after that, as an outsider with frequent contact with FBI personnel throughout the United States and the world.

Personnel

In 1924, when J. Edgar Hoover agreed to take over the Bureau of Investigation, then riddled with political hacks and which eventually became the FBI, he did so under certain circumstances and conditions. He insisted that his personnel would be selected and hired based on merit. They would adhere to the highest standards of morals and ethics and would avoid becoming involved in any political issues or activities as members of the Bureau. Along those lines, I can't speak for others, but I can personally attest that during my entire career, both in the field and at FBI Headquarters (FBIHQ), not once was I ever directed or asked to engage in any activity or investigation that I considered political in nature.

During the early years, there were basically two types of FBI employees. We had Special Agents (SAs), who carried guns, badges, and handled investigations. All other employees were support or clerical, and included stenographers, file clerks, auto mechanics, radio engineers, laboratory assistants, and a plethora of others with support responsibilities.

With a few exceptions, only SAs were normally eligible for all of the supervisory and management positions in every one of our administrative and operating divisions. Eventually, it became clear that the Bureau needed to make some changes. To maintain the most qualified and professional expertise in specialized operating positions, such as the FBI Laboratory, computer technology operations, finance and budget, and other areas requiring a special expertise, management personnel with that expertise outside the SA ranks would really need to be selected and hired.

Likewise, for a long time, it had been clear to some SAs conducting many functions such as physical surveillance, collecting fingerprints, doing photography, or even making a plaster tire cast, that a different kind of expertise from theirs was probably necessary and preferable. Gradually, through the years, the Bureau reached out, recruited, and hired some of the most qualified experts for these positions, regardless of their gender or national origin. I'm sure the FBI's overall professionalism took a step forward, and is much better off in most areas today, for that change. Of course, the proliferation of nonagent specialty hires became a virtual deluge after the disaster of 9/11 in 2001 and the pattern of extreme terrorist acts against the United States that followed. After 9/11, an army of analysts were recruited and hired to "connect the dots," especially in our counterterrorism investigations.

For a number of SAs, it is probably fair to say that there was a major downside for them in the FBI hiring of specialty nonagents for supervisory, management, and higher grade positions. It resulted in a situation that meant fewer promotional opportunities for SAs, who had traditionally occupied those positions in the past, as steps in their career advancement. Fortunately for the SAs, the situation was ameliorated substantially in subsequent years, as additional SA supervisory grades and positions were created to lessen the number of subordinates and tighten the span of control for the burgeoning responsibilities of the FBI. Efficiency and effectiveness were improved through creation of additional squads, units, and Headquarters divisions to be led by additional Supervisory SAs and other FBIHQ executives, as well as additional Assistant Special Agents in Charge to assist the Special Agent in Charge in the FBI Field Offices (FOs).

At this point, I think it important to interject a piece of personal information. In previous chapters I identified and described my units and positions held at FBIHQ during my various assignments there. Because of constant mission changes, reorganizations to accommodate the missions, and gradual but constant growth, most of the units and sections have been merged and/or renamed. The other major change would be the substantial increase in the actual number of units, sections, and even divisions in today's FBIHQ.

Culturally, the continued interest and enthusiasm of Americans desiring to become FBI SAs have allowed the ability to select a true microcosm of our population who rank among the most qualified for the position, including women, African Americans, Asian Americans, Native Americans, and Arab Americans, just to name a few.

Sometimes in casual conversations with retired SAs, and even some of the most senior, long-serving active SAs and managers, the topic of a changing work ethic in today's FBI SAs comes up. They reminisce about the "good old days" when working for the Bureau was not just a job, but nearly a way of life. The Bureau came first, even before family, and seldom did an SA ever think about leaving the service before completing a career of twenty, twenty-five, or even thirty years. They occasionally bemoan current-day SAs who don't put in long hours well into the evenings but instead opt to leave the office in time to take a son or daughter to a soccer game, or some other event or activity. They don't understand an SA who looks forward to spending his or her Thanksgiving or Christmas holiday with the family, instead of jumping on an opportunity to apprehend a federal fugitive sneaking home to visit his family.

Of course, what we all need to realize is that today's FBI SAs and other employees are human members of a changing American generation, with their own values and priorities, influenced, for better or worse, by many factors. In a true cultural sense, we really can't expect respected members of our current generation to be effectively out of step with their peers. However, what we can and should expect is that candidates for FBI positions be on the leading edge of their own generation in every respect, excelling in leadership, education, morals, and ethics. Based on my contacts and experience, I believe our current SAs and other FBI employees remain the "best of breed" among their own generation. My consulting assignments and travels have kept me in contact with FBI SAs either somewhere in the United States or in a foreign assignment, almost weekly.

In all sincerity, I continue to be impressed with the knowledge, expertise, and innovative approaches to their work demonstrated by today's SAs. Moreover, they always display courtesy, friendliness and, most of all, a sincere dedication to giving back to their country and upholding the traditional tenets of fidelity, bravery, and integrity on which the FBI has been built.

It is also important to note that many changes have been introduced by the Bureau internally to help employees deal with the stresses caused by family problems, illnesses, alcohol excesses, and even traumatic incidents such as involvement in law enforcement shootings. For example, in the 1980s in North Carolina, an SA was involved in a shopping mall gunfight with a bank robber in which the robber was killed. I asked if the SA was okay, gave him the afternoon off, and told him to let us know if he needed anything. By the early 1990s, a team of SAs apprehending a dangerous fugitive in Colorado were also involved in a gun battle, during which the fugitive died. This time, peer counselors and myriad other services were available to ease the trauma experienced by the SAs, and to provide support for them in any way possible.

Unfortunately, regardless of the support level and the high bar of professionalism and ethics maintained by FBI employees today, there will still be occasional "bad apples" found in the barrel. Since FBI SAs and other employees have not risen above or slipped the bounds of common humanity, there is an infrequent case in which a fracture in their humanity results in a turn to the dark side. It can cascade from a family problem, mental illness or other health breakdown, financial stresses, drug problems, or various other sources. Understandably, the result can be disastrous personally for the employee, but also very damaging to the FBI and its reputation. Furthermore, a failure can cause inestimable damage to the country, as in the case of an FBI SA turned Russian spy named Robert Hanssen, who will spend the rest of his life in prison.

Fortunately, most often, a violation of the FBI's strict rules and policies is a minor issue but can still leave an employee with a written censure or suspension. The important fact to remember is that these incidents are rare, considering the nearly forty thousand current FBI employees, and constitute a relatively small problem. Based on what I saw in my career and experience now in interactions with FBI employees, I would rank them for ethics, honesty, professionalism, and performance at the very top of America's government and corporate ladder. In fact, with the level of competition among Americans interested in becoming FBI SAs today, and considering their skills, competencies, advanced education degrees, and overall résumés, I frequently hear conversations among retired SAs who make a familiar claim to each other – "If I had to apply to be an FBI Agent today, I would never make it."

Communications

Quality communication, internally and externally, for an agency such as the FBI is absolutely vital. Nearly everything the Bureau does is documented and in the early years, that meant a ton of paper. Inside a Field Office (FO), this documentation occurred in an assortment of various forms. Written communications from a FO to other offices and to FBIHQ took on different colors, depending upon the importance of the information. Routine or normal traffic was handled by letters or memos on white paper. More important information with requests moved between FOs by blue paper called airtels. More important directions from FBIHQ to the FOs were placed on green paper, affectionately known as "greenies." The most important urgent requests and information between both FBIHQ and the FOs were relayed by teletype, which normally required some sort of expedite or immediate action. (Teletype messages were sent from, and received by, typewriting machines operating on the recognition of electrical pulses over phone wires, radio or microwave links). Simply put, in today's computerized digital age, nearly all correspondence moves by email.

Early mobile communications, both by handheld radio or vehicle-mounted units were normally very spotty at best, depending on the radio, repeater locations, weather, and other variables. SAs covering large geographical areas normally had to depend on radios connected to the state police or the state highway patrol in order to stay in contact with their FO. Call-ins by pay phone gradually yielded to use of pagers, brick-like cellular phones with very limited coverage areas, and ultimately to smaller cell phones, Blackberries, and the popular (nearly magical) smartphones. Today's small, and getting ever smaller, digital devices, with voice and text capability, provide the best, and most popular, personal communication service for today's FBI SAs.

To be sure, the age of the computer, with its accompanying internet, has changed forever the way law enforcement communicates and conducts investigations. In the 1960s, nearly every investigation commenced with a visit to the local credit bureau and the police department to conduct an initial background check on a new subject with what we called a "credit and criminal" check. Today, much more detailed background information can be assembled from the internet, not just by law enforcement but also by private detectives and citizens alike, without leaving their office or laptop computer.

New FBI SAs leave the FBI Academy in Quantico, Virginia, with expert computer training these days, and hit the ground running to utilize their new tool to fight crime. Herein lies the one caution and concern, voiced by both retired and senior active SAs, which is hopefully imparted to the new cyber sleuths. The FBI, over the years, has prided itself in gaining the trust of our loyal citizens, and also the cooperation of criminal informants, by expert interviews, contacts, and personal interaction with people on the street and in the community. The former SAs and current senior SAs seriously believe that regardless of the laptop's value, it cannot replace human intelligence, source information, and evidence developed by SAs leaving the office and visiting the streets for the time-proven and vital personal communication with the general public.

Weapons and Tactics

Certainly, FBI technology must include placing the best possible weapons at the disposal of its SAs. As with all my fellow SAs, for the majority of my career, I holstered a Smith and Wesson .38 caliber model 10 revolver, with a four-inch long barrel and six bullets. During my last few years, I began using a Smith and Wesson .357 Magnum revolver with a three-and-a-half-inch barrel, and still holding only six rounds. Just in case, I also carried two bullet pouches on my belt, each with six additional rounds. Our main backup weapon was a Remington .870 shotgun, which I shot in practice regularly but never had to use. During my last year in the Bureau, we were transitioning to heavier weapons, and my new handgun was a Sig Sauer 9mm semiautomatic pistol with a fourteen-round capacity. To be honest, however, much of the time during those last days, I carried both my .357 Magnum, in which I had the most comfort and trust, as well as my new 9mm semiautomatic pistol.

Due to the increasing violence on the part of offenders in the 1980s, the FBI had been experimenting with more powerful handguns. Then, finally, it was the disastrous shootout in Miami on April 11, 1996, that left two SAs dead in the face of far superior firepower, that played heavily in the final decision to arm the SAs with semiautomatic pistols. For sensitive and higher risk operations, FBI FOs also have tactical or SWAT teams with varying types of heavier weapons. For the most sensitive, difficult, and dangerous situations, FBIHQ maintains a specially trained and full-time Hostage Rescue Team which is available to rapidly deploy and support any FO experiencing a serious emergency situation.

As weapons changed, so did circumstances and tactics. Probably the most dramatic change involved the realization, in possible hostage situations, that the old practice of first containing the area, and then negotiating with the hostage taker, might not be the best practice. A spate of school shootings brought about findings that quicker action was necessary, and could have saved lives. Eventually, "active shooter" tactics have proven to be the best solution to save victims' lives. The new tactical approach calls for the first law enforcement responders to immediately engage an active shooter to save lives, rather than wait for an opportunity to negotiate.

In connection with other arrest or raid situations, I believe, generally speaking but with certain definite exceptions, that FBI SAs usually enjoy a tremendous advantage over the unknown, and often extremely dangerous, situations faced by their fellow state, county, and local law enforcement officer counterparts. Many times, the SAs have the opportunity to know much about the subjects or criminal operations they are facing. They have conducted investigations, gathered considerable background information, and are less likely to encounter surprises. In my experience, we frequently had time and opportunities to have ambulances or fire apparatus alerted and at the ready. Hopefully, we also had time to prepare cover by FBI aircraft, and the opportunity to alert local law enforcement to provide backup and other pertinent coverage if necessary.

It is very important to note that today's police officers, sheriffs' deputies, and state troopers frequently have none of these advantages when they stop a suspicious person or vehicle or respond to a residence or location. They usually do not have the advantage of knowing that an individual might well be a dangerous and heavily armed fugitive, suffering from some mental illness, lying in wait for an ambush, or using drugs and/or alcohol to the degree he or she is ready to take aggressive, even lethal action against the officer.

Take, for example, a case in point demonstrating the advantage that we had in North Carolina during the arrest of an extremely dangerous fugitive in Charlotte.

In March 1983, a fugitive named Patrick Cecconi was a badly wanted escapee from the Illinois State Penitentiary in Joliet, Illinois. He had been serving forty years for armed robbery and attempted murder, and escaped in January. We received information that he would probably be receiving a money order the following day at the downtown Western Union office in Charlotte. A stakeout was set up in the morning to cover the office, and included air support.

Around 10 a.m., SAs outside the office spotted the arrival of a suspect vehicle with three occupants. One of the occupants entered the Western Union office, attempted to receive the money for Cecconi, and was arrested and eventually charged with harboring an interstate fugitive. Due to the heavy vehicle and pedestrian traffic outside, SAs considered the risk to public safety and allowed the aircraft to follow the fleeing vehicle, thus avoiding a high-speed chase.

The air surveillance headed north on I-77 and ended at a trailer park, directly off of NC Route 115. The trailer was located, and the location passed off to the ground units, who arrested the second occupant in the vehicle, who happened to be another Illinois fugitive wanted for parole violation. Cecconi made a run for the woods behind the trailer. Mecklenburg County Police arrived to help surround the area, and we called for "Barney," an eight-year-old Bloodhound, to help sniff out Cecconi. Shortly thereafter, Barney zeroed in on Cecconi lying facedown behind a dead, fallen tree log. The advantage we had that day allowed us to capture not only Cecconi but two other subjects as well, and without any incident or injury.

Science and Technology

While virtually every facet of FBI personnel and operational activities has changed in substantial ways since my career commenced in the 1960s, arguably, the technology itself has changed the most. The FBI Identification Division (fingerprint division) was initially the principal reason for a new site located in Clarksburg, West Virginia. This large center now houses the Criminal Justice Information Services (CJIS) Division, which is one of the largest, if not the largest, FBIHQ Divisions. SAs and support specialists there are now involved in research and development in such emerging technology areas as metric identification measures, which involves iris, retinal, and facial recognition to complement and

supplement the fingerprints used for years as our principal identification tool. To be sure, if there are any new initiatives in the criminal
science and investigative areas, personnel in the CJIS Division are
actively pursuing them.

As stated previously, for decades the best tool for the positive identification of criminals had been through comparison of fingerprints. The
FBI files are massive, and for years, matches were made by hand, and
sometimes involved hours or even days of meticulous examination. For
example, during the investigation that followed the assassination of the
Reverend Martin Luther King, Jr. in Memphis, Tennessee, on April 4,
1968, a single fingerprint, located on the rifle responsible for striking
down Dr. King, was run by hand through the thousands of prints on
file. Amazingly, the fingerprint was positively identified as belonging to
James Earl Ray, leading to his arrest, trial, conviction, and imprisonment.
Eventually, the fingerprint examination system became automated, and
now allows a comparison and identification almost immediately.

Probably by now, all TV crime drama viewers, as well as followers
of real-life criminal justice developments, know of something that has
become quite familiar – DNA. DNA is the abbreviation for the not-so-
easy-to-pronounce Deoxyribonucleic Acid, which exists in all living
things, including people. Most important is the fact that it is different in
every single person, similar to fingerprints. For obvious reasons, its development has been critically important in identifying subjects of criminal
acts, and its progressive use as a criminal investigative tool has been rapidly expanded and further developed by the FBI. Its application in cases
has cleared many innocent individuals, wrongly convicted and sitting in
prisons based on faulty eyewitness or other erroneous information. Con-
versely, it has aided in solving numerous unsolved cold cases, for which
existing evidence was previously absent or insufficient to sustain an arrest
or conviction. Therefore, in recent years, DNA has joined fingerprints as
one of the two most important positive sources of evidence in identifying
and convicting those guilty of criminal activities in our country.

That brings me now to one of today's most omnipresent and valuable tools for crime solutions, as well as prevention, on our streets and
in our communities, and that is video. A few decades ago, still cameras
were bulky and their products grainy, while video cameras produced
inferior results, and were very expensive to operate. I recall working

the streets of New York City with the best 35mm camera that we had available, concealed in a briefcase. Discreetly trying to photograph a subject was somewhat of a joke, since you had to practically lift the briefcase up to his face level, as you approached your target on the street. So much for discretion!

Today, video cameras are almost everywhere, inexpensive to operate, and extremely helpful for users, both in the public and private sectors. They assist, across the board, everything from traffic control to crime prevention and solution. They are mounted in police cars as "dash cams," and more often now are finding their way onto the bodies of officers themselves. Smart police agencies countrywide are noting the locations of video cameras, placed not only by public law enforcement and other government agencies but also by private security and corporate entities. Checking the results of these twenty-four-hour electronic eyes, set at strategic locations, is becoming the very first step taken by law enforcement after a criminal act occurs.

In fact, the state of the video market for overt as well as covert photography has advanced to the point that commercial magazines of fifty or more pages are printed and distributed regularly, advertising and marketing the sale of various video and camera devices. They range from large to minuscule and can be concealed in every possible garment or piece of furniture. Further, these magazines and their products are openly available for purchase by not just government agencies, and not just private detectives, but by anyone. I mention here video-capable devices, but the same availability is there for concealed audio-recording devices. Obviously, with today's advanced technology and commensurate with their responsibilities, the FBI must also develop and maintain such sophisticated and state-of-the-art technology in order to conduct the legally warranted and required investigations authorized by Congress and the public laws.

In this connection, it might be interesting to note one specific situation that occurred in New York City during my assignment there in the late 1960s, to point out just how the incredible development in video technology could have made a big difference in one of our cases. It so happened that it became very important for us to identify some bad guys who planned a meeting at a park in Brooklyn. We had information about the specific location in the park, but no information about when the meeting would occur, or who, specifically, would be making the meeting. Unfortunately, the meeting site was in an area almost impossible to stake out or cover discreetly on a twenty-four-hour basis, for however long it might be necessary.

One innovative approach involved moving in a construction trailer, which could be manned inside, and surrounding it outside with some lumber and some other miscellaneous construction material. While this plan offered a workable observation site, it brought an unexpected downside. Nearly every night during the several-day operation, we were fighting off would-be young burglars and thieves, attempting to break into the trailer or steal the lumber outside. We tried to outfit an SA as a private security guard to patrol outside intermittently, and occasionally, even resorted to having SAs inside the trailer emit some ghostlike shrieks and sounds to ward off the thieves.

On one occasion, we tried another novel approach involving a nearby zoo building, which would have offered a reasonably good observation post. A lion's outdoor cage was positioned in the direction of the target site, and with the cooperation of the zookeeper and manager, we were able to position an SA in the lion's cage one night after the lion went inside. This worked well for that overnight coverage, but, unfortunately, the plan was not relayed from the night zookeeper to the morning shift. As the lion ambled outside the next morning, loud yelling and desperate appeals could be heard from inside the cage. Fortunately, the lion was as surprised and stunned as the SA occupant and gave the day-shift zookeeper the opportunity to get him back inside and secured. Needless to say, the incident thwarted our efforts to find another volunteer for that particular plan.

Eventually, we worked our way through several days and nights, with our best possible efforts to accomplish our mission. Ultimately, we succeeded in making the needed identification. The bottom line was that the operation cost us hundreds of SA hours, and very expensive vehicle and other support costs. With today's technology, our mission probably would have succeeded much more economically, efficiently, and effectively. It would have taken just one or two video cameras, strategically concealed and monitored remotely, with minimal surveillance support.

CHAPTER 15

FBI in Transition

Investigations

OF COURSE IT IS VITAL AND ENVIABLE that the FBI is staffed with a corps of highly educated, knowledgeable, and capable Special Agents (SAs), both male and female, and made up of US citizens from widely diverse cultural and national backgrounds. Yes, it is equally important that SAs are backed up by nonagent experts in many essential administrative and operational support areas. It also helps that the FBI has the research and training capability to employ the latest strategy and tactics in their operations, with SAs armed with the most advanced weapons and weapon systems. Of equal importance, they can communicate almost immediately among themselves and with other agencies, using the very latest smartphones and digital electronic technology, to assist in accomplishing their mission, both in the United States and throughout the world.

However, with all of the above, there still remains the same ultimate challenge that has always been there for the Bureau – effective and efficient investigations. All of the lessons learned, innovations, and current positives listed above must dovetail into meaningful and successful investigations. That's the "name of the game" or the "proof of the pudding," so to speak, and will allow the FBI to stay on top of its game. Whether it is preventing a major terrorist act, capturing an enemy spy, catching a criminal fugitive, or solving a major cybercrime, the FBI should always be measured by how well its SAs use their many resources to play and win the endgame, with a thorough, aggressive, legal, and nonpolitical investigation.

Changing Investigations

Back at the end of 1962, as a brand-new FBI SA, freshly graduated from the FBI Academy, I was driving my personal vehicle to my first Field Office (FO) assignment in New Orleans, Louisiana (NOLA). En route, I was excited and couldn't stop wondering what key assignment and major challenges were awaiting me in my first case. Upon arrival in NOLA, I immediately reported in, got my squad assignment, met my new Supervisory Special Agent (SSA), and then found my desk along a row of desks in the squad area. Then, after meeting with my other squad members, I couldn't wait to get to the metal file cabinet and my own personal drawer, which held the case folders launching my investigative career.

Opening the drawer, I noted a number of case folders and, with a whetted appetite and eager anticipation, I began to read. Expecting to be working the most complicated and major crimes depicted on the radio shows and in movies, it was more than a bit surprising and disillusioning to see a case involving a $35 bad check that had traveled interstate and was drawn on a New Orleans bank. Another case involved a stolen car out of Mississippi, which was recovered in Louisiana and had obviously traveled interstate. True, these were bona fide federal violations over which the FBI has jurisdiction. The bad check was a clear-cut violation of the Interstate Transportation of Stolen Property statute. The stolen car would be a definite violation of the Interstate Transportation of Stolen Motor Vehicle statute. They were not, however, in my humble estimation, of the quality and magnitude that the legendary FBI SAs should be working. There were other similar cases, lots of them, which meant a caseload bulging from thirty to fifty. I soon determined that more experienced SAs were carrying loads of nearly one hundred cases.

This certainly did not mean that there were not vastly more important major cases being worked by SAs of the New Orleans FO. What it did mean was that the FBI, in those years, was working literally every violation of federal law coming under the Bureau's jurisdiction, whether it had high merit or virtually no merit. Normally, the SA assigned would cover the leads essential to outline and determine the minor nature of the violation, and then make a presentation to one of the Assistant US Attorneys in his federal district for a prosecutive opinion. Since I was to be based in NOLA, in the Eastern District of Louisiana, I would make my presentations for prosecutive opinions in NOLA, to an assistant US attorney of the Eastern District. Almost without exception, the attorney would then decline prosecution due to the minimal amount of loss involved, or due to a lack of merit, and we would then close the case.

In addition to the resources and hours dedicated to covering heavy caseloads, with a substantial number of those cases being of questionable value, SAs fielded some rumors and heard some outside criticism that Director Hoover refused to recognize and tackle organized crime and the Mafia. In this connection, I can personally attest that we did indeed work cases and leads on organized crime mob bosses around the country. While in the NOLA FO, I assisted with leads and participated in the surveillance of Carlos Marcello, the Mafia boss of New Orleans and virtually all of Louisiana. While the FBI definitely worked organized crime cases, it probably would be accurate to say that Mr. Hoover disdained and largely refused to authorize undercover operations (UCOs). The SAs believed that only a UCO would allow the Bureau to effectively penetrate organized crime and collect the firsthand evidence necessary to bring about federal convictions. The popular feeling and assumptions were that the Director hated corruption deeply and feared his SAs, in an undercover role, could not be properly controlled and might develop an alternative lifestyle and become corrupted. In fact, it was probably this same mindset and concern that kept the FBI out of drug investigations early on, as the ugly underworld of drug trafficking took off in the 1970s. Mr. Hoover, perhaps rightly or wrongly, probably feared SAs might succumb to bribery and corruption when faced with the huge amounts of money involved in massive drug operations.

The First Sea Change: "Quality Over Quantity"

With the passing of J. Edgar Hoover in 1972, investigations conducted by the FBI underwent a number of significant changes. After a period of time under the leadership of an Acting Director, President Richard Nixon nominated Clarence M. Kelley to be the second Director of the FBI. He was easily confirmed by the US Senate and sworn in on July 9, 1973.

In so many ways, with the selection of Director Kelley, in my mind the FBI really "lucked out." He knew the Bureau well, having touched every base personally in his prior career as an FBI SA from 1940 until retirement on October 24, 1961. He had served in the smaller FBI Resident Agencies (RAs), FOs, FBI Academy at Quantico as a firearms instructor, and at FBI Headquarters (FBIHQ). Further, he knew what the FBI needed, since he held several important posts, starting as an SA, then promoted to SSA, Assistant Special Agent in Charge, Inspector, and eventually to Special Agent in Charge (SAC) in the Birmingham FO, and then the Memphis FO at the time of his retirement. After retirement, he went on to become Chief of Police of the Kansas City, Missouri, Police Department for a dozen more years. After serving nearly five years as FBI Director, Kelley left in February 1978 to return to Kansas City and start his own security organization, which ended up being very successful. He peacefully passed away in his sleep in 1997, at the age of eighty-five.

As FBI Director, Kelley did nothing to denigrate or criticize the reign of Director Hoover but instead moved to encourage innovations that would allow the FBI to flourish in the contemporary criminal justice world. He quickly earned the respect of FBI employees, and will always be remembered in the FBI and the Kansas City Police Department as the leader who encouraged and allowed the concept of Quality over Quantity in investigations.

FBIHQ in Washington, D.C., which had formerly been referred to as Seat of Government, was changed to FBIHQ. Efforts increased to begin hiring additional female and minority SAs, and especially SAs with accounting skills to initiate more complex and complicated investigations in the White Collar Crime (WCC) area. Other initiatives began that would foster more cooperation and open relationships with our sister federal agencies, such as the Central Intelligence Agency (CIA) and the National Security Agency (NSA) in the counterintelligence field, and the major state, county, and local agencies vital to the FBI in criminal investigations. In special cases, UCOs were authorized, under heavy supervision by FBIHQ, both from legal and investigative perspectives. The UCOs would be employed in efforts against crime and corruption, wherever it was found, both in organized and traditional crime. Into the 1980s and 1990s, UCOs made significant inroads in taking down the major leadership of La Cosa Nostra (Mafia), as well as outlaw motorcycle gangs and other criminal organizations.

FBI SAs, both independently and jointly with the Drug Enforcement Agency (DEA), fought the withering battle, which continues to this day, against well-organized and violent drug cartels and other major drug trafficking organizations. However, the most significant and positive transition was the realization that FBI SAs must work the most important cases coming to their attention, rather than every case that technically involved a federal violation within the FBI's jurisdiction. Eventually, the Quality over Quantity concept took hold and, with the concurrence of the Department of Justice and the prosecuting US Attorneys around the country, allowed SAs to concentrate on major investigations that could make the most difference in assuring public safety. No longer would one SA necessarily be assigned to work one case, but a major case might be assigned to one SA, who would be assisted by a few additional SAs, or several, or perhaps even one hundred. US Attorneys set parameters for financial losses in crimes, below which there would be an automatic declination for prosecution. This further assisted the FBI in narrowing the number of cases and focusing on the worst offenders.

Into the 1990s, I think it would be fair to say that a vast majority of the major cases were being handled jointly by the FBI and a variety of other federal agencies, such as the DEA, Bureau of Alcohol, Tobacco, Firearms, and Explosives (BATF), and US Secret Service to name a few, as well as state and local authorities. Task forces have become a standard, and represent critical, essential, and effective vehicles for addressing serious public safety problems. The task forces allow the sharing of important information, as well as taking advantage of the skills and knowledge of other experts from the various agencies represented. They run the gamut from Joint Terrorism Task Forces and Safe Streets Task Forces to others involving cybercrime. They strive to bring together the best combination of resources that any FBI FO can muster. Where necessary, they are also able to address national security issues by providing background investigations for non-FBI members, allowing them to acquire security clearances to accommodate federal rules for handling classified material. Certainly, there are exceptions in which special cases are still being worked only by FBI SAs, individually or by teams, in specific areas such as counterespionage or complicated white collar crime. However, in today's FBI, important cases that do not involve a federal, state, or local partner agency are relatively few.

It is frequently remarked that we truly live today in a global society. The accuracy of this is easily seen in our worldwide financial markets, commerce, travel, and communications, thanks to computers and the internet. To those, you can add quick and cheap worldwide telephone access and ever-increasing global personal mobility, whether by air, sea, or land. As society expands, we need to remember that everything about it, including crime, follows its trail. The FBI is constantly working to protect American interests worldwide and has dramatically upgraded, in recent years, the presence of FBI SAs and offices across the globe. In more than seventy-five foreign locations, SAs, called Legal Attachés, are assigned to diplomatic offices and, while not empowered to conduct independent investigations, act as liaison with the law enforcement agencies of their host governments in a mutually beneficial relationship.

Undeniably, the Quality over Quantity practice, the efficient employment of UCOs, and task force investigations have changed for the better the way the FBI conducts investigations. However, another real sea change was to come right after September 11, 2001, and involved the term "terrorism."

A Second Sea Change: Prevention

During the 1970s and early 1980s, investigations categorized with the "terrorist" label were not unknown or outside the FBI's experience. However, with a few exceptions, it seemed to me that the incidents followed a familiar pattern. It was one international terror group committing an act of bombing, shooting, arson, and so on against a representative or organization of their own country. For example, the anti-Castro Cubans were fighting the pro-Castro Cubans, and the Irish Republican Army was fighting over Northern Ireland issues. Then, there were Serbo-Croatian factions, Puerto Rican independence factions, and others involved in violent incidents over their own separate issues. The incidents frequently occurred on American soil, but did not necessarily represent a terrorist act against America.

However, by 1983, we should have begun to get a clue that the target had indeed shifted for the Islamic terrorist fanatics to the United States, when the US Marine barracks was bombed in Beirut, Lebanon, killing 241 troops. Then, in 1993, it became clear again with the first bombing of the World Trade Center in New York City, with seven killed. In the year 2000, we got yet another dramatic clue when the pattern continued in the harbor at Yemen, with the bombing of the

USS Cole, leaving behind seventeen dead sailors. But if mainstream America had any lingering doubt, it was finally resolved and brought home to every American on September 11, 2001, with stark, shattering and horrific reality, when the Twin Trade Towers in New York City were leveled, bringing a loss of nearly three thousand innocent lives. It changed America, and the FBI along with it, forever.

At this point, it is important to remember that the FBI was created and commissioned to act as the principal law enforcement agency of the DOJ. FBI SAs are charged with ensuring the public safety of Americans by enforcing the more than two hundred federal statutes that fall under their jurisdiction, and investigating those persons or groups who violate those laws. Traditionally, and certainly during my experience, it was normally not until the law was broken and a crime committed that SAs sprang into action immediately to solve the crime. This was the usual process, whether it was responding to a bank robbery, working to catch a kidnapper, attempting to arrest fugitives, or chasing an identified spy or terrorist.

The "I" in the FBI stood for our first priority, and that was "investigation." SAs were normally assigned cases on specific subjects, groups, or incidents in the criminal or national security fields, and it was their responsibility to focus on their cases until resolved. Their focus was primarily on leads to develop evidence, essential to solving their own cases, and getting them prosecuted, if appropriate. Of course, if while working their cases, SAs developed information of importance to cases worked by other SAs, or developed information that was a basis for opening new cases, they would share it or report it immediately. In my experience, networking with other SAs regarding possible relationships with other subjects would usually occur only if specific information was developed to connect the cases.

The point is that, in those years, to the best of my knowledge and recollection, the FBI was not commissioned, organized, or equipped for an overarching intelligence approach to "connect the dots" in such a horrendous international terrorist attack as happened on 9/11. This would have taken an analytical approach, involving a tremendous volume of information and much closer relations with other US intelligence agencies, as well as those around the world. That said, it did not mean that FBIHQ and FOs did not value the development of intelligence information in their operations. Live informants and other sources and methods have been employed successfully in both criminal and security operations. Spies have been identified, and plans for future crimes such as bank robbery, murder, bombing, and so on have been detected and successfully averted. However, what was missing and needed to be developed, obviously and urgently, was the analytical capability, on a national level, to be able to anticipate, detect, and prevent another diabolical and conspiratorial attack like what occurred on 9/11, and ensure it did not happen in the future.

In response to the 9/11 incident, as expected and in accordance with their heretofore understood mission, the FBI immediately launched a massive investigation. Hundreds of SAs were assigned and worked quickly, tirelessly, and successfully to identify those responsible. But then what reportedly changed everything for the Bureau was a meeting held shortly after the incident between then FBI Director Robert Mueller and US President George W. Bush. I've heard several FBI speakers in years after 9/11 relay to public audiences a portion of what was discussed between the two men, and it is very important to note since, in my mind, it launched the next sea change for overall FBI operations.

As the story goes, President Bush was inquiring of the Director what the FBI was doing about the disaster. Director Mueller reportedly responded with details of the ongoing investigation, involving hundreds of FBI SAs, and with very encouraging results toward a solution. President Bush reportedly responded that he appreciated that information, but really what he meant, and really wanted to know, was what the FBI was doing to ensure such an incident never happens again. I believe the meeting was key to a major transformation, which then catapulted the FBI into the additional role of prevention. Although the iconic FBI name would not change, I could picture in my mind's eye a new appropriate title of FBIP, for the "Federal Bureau of Investigation and Prevention."

With little delay, additional SAs would be reassigned from lower priority investigative areas, and counterterrorism would rise to the highest priority for the FBI. As of this writing, counterterrorism remains at the top of the FBI priority list, with necessary internal structural changes made and new units and divisions created. Probably the most dramatic personnel change has been the hiring of hundreds of intelligence analysts to populate both FBIHQ and the Bureau's fifty-six FOs. Obviously, their main mission is to analyze the incredible volume of information that is constantly incoming, attempt to "connect the dots," and fulfill the new mandate to prevent any future such terrorist acts against our country.

Certainly, the FBI well understood that successful prevention would require efforts well beyond the walls of FBI offices, and FBIHQ reached out to make good relations even better with other agencies of the intelligence world, including the CIA and NSA. Also aware of the intelligence complexities involved in world terrorism, FBI leadership increased the resources available in Legal Attaché offices around the world, for the maximum level of cooperation with other nations' law enforcement and intelligence services.

It is also important to note that the FBI is well aware that all terrorism does not necessarily involve bombs and guns. In the cyber world, would-be terrorists could well attempt serious damage to the United States infrastructure and protective systems without ever setting foot inside the country or firing a single shot. Cybercrime and cyberterrorism can be considered extremely serious threats, and the FBI is taking every precaution to counter them, both in the United States and through cooperation with law enforcement and security agencies around the world.

Well, in the United States after 9/11, and with all the resources and structural transformation of the FBI in its additional prevention role, you might ask the question, "How is it going?" Obviously, in a retired capacity as an outsider, I would have to refer that question to the practitioners in the FBI and the employees working hard every day on the inside. I could only add, as a devoted follower of American current events, that it is refreshing and reassuring to note, with all the bad things that might have happened, so far major bad things have not occurred – that is, at least, so far! From my best outsider view and perspective, it certainly appears the new prevention role is working.

CHAPTER 16

Women in the FBI

THE DECISION TO RECRUIT, HIRE, TRAIN, and deploy female FBI SAs into the all-male Special Agent (SA) workforce was neither an easy nor a popular one. The process constituted a story, or more aptly a saga, in and of itself, and I experienced it firsthand during my years of service.

Considering minority representation in the Bureau through the year 1962, when I entered the FBI, records indicated that there were thirteen African American male SAs, but no female SAs. Director Hoover steadfastly believed that women had no place serving in the FBI as armed SAs. In fact, from its very creation as the Bureau of Investigation in 1908, and definitely from Mr. Hoover's term starting in 1924 through his death in 1972, there were basically two types of FBI employees – male FBI SAs who carried guns and badges, and FBI support personnel, both male and female, who handled all the other roles from file clerk to stenos, automotive maintenance experts, radio operations, lab technicians, and virtually everything else.

Bureau history will show only two exceptions to this policy. At the very beginning of Mr. Hoover's term as Director, two female SAs were already on board, but quickly resigned as he reduced and restructured the SA workforce. Records show that later that same year, Director Hoover, for some reason, upgraded a woman in the New York Office from "special employee" to Special Agent (SA). Her name was Lenore Houston, and she continued to serve in this position until her resignation in 1928. After that, the ranks of FBI SAs were closed to women until 1972.

In the early 1970s, the American workplace was buzzing with programs and names like "Equal Employment Opportunity," "diversity," and "affirmative action." Pressure was on the FBI to have a more fair and balanced workforce. Therefore, it was probably not surprising that the first two female SAs were hired literally a few weeks after Mr. Hoover's passing in 1972. By the end of that year, eleven women had taken the oath to become FBI SAs. Unfortunately, the manner in which the FBI and its SAs handled the process of assimilating females into the SA ranks did not constitute or represent its "finest hour."

Recruiting was certainly not a problem, as any number of young qualified women were outside, waiting to get through the door, processed, and off to the FBI Academy in Quantico, Virginia, for the several-week training process to become FBI SAs. As might be expected, a number of modifications in the overall training program were necessary to accommodate training both men and women together. In addition to the obvious necessity to provide separate lodging and other facilities for the women, some modifications were necessary in the physical training program, to include, for example, allowing a modified pull-up that would not require pulling up to the horizontal bar from a dead hang.

In connection with the very important firearms training, I was told that some women, in the very beginning, were having difficulty with sufficient strength in the arms, wrist, and fingers to pull triggers on the FBI weapons. This required some corrective action, which was accomplished, and ultimately created a need for testing "trigger pull" on the part of all candidates (male and female) as a prerequisite and qualification for the SA position. After successful completion of training at the FBI Academy, female SAs were issued a lighter Smith and Wesson .38 caliber revolver with a two-and-a-half-inch barrel, while the male SAs received the heavier revolver with the longer four-inch barrel. Female SAs were also given a few options as to where they could carry their weapons, one of which was not available to the men – a purse they were issued.

So the first challenge of training the new female SAs was accomplished through the flexibility and dedication of a professional FBI Academy staff. However, unfortunately, it was only their first challenge. Little did they know what new challenges were awaiting these eager new SAs as they arrived at their first FO assignment.

From various anecdotes, stories, rumors, and firsthand accounts, it appeared a number of their male counterparts harbored the same reluctance for the presence of female SAs as did their former boss, Mr. Hoover. Comments were widely reported such as "you girls belong back home in the kitchen" or "you should be back in your house making babies and taking care of them." Varied accounts have them being subjected to a steady stream of derogatory and unflattering harassment, both from fellow SAs and some supervisors. Reportedly, some supervisors even made comments to the new women to the effect that their work was fine, but they would not be rated highly, since they should not be promoted to supervisory positions and take the jobs of male SAs. Some women complained that sometimes they were just plain ignored and left out when assignments were given, such as responding to a bank robbery or other fast-moving tactical situation.

Then there was the question of what type of case assignments they would receive. Apparently, most of the women were being assigned the lowest-risk cases, such as applicant matters, which were the least exciting, created the most voluminous paperwork, and were the least likely to result in any violent encounters. To be fair, I'm sure there were many instances in which the assignments were based on an honest attempt by the supervisor to protect the women. However, in their minds, it was not a fair approach, and certainly not one that our female SAs wanted or expected. The net result of this treatment in those early days probably explains the short few years that many of our first female SAs remained and served in the Bureau.

One of the women who obviously felt victimized by the treatment received in her first office assignment, and one of the first eleven women hired for the SA position in 1972, was Christine Hansen. She resigned in 1977, and filed a sex discrimination complaint with the Department of Justice (DOJ) against the FBI. In 1981, she won a ruling from the DOJ that indeed the Bureau had discriminated against women in hiring, training, and case assignments, and called for sweeping changes in the agency proceedings. This ruling brought a number of changes to improve the Bureau lives of the female SAs, but only time would lessen and curtail some of the teasing and unflattering comments that they unfortunately had gotten accustomed to hearing.

For those who persevered, the advancement pathway began to crack open. Burdena "Birdie" Pasenelli entered on duty as an SA in January 1973, and was the first female to reach the status of Assistant Special Agent in Charge (ASAC) in 1989, and then the coveted Special Agent in Charge (SAC) position in 1992. Still ascending, she attained the title of Assistant Director of the Finance Division of the FBI in 1994, and then retired in 1999. By 2001, SA Kathleen McChesney had climbed the ladder all the way to the third rung as Executive Assistant Director, only beneath the Director and Deputy Director in positions at the FBI.

My first personal and official contact with a female FBI SA came in the mid-1970s, when I was assigned as the ASAC of the Louisville, Kentucky FO. She was under my general supervision, and as it turned out, within a very short period of time, I realized just how valuable she was.

Early one afternoon, during that time, we received an urgent call in Louisville from the FBI in Virginia. They reported that, a few days earlier, a heavily armed and extremely dangerous fugitive had kidnapped a young girl, elementary school age, from a residence in Independence, Virginia, which is located right along the North Carolina–Virginia border. A ransom call from the fugitive to the family had just been traced to a pay phone in the vicinity of Lake Cumberland State Resort Park in extreme southern Kentucky, just north of the Tennessee border and about one hundred and fifty miles southeast of Louisville.

SAs from our Bowling Green Resident Agency (RA) and other southern Kentucky RAs were dispatched, as well as other key resources from Headquarters in Louisville, including our female SA, Laura Sullivan. Since the crime of kidnapping occurred in Virginia and the victim had obviously been transported across state lines into Kentucky, the federal statute was triggered, and a federal kidnapping crime was in progress. The SAC flew to the scene in Bureau aircraft, and I expedited the one hundred and fifty-plus miles with emergency lights and siren activated during the entire trip. Our SAs from Bowling Green were the closest and arrived on the scene first, and quickly located the fugitive with his young victim, walking in the park. They followed them through the park, and then back to the fugitive's vehicle.

As darkness was fast approaching, a decision was made to take action before we might lose control of the situation. As the additional resources arrived, the arrest and rescue plan was prepared. Rather than trying to approach the subject and the victim with law enforcement vehicles and emergency equipment, the plan was created to ensure the safety of the young victim. It was decided to dress one of the male SAs and the female SA in park maintenance outfits and approach the vehicle from behind in a park maintenance truck. The two FBI SAs exited their vehicle and approached the fugitive's vehicle from both sides, using the pretext of inquiring if they needed some help. Then, before the fugitive could utter a single word, the male SA loudly announced the arrest and quickly raised his service revolver to the fugitive's head. Simultaneously, the female SA, in one lightning-like move, lunged into the open passenger-side window, grabbed the young girl, pulled her out of the car and onto the ground, covering her body with her own. The heavily armed fugitive began to reach behind him for one of his weapons, which resulted in an immediate and effective tap to his head with the SA's handgun, completing a very successful arrest.

After we notified the FBI in Virginia of the arrest and rescue, I waited in a hotel room at the park lodge with the young girl. While she watched television (cartoons as I recall), I began to realize two things that I had never really considered before. First, I was very proud of the courageous actions of both SAs and became a true believer, at that point, in the value of female SAs as indispensable to the FBI. Frankly, I maintained that belief throughout the rest of my FBI career. Still, something else happened that night that I probably always took for granted, but saw it up close and personal for the first time – and that was the incredible value of a single human life.

After a few hours alone with the little girl while she tried to relax and recover, I was notified that a large convoy was arriving from Virginia. They literally burst through the hotel door and included not just the parents, and not just the Virginia State Police, but also the school superintendent, who claimed that school and most other activities of the small town had ceased during her absence. I also believe the mayor was in the entourage, and many others from her community. It suddenly occurred to me what this single solitary young life meant to so many people. The victim, the overjoyed family, and welcoming party stayed in the park hotel overnight as guests of park management before returning to Virginia. The next morning I asked the little girl if she needed or wanted anything before she left for home. She paused and thought for a few moments, then sheepishly and reluctantly whispered something to me. She said that the previous day, while walking with the kidnapper through the gift shop, she saw a replica of a "Daniel Boone" raccoon-skin hat that she really liked. I looked at the park manager, and it took him hardly a moment before, without hesitation, he was leading the delegation back to the gift shop. Through his courtesy and generosity, the little girl returned to Virginia, thrilled to be the proud new owner of her own "coonskin hat." That morning, I returned to Louisville at a much slower speed, and with a lasting respect for the women who had joined our SA ranks.

A few years later, probably around 1982, I had an interesting additional experience relative to the position and feelings of women in law enforcement. By then, I had been promoted to SAC of the North Carolina FO with Headquarters in Charlotte, and was in Wrightsville Beach, North Carolina, speaking to a convention of Women in Policing. I praised the performance of the female FBI SAs with whom I had worked, and expressed my true appreciation for their efforts. I also commented honestly that, at that time, I was still not sure it would be the best policy to have women located on the front end of a battering ram, or in a potentially heavy tactical combat situation. I learned another lesson, when a few of the women met me at the podium after my presentation with some icy stares and stern faces. They proceeded to politely chastise me for my exclusionary comments. They wanted to express their strong belief that women should be involved in all police activities, no matter how dangerous, the same as men. I offered my apology for any statements that offended the women. Then, about an hour later, while walking outside the auditorium, I was approached by a larger delegation of the women attending the conference, who wanted to apologize to me and offer their assurance that my comments were right on target and summed up exactly what they felt. They went on to say that they believed most of the other women attendees felt the same. That day I learned firsthand just how complex and controversial the issue of women serving in law enforcement assignments had become.

Returning to the issues faced by our own female FBI SAs, it was further frustration for them that despite the fact that the women had met and begun to work through the early challenges from inside the Bureau, they started to encounter a few from the outside world. I recall at least two incidents in the early 1980s, while I was still assigned in North Carolina, when I was called by either one of the female SAs or an airline representative at some airport, relative to authority for our female SAs to carry firearms aboard an aircraft. Pilots were reluctant to allow female SAs to fly carrying their Bureau-issued weapons. In one instance, the SA held her ground and refused the pilot's demand that she surrender her weapon to him. She called me, and the standoff was eventually resolved when I was connected to the chief pilot for the airline (to the best of my recollection it was US Airways or one of its predecessors). I reminded the chief pilot that the Federal Aviation Administration specifically permitted all FBI SAs, both male and female, to fly armed. He was aware of the rule and relayed the information to the reluctant pilot, who still refused to fly the plane with the armed female SA, and walked off the plane. Unfortunately, the passengers on that flight were inconvenienced for a while, but, fortunately, a replacement pilot was found relatively quickly, and the flight continued with our SA on board and in rightful possession of her weapon.

The second incident was similar, but, as I recall, in that case the pilot only demanded that the SA empty her weapon and surrender the bullets to him. However, as in the other case, there would be no bargaining or compromise, and again I had a conversation with the chief pilot of that airline. He was advised that if that flight departed, the female SA would be on it, and she would be armed. That particular incident was then de-escalated, and the pilot reluctantly agreed to fly the plane.

Later, a retired female SA related to me her experience in being challenged by a pilot for trying to board his plane with her weapon. According to her, he stated she could board the plane if her weapon was safely resting in his lap, to which she quickly responded, "Okay, as long as I'm comfortably seated up there with it." As the story went, this situation was then resolved reasonably and peacefully, and she was permitted to board with her Bureau-issued firearm.

Regretfully, even as acceptance of the female SAs progressed both inside and outside the FBI, it was still a lengthy process. For example, by the late 1980s, I had received my transfer from North Carolina to head the Denver FO of the FBI. On one occasion, I recall a discussion with one of the squad supervisors, who appealed to me not to have a female SA under transfer to the Denver FO assigned to his squad. The arguments he made did not rise to any reasonable level that would convince me not to assign her there. As a matter of fact, there was a vacancy on that particular squad, and that is exactly where she was assigned. By the way, she performed extremely well, and was soon warmly welcomed as an integral and important asset to the squad.

Sadly, but in the FBI world probably not unexpected, as the female SAs joined the frontlines with their male counterparts, they exposed themselves to the same risks from deadly criminal violence. As of this writing, two female SAs have made the supreme sacrifice, falling as service martyrs in adversarial action, and joining nearly forty of their fellow male SAs in the FBI Hall of Honor. SA Robin L. Ahrens had just completed her FBI training in June 1985, and was then assigned to the Phoenix FBI FO. On October 5, 1985, a short four months later, she died from gunshot wounds received during the apprehension of a fugitive armed robber in Phoenix. She was the first female SA killed in the line of duty.

SA Martha Dixon Martinez had become an SA in 1987, and after a tour of duty in the Knoxville, Tennessee, FO, transferred to the FBI's Washington, D.C., FO. She was assigned to a homicide squad, and on November 22, 1994, happened to be in a meeting along with a fellow SA, Michael John Miller, at the Washington Metropolitan Police Department. Suddenly, a gunman burst into the squad room where they were meeting and shot and killed both the SAs, as well as a Washington, D.C., police officer. That day, Martha would become the second female SA to die from adversarial action in the line of duty, and inherit a permanent place in the Hall of Honor.

Although SAs Ahrens and Martinez have been the only female SAs to die as a result of adversarial action thus far, there have been others who made the supreme sacrifice in the line of duty while engaged in FBI business. SA Sheila Jean Regan perished in an accidental plane crash in Virginia on December 1, 1974. Others, sadly and indirectly, have become fatal victims of the 9/11 terrorist disaster. They are among the many law enforcement officers who were exposed to poisonous materials during assignments to search the massive wreckage and destruction left after the attacks, and have succumbed to fatal illnesses contracted during their extended exposure.

I believe we should salute and thank all of the female FBI SAs who have labored against the challenges, and served so well, once the window opened for them to join the SA ranks in 1972. They have been truly impressive, and I will offer two thumbnail examples of their high caliber from my own experience.

SA Sharon Smith was one of the first female SAs with whom I was associated. I met her early in her career when she was assigned to the Charlotte, North Carolina, FO. She eventually worked a variety of criminal and other matters in a number of FOs, and then spent a number of years teaching at the FBI Academy in Quantico, Virginia. She served from 1978 to 2003, and worked for her master's and PhD degrees along the way. She served loyally and professionally, and upon retirement, developed her own successful forensic psycholinguistics company called Threat Triage.

SA Suzanne Mencer was one of the last female SAs I had the honor and pleasure to work with prior to my retirement. Sue came to the Denver FO in 1990 to serve as a Supervisory Special Agent to supervise counterterrorism and counterintelligence matters. Her Bureau career lasted from 1978 to 1998, after which she further distinguished herself with an appointment from the Colorado governor to the position of Executive Director of the Colorado Department of Public Safety, followed by her appointment as the Director of the Office for Domestic Preparedness of the US Department of Homeland Security, in Washington, D.C.

Currently, women are not only assigned to investigative roles but also operate in literally all facets of FBI operations. They are active in undercover operations, perform as firearms instructors, and have risen to leadership positions throughout the Bureau, not only as squad supervisors but in executive FBI Headquarters positions, and into those most coveted ASAC and SAC positions – commanding FOs. Further, they are not only assigned in all of our domestic offices in the United States but also in many FBI foreign posts throughout the world. In fact, by now most of the SA workforce in the FBI looks at each other as neither male nor female, but just as FBI SAs, accepting the fact that some are women. By September 2019, there were 13,391 FBI SAs in the Bureau, and 2,772 (approximately 20 percent) were women.

CHAPTER 17

The FBI
and Bank Robbery

RECOUNTING MY CAREER IN THE FBI, the investigation and solution of bank robberies played a major role in the working lives of Special Agents (SAs) in virtually every field assignment. I could probably go further to say it is probably for many SAs their favorite crime to investigate. Coincidently, for many misguided criminals it also seems to be one of their favorite crimes to commit. It is really a story of its very own, so let's go back to the beginning and set the stage.

Banks and most financial institutions are insured by the federal government, making bank robberies felonies that fall under the jurisdiction of the FBI. If you wonder why anyone would want to rob a bank, I like to refer to a question once asked of Willie Sutton, one of America's classic master bank robbers. Asked why he robbed possibly one hundred banks in a period of more than forty years, he reportedly answered, "Because that's where the money is." Willie was unique and prolific as an American robber, who was a master of disguise, carried an unloaded gun since he was afraid someone might get injured, and was always polite and nonviolent. Once arrested and in prison, he would soon manage to escape. He was born in 1901 and first arrested in 1931, escaped from prison in 1932, and did the same thing two more times. Arrested finally in 1952 after a bank robbery, he went to prison and got paroled in 1969 to go on to advise banks on how to avoid robberies. At the age of seventy-nine in 1980, he passed away peacefully in Florida.

However, the story certainly doesn't start there. The FBI and bank robberies have been a major competing duo even before the agency got its name in 1935, and probably as early as the original Bureau of Investigation started in 1908. They certainly were prevalent when Mr. Hoover took the helm in 1924. They are still dueling today, and the interaction through the years has much to do with the development and transition of the FBI as arguably the nation's premier crime fighting agency.

After the Great Depression erupted in 1929, the following decade left the nation in economic chaos and gave rise to a group of lawless and murderous bank robbers whose exploits in the 1930s would make them famous or, more appropriately, infamous. Newspaper and radio headlines across the country reported the daring robberies of such familiar names and monikers as John Dillinger, Baby Face Nelson (whose real name was Lester Gillis), Bonnie (Parker) and Clyde (Barrow), Pretty Boy Floyd, Ma Barker, Alvin Karpis, and Machine Gun Kelly. In fact, it was Kelly (real name George Kelly Barnes) who first gave SAs the slang name "G-men" (government men) before the Bureau became the FBI in 1935. Kelly and his wife, Kathryn, were hiding out in Memphis, Tennessee, when SAs surprised them in 1933. Kelly dropped his weapon and yelled out, "Don't shoot, G-men." The nickname for the FBI SAs stuck at least through the 1940s.

At the same time, the media started picking up and reporting tales of the law enforcement agency that was leading the charge to track down and arrest the perpetrators. Frequently, the end results were blazing gun battles in which the bad guys were either arrested or killed by the newly named FBI or G-men. The war effort was being led by J. Edgar Hoover, who had labeled the bank robbers "public enemies," since they were all fugitives and notorious gangsters. Incidentally, naming one of the worst robbers Public Enemy #1 until he was caught, and then giving a number to the next worst one eventually led to the FBI's Ten Most Wanted program in 1950.

As celebrated as the FBI became during those years, there was a terribly sad downside. The seemingly unending violence with gunfights and shootouts during the arrests or encounters with these robbers left the 1930s with an inordinate number of FBI SAs making the list of service martyrs, who gave their lives in the line of duty.

Jumping ahead to the 1980s, it was a bank robbery shootout again on April 11, 1986, in southwest Miami, Florida, that caused a major change in weaponry for the FBI. SAs in three FBI vehicles became involved in a gun battle with two robbery suspects, who emerged from their vehicle firing automatic shoulder weapons. The SAs with revolvers and one shotgun were seriously outgunned. SA Jerry Dove and SA Benjamin Grogan were killed, and others were wounded.

Although the suspects were also killed in the incident, the FBI decided that violent crimes and heavily armed criminals of a new age would dictate more powerful weapons for SAs. Thus, the six-shot revolver gave way to semiautomatic pistols and semiautomatic shoulder weapons for SAs to carry and have available.

The risks notwithstanding, in my years in the Bureau, working bank robberies was probably the most coveted assignment possible. Many SAs actually entered the FBI for the ultimate "cops and robbers" experience they believed it to be. There was always heavy competition to be assigned to the bank robbery squad in larger offices like New York and Los Angeles, or a reactive squad in smaller offices, which would handle these robberies along with kidnapping, fugitives, bombings, and other miscellaneous reactive matters. These crimes are clear-cut violations and create an immediate reaction. Sometimes, they also allow swift results with solutions and very active arrests. I think any SA appreciates the energy high and adrenaline rush in taking down and handcuffing a badly wanted fugitive, terrorist, or bank robber.

However, to be sure, just as important to the FBI and the American public are the SAs who dedicate months, even years, to a complicated white collar crime case, involving thousands of documents, or when the subject may be a corrupt politician or highly placed crooked banker or business executive. When an indictment finally comes, the arrest might not be as dramatic or exciting, and might not even involve handcuffs, but the ultimate conviction is every bit as meaningful for American justice. Similar are the cases with vital efforts and endless hours of physical surveillance, by scores of FBI SAs, with justification or probable cause, but without the actual knowledge many times as to whether their quarry is really a spy or terrorist. These assignments are among those that can require exhaustive patience and still yield nothing but frustration.

Even though some SAs might be assigned to a squad or a special investigation with fewer reactive responsibilities, the important takeaway is to understand that all SAs are trained in the full investigative jurisdiction of the FBI and available to respond as necessary to the many special and unexpected emergency situations that occur with some regularity in every FBI FO.

Back on the relevant topic of bank robberies, probably the most common incident in my experience was what we called a "note job." The robber would enter the bank, walk up to a teller, and present a piece of paper with a handwritten demand for "all your tens and twenties" or other similar wording. The notes frequently added a warning not to trip an alarm or alert police. Some went a step further and claimed they had a gun or even a bomb as an added threat to their demand for cash. We have seen just about any possible scenario, and I recall one bank robbery in which the demand note was written on a deposit slip from the robber's own bank account. Needless to say, that case had a quick solution!

Our bank robberies were committed for all types of reasons by males and females, young and old. Most were nonviolent, but many were far from routine and potentially very dangerous. One interesting characteristic I've noticed with most bank robbers is that, for them, it is a career. You could almost use the expression "once a bank robber always a bank robber." One of our early normal leads in any unsolved bank robbery was to determine whether any convicted bank robber had recently been released from prison and whether he or she matched the description of our latest robber. Perhaps, as Mel Dellinger, the Gentleman Bandit, believed, bank robbery is the "ultimate crime" and worthy of making it a career.

For me and my career, bank robbery violence came early after I arrived in North Carolina. In March 1981, responding Fayetteville Resident Agency (RA) SAs encountered a robber leaving The First Citizens Bank and Trust in the Fayetteville Cross Creek Mall and were fired upon. An SA returned fire, and the robber's life ended fatally from a shotgun blast.

Between 1981 and 1982, SAs in both the Fayetteville RA and Raleigh RA were contending with a robber hitting banks in both their territories. In May 1982, after a robbery in Hollywood, South Carolina, SAs were in hot pursuit of the robber and were fired upon by the subject, using a .357 Magnum revolver with armor-piercing rounds. The SAs were not hit, but their FBI vehicle was disabled.

About ten days later on May 18, 1982, SAs developed information that the fugitive from that bank robbery, Huel Locklear, was hiding in the trunk of a vehicle and being transported out of the area. They located the vehicle near Dillon, South Carolina, stopped it, arrested the driver, then surrounded the car. The SAs carefully tapped on the trunk lid, and then with their vehicle public address speaker, welcomed Locklear to come out when he was ready, noting the temperature was well over ninety degrees in the South Carolina afternoon heat. He soon yelled his desire to surrender and came out for a badly needed drink of water. He had evidence of a superficial bullet wound in his rear end, apparently received in the earlier shoot-out when he disabled the FBI vehicle. A search of the trunk located weapons, including the .357 Magnum and a supply of armor-piercing bullets, as well as the bag of bank robbery loot. Locklear was eventually tried, convicted, and sentenced to thirty years in prison.

One of my favorite bank robbery stories is particularly memorable to me for two special reasons: one, it involved the longest drive in my career with emergency lights and siren operating (nearly three hundred miles); and two, it involved the nicest compliment I ever received from a bank robber. To set the scene, Thomas David Dixon was a serial bank robber from North Carolina who led the Dixon gang, usually made up of Dixon and one of a number of his associates. Dixon had been robbing banks most of his adult life (when not in prison), and most recently in South Carolina, North Carolina, and the Atlanta, Georgia, area. He was extremely dangerous, heavily armed, and known to carry explosives. He had reportedly made the claim he would never be taken alive, and if cornered by the FBI, would take as many SAs down with him as he could. Unknown at the time, Dixon and one of his associates, Guy Leslie Graesser, of Marietta, Georgia, were responsible for the October 19, 1984, robbery of a bank in Candler, North Carolina, in the extreme southwest portion of the state. They were armed with machine guns and also fired pistol shots into the bank ceiling.

On Halloween in 1984, I was in Rocky Mount, North Carolina, at the extreme eastern portion of the state, having lunch with the police chief. I got paged for an urgent call from my office in Charlotte. We had received a reliable tip from the Atlanta FBI FO that the Dixon gang was responsible for the Candler robbery and were hiding out in a cabin near Andrews, North Carolina, waiting to hit another bank. The Atlanta FBI SWAT team was en route to the location, as were SAs from our Asheville, North Carolina, RA, the Charlotte FO SWAT team, and other necessary support SAs, including air support. Since we would have some preparation time, I also invited a member of the newly organized special National FBI Hostage Rescue Team from Quantico, Virginia, to join as an observer/advisor. I left Rocky Mount and expedited, with emergency equipment operating, the approximate three hundred miles west across the entire state of North Carolina.

We all met at a strategic location down the mountain from the target cabin and organized our plan. Darkness had fallen, and our intelligence indicated both Dixon and Graesser were in the cabin with two women. Due to the presence of possible female hostages and considering the darkness, we decided to move SAs into positions around the cabin's perimeter, seal off the cabin, and wait for morning.

Later in the evening, we caught a break when Graesser and one of the women left the cabin and went down the mountain to a convenience grocery store. SAs of the Atlanta SWAT team carefully followed and surprised Graesser in the store. Although armed, Graesser was unable to use his weapon, and a physical struggle took him into custody. The SAs did say that potato chips and other grocery goods were literally flying as they wrestled him down. We were then concerned what action Dixon might take up in the cabin if he missed Graesser, but fortunately all remained quiet there through the night.

With the terrific assistance of the cabin owner throughout the incident, any nearby residents were quietly evacuated before morning. The North Carolina State Highway Patrol also assisted by blocking critical roads and rerouting traffic. As dawn broke on November 1, 1984, one of our surveillance planes was in the air patrolling the area around the cabin, and the SWAT teams were concealed and lying in wait. At about 9:15 a.m. a radio call came from our pilot: "He's out, alone, and only wearing jogging shorts, no way he can be armed." With that, SAs pounced on Dixon from every direction, and he was taken to the ground without any resistance and no shots fired. SAs radioed down to the command post that Dixon had a message for me. "Tell your boss, this was a damn fine bust."

The search of the cabin found the second woman, who was not charged, along with a veritable arsenal of weapons. Located under every piece of furniture and nearly everywhere else were blasting caps and several sticks of dynamite, automatic weapons, rifles, and 9mm semiautomatic pistols. The only downside to the operation, which turned out to be only temporary, was the loss of one of our radios during the chaotic activity. However, before long an anonymous call came into our Charlotte FO that the FBI radio could be found at a very specific location in the river in the Atlanta area. The FBI does not like to lose equipment, and sure enough, one of our dive teams located the radio. That made a safe and successful arrest scenario totally complete.

As a postscript, I later learned that, after getting paroled from ten years in prison for our bank robberies, Dixon started again, was arrested in Tennessee, and went back to prison where he later passed away. Another interesting fact or coincidence, although totally unrelated to Dixon, involved the location of the Dixon arrest in the remote cabin area near Andrews, North Carolina. Andrews is located just up the road from Murphy, which is close to the similarly remote area where FBI Top Ten Fugitive Eric Rudolph was arrested on May 31, 2003. Rudolph received life in prison for the 1996 fatal bombing in Centennial Olympic Park in Atlanta, Georgia, during the 1996 Olympic Games.

In North Carolina, a year or so earlier than the Dixon gang arrest, we were struggling with another bank robbery gang in a different part of the state. In the southeast region of North Carolina we were experiencing an increasing number of robberies allegedly being perpetrated by members of the Lumbee Indian Tribe, who lived in and around the area of Lumberton, Maxton, and Laurinburg. The banks were normally entered by more than one heavily armed and masked individual carrying a bag draped around their shoulders to carry the loot.

We made this a priority investigation and assigned a number of SAs to the area to attempt to determine the identities of the robbers and get the rash of robberies stopped. Eventually, we developed information from our sources that the bank robbers would leave the bank in one vehicle parked nearby, and after driving a short distance everyone would be dropped off except for the driver. The other robbers would then hide in a wooded area and wait for dark. After dark, the driver would return to the drop-off spot and look for some prearranged signal or symbol left by the others to indicate they were ready to be picked up.

Although we did have some idea of the suspect robbers' identities and the vehicles at their disposal, we did not have enough evidence to make any arrests. When information was developed about a possible robbery planned for a certain area, SAs were dispatched throughout the area that particular day. When the bank robbery notification was broadcast over FBI radio, responding units got to the victim bank early enough to determine which road the robbers took as their escape route.

There happened to be two masked robbers involved in that particular robbery, and intelligence had indicated which highway would be used by the driver to return to the Laurinburg, North Carolina, area, after dropping off the other robber. Upon initial notification of the robbery, other SAs were already en route east on US Hwy 74 to hold short along the highway west of Laurinburg, park, and wait for the expected getaway car. Right on schedule, one of the gang's known vehicles appeared heading east toward Laurinburg and Maxton. SAs pursued the vehicle, made a felony stop, and placed the driver under arrest. The next part of the plan was to have an SA drive the vehicle back to the victim bank vicinity and wait until dark.

That evening was very dark and rainy as SA Howard Burgin of our Fayetteville RA drove the bank robbery suspect's tan car from the bank area down the same road that had been taken on the escape route earlier that day. He drove back and forth through the area slowly, until on one pass he noticed a large tree branch on the road, which definitely had not been there earlier. Returning to the site and slowing down, SA Burgin heard a voice from along the road yell, "Stop," and the dark outline of the robber approached. SA Burgin challenged the robber with "FBI – stop," and a gun battle ensued. SA Burgin was not hit, and in the darkness, the robber retreated back into the trees. We called in additional SAs, requested fire engines and other equipment to light the scene, and sealed the area as best we could until daylight.

Early the next morning, we moved into the area the robber had entered and located a cache of weapons, the bank robbery loot, and a number of other items that were there to make him comfortable until he would have been picked up later the previous evening. Through-out the day, SAs canvassed the entire area, and eventually a tip came in that an individual had approached a house in that immediate area earlier that morning. SAs responded, located, and arrested the other bank robber. Based on those arrested, the entire gang was ultimately identified and effectively put out of action. When we figured out their method of operation and worked a strategy to defeat it, the situation brought home to me initially the famous quote of US Army General George Patton (stated earlier in this book), when he defeated his German nemesis General Erwin Rommel, the Desert Fox, in World War II. It took us a while but we also "read the book" of this bank robbery gang, just as we would do later in Colorado when we caught up with the Gentleman Bandit, Mel Dellinger.

In North Carolina, our bank robbery experiences were not limited to just the familiar "note jobs" with a demand for money, or the more violent gangs and other robbers with guns. Some robbers were innovative with their techniques and frequently just as dangerous.

In October 1984, a would-be robber walked into a Charlotte, North Carolina, bank with a small box attached to his belt. He told the teller that the box contained a bomb that would be detonated if he didn't come out with money. The teller flatly refused, and the man became frustrated, turned around, and left the bank. Of course, that was a gutsy reaction from the teller, but probably not the smartest move considering the potential consequences (and certainly not in conformance with training given to bank employees to comply with the robber's demand in the event of a robbery).

In June 1985, a robber entered the Central Carolina Bank in Butner, North Carolina, carrying a satchel filled with twenty-two sticks of dynamite, a timer, and a detonator. He demanded money, and the scene developed into a tense one-and-one-half-hour standoff, with SAs eventually convincing the perpetrator to surrender, due to the efforts of one of our SA negotiators. Afterward, the bomb was deactivated by a US Army demolitions expert from Fort Bragg.

Then, in April 1986, a bank in Smithfield, North Carolina, got a call, supposedly from a construction company, around the lunch hour when a single employee was in the bank. The caller stated they would be sending over an employee to take some measurements for a renovation that the bank had been considering. Shortly thereafter, a male in work clothes showed up and pretended to be taking measurements before suddenly announcing a robbery and tying up the employee. He waited there until the other teller returned from lunch and was forced to let him into the vault for a sizable loss of several thousand dollars. SAs successfully developed a lead that identified and arrested the robber. He was, at that time, employed with a printing business near Knoxville, Tennessee, but had formerly been with a firm that had worked on the bank's security system.

Transitioning from the Charlotte FO to my new assignment at the Denver FO in 1986, I experienced the same volume of "note jobs" along with the same troublesome and dangerous armed bank robberies. Getting past the Gentleman Bandit in 1987, with his record of fifty bank robberies, we turned our attention toward a new batch of serial robbers. Since we had no names yet for some of our frequent robbers, we found it easier to keep track of them by giving them nicknames.

Take the year 1989, for example. By late December 1989, we had experienced nearly seventy-five bank robberies in Colorado, which outnumbered the sixty-six we worked in 1988. Here are a few of the interesting characters we were chasing in 1989:

- The "Baby Faced Bandit," finally identified as David Lee Martin, was suspected in six bank robberies in Boulder County and the northern Denver Metro area. He was arrested in Salt Lake City after a robbery there on June 20, 1989.
- The "Chameleon Bandit" was a white male, twenty-five to thirty years of age, who always wore a ski mask or nylon stocking over his face. He was suspected in twelve bank robberies in the Denver Metro area, starting in 1988. He usually restrained the tellers and constantly changed his dress and appearance.
- The "Bandaid Bandit" was a Latino male, who wore a patch of gauze over his left cheek and a ball cap. He was responsible for three robberies in the Denver Metro area during 1989. After waiting his turn in the customer line, he greeted the teller with a handgun.
- The "Mary Poppins Bandit" was a white female thirty to fifty years of age who entered the bank wearing a flat-top hat and carrying a very large purse. She used a handgun during four robberies in the region north of Denver starting in 1989.

Probably our most interesting bank robbery arrest of the year, in March 1989, ended the colorful armed robbery career of eighty-two-year-old Jack Kelm. He had been wanted as the "Salt and Pepper Bandit" responsible for a number of armed robberies in the Loveland, Longmont, and Fort Collins, Colorado, area. He was spotted leaving the First Bank of South Longmont on March 28, 1989, by an eleven-year-old boy and his father, who noticed Kelm taking off a stocking mask and climbing on a bicycle amidst an exploding red dye security package inside the bank loot. The father and son followed Kelm in their car until the father was able to exit his vehicle and wrestle him down from the bicycle and wait for police.

Born in Germany on November 21, 1906, Kelm had been involved in criminal activity since he was a young boy. He was robbing banks and supermarkets since the 1920s, and had been arrested and escaped from prison a number of times, including an escape from a chain gang in Florida in 1936. In the 1940s, he was the tall member of a robbery duo dubbed "Mutt and Jeff," and after one Denver robbery he escaped in the squad car of the deputy chief of the Colorado State Patrol. In prison in Illinois in 1963, because of his age they called him the "Bifocal Bandit." In later years, he made his way back to Colorado and was living in Greeley. For some time, he was the custodian at a United Methodist Church in Greeley and beloved by staff, congregation, and neighbors, who described him as loving and caring. He carried a gun, which actually turned out to be a starter's pistol, and there were no records that the oldest bank robber in Colorado history had ever injured any of his victims.

Unfortunately, after a busy bank robbery year, we headed toward the end of 1989 alarmed with what we hoped would not become a future trend. On December 11, 1989, three armed black men, one carrying a machine gun, entered and robbed the Capitol Federal Savings in Denver. This robbery presented two ominous elements that always concern us most: one, multiple perpetrators; and two, automatic weapons. Fortunately, the robbery was solved and did not result in a dangerous trend.

The string of bank robberies continued into 1990, with a few new wrinkles to make things interesting. In February 1990, we arrested a former ordained minister who had developed mental health problems. He adopted a double life as a furniture salesman, and became a suspect in a string of robberies in Denver and Colorado Springs. He was eventually arrested for bank burglary, after an unsuccessful attempt to blow open a Denver bank vault with a self-constructed pipe bomb.

In April 1990, we had an interesting bank robbery in rural Wiggins, Colorado, perpetrated by one of two identical twins, Ricky and Ritchie from Greeley. We had to consider both of them suspects until we were able to verify Ritchie's whereabouts elsewhere on the day of the robbery, after which Ricky broke down and confessed.

In May 1990, we took down another of our robbers with the nickname "Hollywood Bandit," a suspect in at least six bank robberies in the Denver area, including one involving a shoot-out with the bank guard. Allan Bliler, age thirty-three, took such great photos by surveillance cameras (hence his nickname) that he was easily identified and tracked to San Diego, California, where he was arrested by the police and FBI.

The last bank robbery I will mention occurred in Denver the following year in 1991, and was, without any doubt, the most deadly and tragic in my FBI career. It happened on Father's Day, June 16, 1991, haunts me regularly, and will always be remembered as the Father's Day Bank Massacre. That Sunday, Denver Police Department (DPD) Chief Ari Zavaras and I had finished playing golf at the Overland Golf Course in Denver and were having lunch, when our pagers went off almost simultaneously. Calling into our respective offices, we both got the sad message – bank robbery at the United Bank Tower in Denver with fatalities. We expedited immediately to the location at 17th Avenue and Lincoln Street in downtown Denver (now known as the Wells Fargo Bank Building).

A robber had successfully penetrated the closed building, got down to the lower building level and into the bank guard security office, where he executed three of the bank guards. He then entered and robbed six employees in the vault area of nearly $200,000 cash. After a room-to-room search of the lower floors, a fourth guard was found shot to death in a storage room near the elevator on a different floor. An immediate and nonstop joint investigation was initiated by dozens of SAs and DPD detectives, who quickly focused on the strong probability that the robbery was an inside job.

It was established that the robber had gained entrance by calling from a ground level outside phone near a freight elevator, identifying himself using the name of an actual bank officer, and asking to enter the building. One of the bank security guards responded to let him into the building, and was probably the one found murdered in the storage room. The robber then entered and assassinated the other three guards in the security office before entering and accosting the six vault employees. Based on their descriptions of the robber, he was around fifty years of age, graying hair, a white male about five foot ten inches tall, one hundred and eighty pounds, with a mustache and wearing a bowler-style hat. He was also wearing sunglasses and had a bandage over his left cheek. After a few weeks of intensive investigation, the probable suspect continued to be someone with inside knowledge of the bank building, and with possible law enforcement experience. The spotlight began to focus strongly on a retired DPD sergeant named James King.

Investigators amassed a formidable amount of circumstantial evidence against King, including the following items, which were not all inclusive:

- He had worked at the bank for a period of time as a security guard after retirement and would have known how to access the bank on a Sunday morning, when the entire building was closed.
- He basically fit the physical description of the robber and had a mustache before the robbery, which suddenly vanished when he was seen afterward.
- He might have been known to one or more of the murdered guards, which could have been a reason for the four executions.
- With more than twenty years' experience as a police officer, he would know the importance of wiping the crime scene of fingerprints, securing tapes from the surveillance cameras, and taking keys and other records from the security guard room.
- It was reported that King was assigned for a time to the Identification Unit while with the DPD, and that assignment would have been all about fingerprints.
- The robber used a .38 caliber Colt Trooper revolver, and eighteen bullets were accounted for. King carried and owned the same make and model revolver from his police days. Police officers normally carried six bullets in the gun cylinder, and an extra two speed loaders, each with six additional bullets for a total of eighteen bullets. A former police officer would also know the importance of picking up the spent shell casings, which could be used for evidence.
- When questioned as a suspect about his service revolver, King claimed he had earlier disposed of it because it had a cracked cylinder. Most retired police officers, who carried their service revolvers for more than twenty years, would probably scoff at the idea that their weapon would ever be destroyed, no matter what the reason.
- During his time with DPD, it was reported that police officers would reload revolvers from a mixed pot of ammunition, since DPD would purchase mixed brands of ammunition from several different vendors. Bullets recovered from the victim guards were of several different brands. The average robber would very likely have in his revolver bullets from the same box or source.

- King had no good alibi for the time of the bank robbery. He claimed that on that morning he went from his home in Golden to downtown Denver to play chess. However, he had not played in some time, and the club he wanted to visit had been closed. Investigators believed he made up the story to explain his presence in downtown Denver, if someone had happened to see him there.
- Before the robbery, he had filed for bankruptcy and had heavy credit card and other debts.
- Just after the robbery, he secured a larger bank safe deposit box than he had rented previously.
- Inside the security guard office there was a locked room that formerly had a surveillance camera (possibly when King worked there), but which had since been removed. The robber apparently had tried unsuccessfully to enter the room by kicking the door. There was a clear shoe print on the wall near the door handle. A pair of shoes recovered from King after the arrest had the same tread pattern, but the FBI Laboratory determined they were not identical only because the pattern showed less wear.
- Of the six bank employees in the vault who actually observed the robber, five of them either positively or possibly identified King as the robber.

King was arrested on July 4, 1991, and tried on state charges of murder in the summer of 1992. As strong as the circumstantial evidence might have been, the case ultimately turned on the eyewitness testimony. During defense examinations of the eyewitnesses, enough questions were raised about who and what they had actually observed that the jury had apparently developed reasonable doubt that King was responsible. He was acquitted of all charges.

Some leads questioning the possibility of other suspects had been covered earlier, but the prosecutors, as well as most of the investigators, remained firmly convinced that King was guilty. The money was never recovered, and the case remained officially unsolved. It was reported that after the trial, King lived a quiet, hermit-like life and passed away from dementia on May 21, 2013. If he was indeed the one responsible, justice will now have to come from a much higher authority than we ever expected. I think about this case often and sincerely regret the loss of lives and missing justice for the four guard victims: Phillip Lee Mankoff, forty-one years of age; Scott Raymond McCarthy, age twenty-one; William Roger McCullum, age thirty-three; and Todd Allen Wilson, age twenty-one.

Bank Robbery: Observations and Conclusion

While Willie Sutton, the prolific career bank robber, might have been correct when he allegedly noted that he robbed banks because that is where the money is, the fact is that stealing the bank's money successfully is not so easy to manage, and in my opinion, a really stupid idea. I always tried, through press releases and comments during speaking engagements, to convince the public why crime doesn't really pay when considering a bank robbery:

1. It is a frequent pattern crime, which has one of the highest solution rates of those cases investigated by the FBI.
2. The average amount of loot taken by the robber is usually a few hundred or a couple thousand dollars, but seldom a large amount of money.
3. The bank robber is usually tried in federal court, and the conviction brings him or her many years in prison, especially if a weapon was used.
4. Bank robbery is both a state and federal crime and will bring an immediate response from the FBI, as well as state, county, or local law enforcement within the jurisdiction where the robbery occurred.
5. Use of multiagency task forces for fighting violent crime in today's society will bring the resources of even more agencies into the search for a bank robber.
6. Banks employ a number of security devices and measures to assist in solving bank robberies at their branches.

The bottom line – if someone wants to consider bank robbery as an occupation, they should do it only if they want to score less money than they expected, if they want to risk very heavy odds of being arrested, and if they want to plan on spending many years in a federal prison after their trial and conviction.

CHAPTER 18

The Media and
the FBI

IN THE WORLD OF LAW ENFORCEMENT, no matter how small or large the agency or department, and fully on a global basis, there will be an entity close by focusing on their every move – the various video, audio, and print arms of the news media. It seems to have been that way since the two institutions found their very beginnings. Whether one was to serve as a conscience for the other, to provide accountability, or to merely inform the public about their activities, the relationship has been there. Sometimes, it's a love or hate relationship and frequently contains some tension over the tenor or accuracy of the reporting, yet the beat goes on. Moreover, it has become a twenty-four-hour per day, seven-day-a-week affair.

Technology has developed to the point that breaking news can be conveyed to a waiting public almost instantly, not just in the United States, but around the world. This blanket coverage has been invented and cannot and will not be uninvented into the future. In fact, if possible, going forward it will probably become more intense and detailed, instead of less. Furthermore, it is not at all difficult to explain the "why" of what is happening. It's what the public wants! The news media is producing and pushing out a product that is of immense interest to the American public, and arguably their most important source is American law enforcement.

News media management as well as reporters often cite the rule they live by, "If it bleeds, it leads," in describing their news coverage. I think it fair to assert that a majority of Americans are more atten-tive to news stories that describe "bad things" that happen, whether they involve crime, violence, accidents, or natural tragedies. Perhaps the "good things" in our society are considered business as usual and are simply taken for granted. Regardless of the reasoning, in my expe-rience, most of the investigative or enforcement activities of the FBI have been of significant interest to the news media.

Dating back to 1924, when J. Edgar Hoover accepted the appoint-ment to head the agency, our activities were closely followed by the major media of the day, basically radio and newspapers. Stories of the early days suggest that, in the beginning, Mr. Hoover was cooperating with the media. However, gradually major leaks by FBI SAs, as well as law enforcement officers working with the SAs, began to interfere with and compromise ongoing cases. The result was a strict "no comment" response ordered for most of Mr. Hoover's tenure. It was made clear that press releases and comments would be made, or cleared, by the Seat of Government (now called FBI Headquarters) before being released to the media, and the actual spokesperson would normally be the Special Agent in Charge (SAC).

After Director Hoover's passing relations with the press were relaxed, and a clear policy developed by which FBI Field Offices (FOs) could handle press releases and contacts with reporters. Contacts were to be made by the SAC, or his or her designee, and limited to content that essentially did not compromise an ongoing investigation or violate the rights of an arrested subject. Common items announced in press releases would include arrests, indictments, search warrants/seizures, and convictions, as well as investigative priorities.

For me personally, dealings with the media started during my assignment as Assistant Special Agent in Charge (ASAC) in the Louisville, Kentucky, FO. Then followed numerous contacts with print, radio, and electronic media as SAC of the Charlotte, North Carolina FO and Denver, Colorado and Wyoming FO. Looking back, after literally hundreds of media contacts, the one and only episode I regretted, and which left me feeling a bit betrayed, occurred as I arrived in Charlotte. As I described in Chapter 10, my introductory press conference, in which I recited the current FBI priorities at that time, got the message misinterpreted. My mention of public corruption as a national priority deteriorated into an assertion by the media that I considered North Carolina a corrupt state. This brought a wave of defensive condemnation from public officials, including the North Carolina governor. Unfortunate and misleading as it was, the ultimate result was a wave of calls and mail reporting information, which, in turn, led to a number of FBI investigations.

I made it a practice to be as available as I could to reporters, to furnish as much information as the FBI press policies and guidelines would permit, and to always try my best to be fair and honest with them. I tried never to play favorites, but infrequently a reporter might uncover important details about a particular investigation that, if aired or reported, could adversely affect a pending case. On those occasions, I would respectfully request that the information be held back for that reason. I can't recall a single instance in which my request was not honored. In return for their understanding, I would give that reporter the first call at the point when that particular information could be made public.

With wholehearted belief in a strong and transparent press policy, I worked eagerly with the press for a number of important reasons: one, to show pride in our work and successes; two, to let the general public know of the widespread scope of the FBI's jurisdiction; and three, to encourage additional support and contacts from the public regarding other illegal matters that might generate new investigations. Taken together, I was hoping to garner the appreciation, trust, confidence, and respect of the public for the hard work of our FBI employees. As an aside, I attribute the mutual respect generated with the media for the fact that I continued, even into retirement, to receive requests for contacts and appearances from the Denver news media and the national TV news networks. For these contacts, I limit my comments to general law enforcement policy and procedural questions and not details regarding any specific ongoing investigation.

Frankly, I appreciate very much the work and stress of individual news reporters, who, in the majority of cases, do their very best under frequently tight and restrictive timelines and guidelines. With the explosive increase of media outlets and the keen competition to be "first" on the story, there are sometimes errors and inaccuracies in their reports. To be honest, I always prefer the "live shots" either on the local or cable news programs, since my comments are being broadcast live and complete for the length of the appearance. As most law enforcement interviewees know, the recorded "hits" in interviews you provide for later airing have some interesting results. The interview might last for several minutes or longer, while the segment that eventually gets aired during the story lasts only several seconds. Furthermore, the chosen several seconds frequently bring a smile or eye roll, since they are probably not the several seconds you would have preferred or expected!

Broadening our scope for a moment to the national picture, and even the world, there is an abundance of excellent training currently being made available to law enforcement public information officers, or press spokespersons, to make them professional players in dealing with the media. The days of "no comment" are effectively gone in favor of timely updates from the highest ranking officers available at critical events. It is ever more important to be as transparent as possible with the public, by offering factual, nonspeculative information without hampering or interfering with a continuing investigation. Of course, one of the main reasons, if not the main reason, is to avoid or stay ahead of the frequently speculative and inaccurate details that can easily pour forth otherwise from the plethora of omnipresent social media – Twitter, Facebook, and Instagram, just to name a few.

In my experience in North Carolina, Colorado, and Wyoming, dealing fairly with the media held other benefits. In both the Charlotte and Denver FOs, we decided to adopt a page out of the famous FBI's Ten Most Wanted Fugitives program and create a similar program locally to capture fugitives in our territory. Most readers have probably heard of what we refer to as the "Top Ten" program, which was placed into existence in 1950, in cooperation with what later became the United Press International, or UPI, to showcase some of the nation's most dangerous and badly wanted fugitives. Director Hoover implemented the list, and to give readers an idea of the caliber of those who made the list, the first person placed on it was Thomas James Holden, who was wanted for the murder of his wife, her brother, and her stepbrother. As of 2018, 521 fugitives have made the list, and 486 have been apprehended or located. Of those located, 162 were located as a direct result of citizen cooperation.

With the success of the Top Ten list in mind, the Charlotte FO inaugurated our Big Six Fugitive Program in 1982, and got excellent support and cooperation from the North Carolina media. So successful was the program that within six months, and by February 1983, we had arrested six of those placed on the list with the help of citizens in North Carolina and elsewhere.

Later, during my assignment in the Denver FO, we implemented the Fugitive of the Month program in May 1987. Again, with the full cooperation of the news media, we named our first fugitive to the program – Charles Allen Atkins.

In May 1981, Atkins was working as a security guard for Purolator Armored and vanished with $1,113,000 in cash from their Denver vault, the largest cash theft in Colorado history at that time. Leads to locate him had dried up, and the case was virtually at a standstill. With publicity from our new program, a flood of calls were coming in, but none of them was responsible for his location or arrest. Frankly, in this instance, the value of naming Atkins to the list was that it proved to be the linchpin to reignite interest from our own Denver SAs to go into a full-court press and craft new leads and start new innovative thinking in the hunt for him.

A successful initiative led to information that his children formerly attended a school in Lakeland, Florida. Florida SAs then developed information from a family who remembered the Atkins family and believed they had moved to the Santa Barbara, California, area around 1984, and then possibly moved on to Hawaii around 1986. The net started to tighten quickly, and on June 10, 1987, Honolulu SAs arrested Atkins without incident in Honolulu and recovered about $300,000 of the missing cash. He was located and arrested about two and a half weeks after ending up as number one on our new Fugitive of the Month list. Others who made the list took longer for justice to come knocking, but, as I recall, we located two of the next four within six months and considered the program very successful, thanks to the media cooperation and the public response.

Timing Is Everything!

An important factor to consider in dealing with the media, and expecting maximum coverage, is timing. Of course, in today's society with widespread criminal violence, terrorism, and other egregious tragedies, the "breaking news" phenomenon knows no particular time period. It creates its own timing, day or night. However, even absent a crisis, selection of a slow news day and early hours (so the media can make their deadlines) for a press conference can still fall victim to unavoidable bad timing. For example, I wrote in Chapter 12 about our long-term undercover operation, called Operation Aspen Leaf, in which we were hoping to advise of arrests involving some commercial companies for the illegal practice of dealing in prohibited products, sometimes classified, and trading them or selling them to unfriendly nations. It was an important case, worked jointly with the US Customs Service, and we had hoped to leverage our efforts to expose the practice of selling prohibited items and serve as a warning to other unscrupulous companies nationwide to abort any efforts or practices to trade with the enemy, so to speak. As this press conference commenced, a terrible bus accident with multiple fatalities occurred in the Rocky Mountains, and the press understandably scattered to cover the tragedy. Unavoidable yet understandable, the accident created terrible timing and nearly obliterated our message.

On the other end of the media spectrum, in what could easily be described as the perfect storm for a media news story to be extraordinarily well covered, the darling young Jon Benet Ramsey was murdered in Boulder, Colorado. On Christmas night in 1996, or early morning of the following day, six-year-old Jon Benet was strangled in her own home in what continues to be an unsolved mystery. Although the facts would have made this a headline media case at any time, the timing and circumstances kept it in the world headlines for months. First, it occurred during Christmastime, traditionally a very slow time for "hard" news. Second, the victim was a sweet six-year-old who had been a contestant in numerous children's beauty contests, leaving a virtual media treasure chest of wonderful photos and videotapes. Third, the family was wealthy and lived in upscale Boulder, Colorado, and the mother herself had been a former beauty queen. Fourth, questions arose as to the quality of the investigation provided by law enforcement and prosecutors. For all those reasons and more, the world news media descended on Boulder and stayed for several weeks.

As time passed, the story took many twists and turns and brewed considerable controversy. It was rich fodder for the cable TV talk shows, and had the necessary legs to stay atop the media's interest for months. Although retired from the FBI by that time, I ended up as an on-air media consultant for a few different TV networks and their local affiliates. In a seemingly unending series of appearances, my role was to try to balance the frequently bizarre statements and opinions of other media contributors with what I hoped were logical, factual, and rational observations based on my experience.

Calculating Level of Interest

As important as good timing can be in conveying your message to and through the press successfully, another factor involves judging the level of interest of the message recipients. Sometimes the topic and details stimulate a fire in the media that lifts a news story above and beyond any limit you might reasonably have expected. One case that springs to mind was reported earlier in Chapter 10 and involved our DIPSCAM investigation to identify and take down the dozens of "diploma mills" selling so-called students graduate level college degrees for little or no academic work.

Starting with a few search warrants executed in multi-FBI FO operations spread across the United States, SAs exposed dozens of phony colleges and universities, and found hundreds of "graduates" employed in industry, government, and the military. At the press conference announcing the investigation, the reaction was immediate and frankly, totally unexpected. Hundreds of inquiries were fielded for weeks. A feature article in *Newsweek* magazine followed, along with a variety of speaking engagements. We also accepted invitations for talk show appearances in major TV markets around the country for the next several months.

The Copycat Syndrome

We've already discussed the kind of stories and news that much of the public decides to read and watch. The big question for law enforcement is what action or reaction, if any, is generated by people in the audience receiving the information. If the news relates a positive story and prompts a similar or like positive action, that's a clear win. However, for some, hearing details of a horrible crime or particularly violent negative act seems to stimulate the need or desire to copy the act, and in some extreme cases, to attempt to increase the level of violence, as if in some sick type of competition. These copycat scenarios seriously concern law enforcement and are a clear loss for our society.

In past cases, critics have tried to blame the media for causing copycat-type criminal acts, but frankly, the media in most cases just reports the detailed facts. Normally, neither legal nor scientific evidence has been successfully developed to prove that the news reporting caused the resulting incident. That said, from a strictly logical, if only anecdotal, standpoint, it is difficult for many of us to ignore what appears to be a clear cause-and-effect relationship in a litany of school shootings, mass shootings, bombings, arsons, and other terrorist acts.

With the mass media reaching the farthest and most remote corners of America with twenty-four-hour coverage, I suspect there will be no simple solution or cessation to the problem. What makes matters even worse, with so many troubled juvenile and adult minds driven so close to the edge of rage or violence these days, it doesn't matter whether that trigger comes from an actual news report or the pervasive violence in dozens of entertainment-type programs.

Meeting with Greg Jbara, an actor from the police TV show *Bluebloods*.

Before examining the relationship between the FBI and entertainment programs featuring the FBI, and since anecdotal narratives seem to be the best proof of cause and effect when examining the copycat syndrome, let me mention a story that I recall from the past. In 1993, MTV, the prominent US cable TV channel, ran a popular animated program called *Beavis and Butt-Head*. In some episodes, the two featured cartoon adolescents played with matches and set fires, explaining how fire was fun. Unfortunately, it was not fun at all for one Ohio family. After watching the programs their five-year-old son found some matches and burned down their mobile home, killing his two-year-old sister. Despite the claims and opinions, there was no proof of fault on the part of MTV. However, MTV did remove all references to fire in those past program episodes and all future scripts, as well as airing the program at a later hour.

The FBI and TV Entertainment Media

How accurate is the portrayal of the FBI on the myriad TV programs and movies featuring the agency? That is a recurring question I have gotten frequently from my speech audiences and at other meetings. The answer is short and easy – not remotely close to reality.

Probably the recurring scenario that bothers me the most is the role relegated to FBI SAs in programs that feature other law enforcement agencies and officers as the main characters and heroes. The FBI or "feds" are customarily pictured as incompetent or arrogant, always walking into the room or onto the scene trying to take over the investigation. In all my years in the Bureau, I never participated in or even witnessed such an exchange in reality. FBI SAs depend so much on the assistance and cooperation of other law enforcement agencies that the negative behavior so frequently aired on the big or small screen would risk terminating any future cooperation from those agencies. That is not to say that differences of opinion and other personality conflicts do not occur from time to time, but, in my experience, they were infrequent and quickly resolved. In fact, in my experience, where there was both a federal as well as a state violation occurring, local authorities were usually very comfortable in asking the FBI to take the lead.

A prime example was highlighted in Chapter 8 describing my assignment in Kentucky. In a suburb of Louisville, county police were involved in a hostage situation in a trailer park. They had the suspect's trailer surrounded, the area evacuated, and the entire perimeter sealed. When they identified the suspect, the incident commander approached me and said, "Bob, he's an escaped federal prisoner – he's all yours. What do you want us to do?" We worked jointly through the night, and eventually the suspect surrendered very early the next morning.

The truth of the matter is that FBI SAs work very well with officers of most other agencies. In fact, today most major investigations are being worked by FBI SAs jointly with officers from various other agencies in a variety of task forces targeting such areas as drugs, terrorism, cybercrime, street crime, and child predators.

My other regret is the extreme and gratuitous violence that permeates most of the FBI television shows, and the fantastic, but unfortunately fantasy, crime scene investigation techniques used to quickly solve the crimes. If there is any truth that the copycat syndrome is responsible for repeating the violence and trying to make it even worse the next time, then I believe the violent TV shows bear some responsibility. With regard to the TV technology employed in solving crimes quickly, in large part it simply does not exist. Sadly, this fact is lost on many citizens and particularly jurors, who expect the same level of evidence to sustain a conviction at trial in a real court. Ironically, to take it a step further, to expect law enforcement to get technology solutions like they are getting on TV today would require super databases so massive they would dwarf the very databases that many Americans already complain about as being excessive and invading their privacy.

Finally, at least from the FBI's perspective, there is the question of investigative jurisdiction in many of the TV shows showcasing the activities of other US federal law enforcement agencies. Unfortunately, many of these shows play fast and loose with storylines showing investigations that tread well outside their agency's jurisdiction and well into that of the FBI. The FBI has primary jurisdiction over more than two hundred federal crimes, and I guess the only important point here is that the various shows continue to have good plots, good actors, good writers, and lots of viewers. From the viewers' perspective, it probably matters little whose jurisdiction is involved.

A good case in point would be the television show *NCIS* standing for Naval Criminal Investigative Service, made famous through the power of the entertainment media. A TV program featuring NCIS started on CBS in 2003, and enjoys a number of spinoffs that have also achieved popularity. Boasting a wealth of excellent acting and scripts with plenty of action, but frequently spilling into the FBI's jurisdiction, this show has been a popular staple for audiences not only in the United States but in TV markets around the world. I'm happy for the NCIS, since I'm sure the program has brought their personnel recognition and has allowed a justifiable pride in their hardworking military investigative agency.

Unfortunately, there is no such popular result for their equally hardworking US Army Criminal Investigative Division or the US Air Force Office of Special Investigations. And you certainly know you've achieved success and popularity with the people when your T-shirts, sweatshirts, hats, and other wearables find a prominent place in our Capital's gift shops. All around Washington, D.C., and its two major airports, you can find wearables of all sorts with the NCIS name emblazoned on them. Yes, the media has helped NCIS get its signature products right up there with the CIA and the FBI, whose wearables have held their prime positions for years in Washington's tourist and visitor outlets. Still, despite the TV fame, to my knowledge the actual jurisdiction of NCIS has not changed, and Americans should probably not hold their breath waiting to see anyone with hats or raid jackets bearing the letters "NCIS" conducting operations or raids on the streets of New Orleans, Los Angeles, or Washington, D.C.

FBI and Reality TV Crime Shows

In my opinion, what really has benefited both the FBI and numerous other law enforcement agencies has been the emergence of reality TV crime shows, which are actually a blend of both news and entertainment. Hundreds of fugitives have been located and brought to justice, and serious crimes solved by featuring the real-crime scenarios or fugitives on TV and seeking the help of citizens for solutions and locations.

In 1988, *America's Most Wanted* hosted by John Walsh debuted as the first crime-fighting TV program, followed the same year by *Unsolved Mysteries* hosted by actor Robert Stack. The resounding success of both programs definitely demonstrated that our citizens are interested and want to be actively involved in fighting crime and aiding the criminal justice process.

As a personal aside, thinking back to the origins of these crime-fighting programs, I feel some personal satisfaction and justification for some action I took in the late 1960s, as a young FBI SA. After returning to the United States from a trip to Germany, I submitted a formal suggestion to FBI Headquarters (FBIHQ) under the FBI Suggestion Program, based on something I had witnessed in Europe. Starting in 1967, there was a wildly popular and successful television show centered in Germany called *Aktenzeichen XY Ungelost*, translated as "File Number XY-Unsolved," which dramatized actual unsolved crime cases and requested assistance from viewers in identifying the perpetrators. They were reporting incredible solution rates with public assistance, and I thought it might have application in the United States and suggested FBIHQ consider a similar media program. Unfortunately, officials at FBIHQ responded that the FBI had never done anything like that, and they would not approve it with the belief that it would not be successful now or in the future. Well, it took about twenty more years, but then, finally, along came *America's Most Wanted* in 1988, and we haven't looked back since.

A very specific and dramatic example of the value of real-life cases presented on TV assisted the Denver FO in September 1989. The case of Leroy Joseph Chasson, age forty-one, had been featured on

America's Most Wanted in June 1988, and again in August 1989. Chasson was a convicted murderer, stemming from the stabbing of the son of a Boston, Massachusetts, police officer in 1977.

While serving a life sentence in Walpole State Prison, he carried out a daring and bizarre plan. After stabbing himself superficially seven times in the stomach in 1982, he was transferred to a Boston hospital for treatment. While there, his wife, Kathleen, dressed as a nurse and carrying a .45 caliber pistol, suddenly entered the operating room and lined up the medical personnel at gunpoint. Ripping away intravenous needles and heart monitors, Chasson and Kathleen fled to a waiting getaway car as pursuing guards fired at them.

They eventually made their way to Denver and settled peacefully in an apartment along East Tenth Avenue in Denver's Capitol Hill area. Chasson adopted the alias of James Garrity and was known as a friendly, charming handyman, while Kate, a nurse by occupation, worked as a health aide to the elderly and disabled in private residences.

As a result of the TV profile, a flurry of calls from Denver alerted Massachusetts authorities to Chasson's probable presence in our territory. We secured a Federal Fugitive Warrant and began to check out leads provided by the Denver callers. An SA dressed as a casual jogger moved through the suspected neighborhood and actually encountered the fugitive in a brief conversation, making a positive identification. Chasson then returned to his apartment and came back outside shortly thereafter, wearing a changed long sleeve shirt.

As the arrest team of SAs closed in, he pulled a handgun from under his shirt and began firing, forcing the SAs to return fire. Unfortunately, the results were fatal for Chasson, and very fortunately, one SA suffered only a grazed finger wound. Chasson's wife, Kathleen, who was later arrested for her role in the hospital escape, was at another residence assisting a patient at the time of the shooting. She claimed she heard about it on the news, and knew her husband would never let himself go back to prison.

It goes without saying that, in my experience, SAs always planned and spared no possible efforts to effect arrests without resorting to using firearms. Regrettably, in this case they had no alternative.

Although both *America's Most Wanted* and *Unsolved Mysteries* have now run their respective courses, their success was a breeding ground for a variety of similar programs, both on the major TV networks and on various cable networks, which work to fight crime or tell real crime stories. Even local TV news programs have gotten into the fight against crime with the brief Crime Stoppers reenactments, which offer cash for citizen tips.

Finally, on the news side, I personally applaud the work of the investigative reporters, who are becoming such an important part of local television news. Their efforts sometimes go where public law enforcement lacks the resources or time to get involved. Their results can frequently benefit either a single individual victim or sometimes an entire group of taxpayers. Importantly, they can expose and resolve problems, whether they lead to a criminal prosecution or just a badly needed peaceful resolution. It has been impressive to watch their evolution and progress.

A prominent example of their results comes to mind among the Denver media in the person of Brian Maass, a thirty-five-year Investigative Reporter for Channel 4, the CBS Denver affiliate. I've watched a number of successful and productive reports presented by Brian, but one clearly stands out.

In 2012, the Denver media routinely reported the death of a female named Toni Henthorn, who had accidentally fallen off a cliff in Rocky Mountain National Park in Colorado while on an anniversary hike with her husband, Harold Henthorn. A few days later, Brian received an anonymous tip that Mr. Henthorn's first wife, Lynn, had also died in a freak accident while out with her husband years earlier, suggesting that both accidents were really not accidents. Picking up on the possibility of foul play, Brian conducted extensive research, interviews, and a variety of other inquiries over a three-year period, which led law enforcement to arrest Harold Henthorn in 2014 for the murder of Toni Henthorn by pushing her off the cliff. His work also led to reopening the accident investigation into the death of Henthorn's first wife, Lynn, in 1995.

In 2015, Mr. Henthorn was convicted of first-degree murder in the death of second wife, Toni, and received a mandatory life prison sentence. As evidence of its significance and Brian's efforts, this case was featured nationally on the CBS's *48 Hours* investigation program titled "The Accidental Husband," which aired on CBS in April 2015.

CHAPTER 19

The FBI
and the US Military

MY CAREER STARTED IN THE MILITARY and it almost remained there. I have described earlier the "how" and "why" my life early on pointed in the direction of public safety as my real passion and goal. After college graduation and by virtue of the fact that I had selected ROTC military courses, I entered the US Army for my obligatory tour of duty as a commissioned officer. As it turned out, for me there could not have been a better choice or development to nurture and enhance my maturity and prepare me for a career in public safety. Nor could there have been a more pure introduction to public safety itself – so much so that when completion of my tour approached, I gave thought, more than once, to staying on for a military career.

Ultimately, in spite of my total respect for the military, I yielded to the pursuit of my first love – that of becoming an FBI Special Agent (SA). Having applied but heard nothing from the FBI on my separation day from Fort Dix, New Jersey, I drove off the base on the long drive back to western Pennsylvania, still wondering if I had made the right choice. Home just a few days, I got the good-news telegram from Mr. Hoover and prepared for my trip to Washington, D.C.

Although my dream job was realized, I never lost my attraction to the military and was fortunate to build and maintain strong bonds with various military branches in years to come. In fact, little did I realize when I started just how close in theory, practice, and mission I would find relationships between the military and the FBI. However, it should not really have been that surprising, considering we are both in the same business – protecting the security of the United States.

After graduating from New Agent Training School and starting my new career as an FBI SA, it was rather amazing how relationships with various military branches presented themselves to me, in both liaison settings and joint investigative capacities. In fact, the first relationship developed even before I graduated from training school! After initially reporting to FBI Headquarters (FBIHQ) in Washington, D.C., for a couple

days of introductory meetings, briefings, and orientations, I quickly realized just how closely the FBI and the military are related. In Washington,
we boarded buses and were transported to Quantico, Virginia, for our
basic training. Our training academy was located directly in the center
of the US Marine Base at Quantico. This gave us easy and frequent ability
to make contact with US Marine Corps members daily at the PX, restaurants, dry cleaners, barbershop, and everywhere else on base.

Later, after completing my first field assignment in the New
Orleans FO, I was selected to attend a yearlong course of instruction
in the Chinese Cantonese language, and transferred to Monterey, California. One other FBI SA and I were once again immersed in training
with a group of military officers and other military personnel at the
West Coast Branch of the Defense Language Institute, run by the US
Army at the Presidio of Monterey.

After graduation from the language institute, I was transferred to the
New York Office (NYO) of the FBI to put my newly-acquired knowledge
of the Chinese language and culture to work. Interestingly, among the
various tasks and responsibilities I assumed while assigned to the NYO
was one that placed me once again in liaison contact with the US military.
In matters involving possible espionage activities against the United States
by Communist China, we wondered about possible intelligence efforts
committed by the large number of Chinese ship jumpers illegally entering New York City, when certain vessels called at the Port of New York.
As a result, I had a continuing assignment to conduct liaison and provide investigative assistance, when necessary, with the US Coast Guard in
New York City. I would normally take the ferry to the base on Governor's
Island for meetings and networking. Periodically, I would ride along on
one of their forty-foot patrol boats doing spot-checks on and around the
vessels docked throughout the extensive piers and expansive territory
covered by the Port Authority of New York and New Jersey.

From the NYO, my next transfer took me back to FBIHQ in
Washington, D.C in 1969. Before long, I got diverted from supervising
counterespionage investigations and was reassigned to help determine if
any of the massive protests against the Vietnam War were being instigated
by leaders whose efforts were in violation of federal law (particularly
federal Anti-Riot Laws). Because of the violence involved and potential for even greater violent activity, the information being developed

was furnished to the highest levels of the US government, including the military. The mood was very tense, and the daily situations were extremely fluid. Again, relationships and information sharing with the various levels of the military proved very important and necessary.

Aside from the urgent protest-related stresses during this time, I also felt privileged to have an unrelated temporary assignment to work with the Defense Intelligence Agency in a very special project. The project involved assistance to the military in locating lost or missing servicemen from the Vietnam War. It involved covering some leads in the United States relating to family locations, and determining other facts pertaining to the missing troops. It was an honor for me to be able to assist, and I'm sure it was also for the other FBI SAs who covered the necessary leads.

In Washington, D.C., there are other examples of the close working relationship between the military and the FBI. For example, FBI SAs are each provided a fitness-for-duty physical examination annually. During my various tours at FBIHQ, these exams were routinely scheduled either at the Bethesda Naval Hospital in Bethesda, Maryland, or the Walter Reed Army Medical Center in Washington, D.C. (In 2011, both of those facilities were merged into what is now called the Walter Reed National Military Medical Center in Bethesda, Maryland.)

While assigned in the Louisville, Kentucky FO as Assistant Special Agent in Charge, I maintained a liaison relationship with command officers at Fort Knox, located near Louisville, Kentucky, and Fort Campbell, located near the Tennessee border and the Kentucky city of Hopkinsville. Fort Knox is a US Army base that hosts mainly armored units, but it is best known as host to the US Bullion Depository, which reportedly secures about $186 billion worth of US gold reserves. Fort Campbell is the US Army base best known as the home of the celebrated and decorated 101st Airborne Division.

During my first visit to Fort Knox, I was given a tour by command officers and invited to play a round of golf at a course on the base. The base held the General George Patton Museum of Cavalry and Armor, with features such as the vehicle in which the famous general was injured in an auto accident leading to his death in 1945, as well as his two ivory-handled revolvers. Other memorabilia there celebrate the history of armor in the development of the US Army. After the tour, we moved to the golf course and a very important briefing.

It so happens that the golf course on base is situated right next to the US Bullion Depository property, with their borders separated at some locations only by a fence – but a very important fence. I was cautioned, very specifically and passionately, that if any ball goes through or near the wire fencing, not to make any effort to retrieve it. Well, during the game, as you might expect, I hit one ball that rolled just under the fence. I could have reached it – and actually was about to, because I thought it would not disturb anything just reaching a couple of inches inside the fence. But then I thought better of it, stopped, and was reassured by my relieved hosts, running toward my location, that if I had reached beyond the line of that fence, the sound and light show would have been "memorable." Needless to say, I was very pleased that I followed their instructions exactly on that particular occasion.

It was on one of my other visits to Fort Knox that I received a wonderful surprise. Unexpectedly, and purely by accident, I spotted the first sergeant who had served me so well back in Fort Dix, New Jersey, in Company F, 3rd Training Regiment. He had been such a helper to me as a young, inexperienced company commander and was truly a mentor from whom I learned so much. He had since retired from the US Army and was working at Fort Knox as a civilian in a support capacity. It was an incredibly special treat for me to see First Sergeant Lloyd Pool again, and enjoy a warm and welcomed reunion.

During my assignment in North Carolina, I had liaison contact mainly with command officers at Fort Bragg, the US Army base in Fayetteville, North Carolina, and Camp Lejeune, the US Marine base near Jacksonville, North Carolina. I especially valued the warm relationship developed with Colonel Charlie Beckwith, founder and commander of the First Special Forces Operational Detachment-Delta, which is commonly referred to as the Delta Force, the elite special forces counterterrorism unit. We had frequent contact, and he was always eager to have me observe how Delta troops were trained, along with showing me the latest and greatest tools, communications gear, and other equipment and weapons the troops had at their disposal. He graciously agreed to travel, on one occasion, and speak about leadership during one of our FBI staff conferences. On a couple of occasions, we invited some of his unit members to observe active FBI tactical operations, but only to observe, since they were prohibited by law from getting actively involved in any nonmilitary, domestic law enforcement activities.

I recall first meeting Colonel Beckwith after he had led the aborted and failed attempt to rescue fifty-two American hostages who were being held captive at the US Embassy in Iran. They were taken hostage in November 1979, and the rescue attempt in April 1980 (code-named Eagle Claw) failed due to command and control, logistical, and communications problems involving the helicopter air support. Colonel Beckwith was extremely upset, and the incident essentially resulted in similar future operations being conducted under one single command (including air, land, and sea, if necessary). It was recommended by Colonel Beckwith and would be named the Joint Special Operations Command. He was a great leader and passed away, after retirement, in Texas in 1994.

Speaking further of Fort Bragg experiences, I remember being invited by the Commanding General's Office to come to Fort Bragg and make a one-hour luncheon presentation to the entire base officers corps on the topic of terrorism. While sitting at the head table with the General during lunch, and just prior to my speech, he leaned over to me and said, "Bob, what's your plan? I never heard a speech worth anything that went more than thirty minutes." I paused and realized that my outline and notes were put together for the entire hour presentation that they had requested. After some very rapid calculations and much mental cutting and pasting, I answered, "I agree, General, I figure that my comments should be just about thirty minutes." They were, and everyone was happy.

Due to the excellent relationship SA Tom McNally and the other SAs of the Fayetteville FBI Resident Agency had with Fort Bragg, my family got invited to an absolutely fascinating annual demonstration at one of the firing ranges on base. The day included troops of the famous 82nd Airborne Division jumping from planes, air drops of heavy military vehicles and other equipment (which landed with pinpoint accuracy in front of the grandstand viewers), and then the main attraction. The highlight of the day was called the "Million Dollar Minute" and demonstrated an incredible amount of firepower. It simulated what the military would refer to as a "final protective line," which might occur if an emergency situation in battle would require all the weapons of an infantry platoon or company (augmented by all the other infantry support units), to fire simultaneously at rapidly approaching enemy targets in front of them – all this at the approximate cost of about $1 million per minute. In addition to live fire from lines of infantry troops, heavy support was coming from the powerful machine guns, grenade and rocket launchers of Cobra helicopters, army tanks, mortars, and other artillery. It was thunderous and exceedingly impressive for all of us viewers.

Upon transfer to the Denver FO, I learned that my new territory hosted some of the most important and critical military installations in the country, most of which were located in the Colorado Springs area. The heavily populated Fort Carson US Army installation is home to the 4th Infantry Division, in addition to several other units, including a military police battalion and a Special Forces Group. It was a distinct pleasure being able to network and conduct liaison activities with many of their command officers. Moreover, it was an honor to be invited as a guest speaker for a number of their meetings and banquet events.

Likewise, I thoroughly enjoyed my contacts and relationships at nearby Peterson Air Force Base, as well as the US Air Force Academy, where I was occasionally requested to address a cadet class as a guest lecturer. In matters involving the air force, probably my favorite contact was General John Piotrowski, who at the time was commander in chief of the North American Aerospace Defense Command (NORAD) operating out of Cheyenne Mountain, and later moving to Peterson Air Force Base. General Piotrowski, who retired in 1990, was a true gentleman and had the reputation of being a great leader.

The city of Denver itself hosted the Lowry Air Force Base (LAFB), which started in 1938 as a US Army Air Corps post and later served as a US Air Force base until officially closing in 1994. Its last runway had closed in 1965, and from that point on the base functioned principally as a technical training base, hosting a number of units and functions. Earlier, from 1955 to 1958, it had served as the first home of the US Air Force Academy. During my time with the Bureau, we had major air force contacts at LAFB with frequent visits and meetings. In fact, I was delighted and honored to have my retirement celebration held on base at the Lowry Officers Club.

Recalling LAFB, one interesting incident comes to mind. On the evening of Saturday, September 14, 1991, the Colorado Society to Prevent Blindness was sponsoring an event to select the winner of a contest called the "Most Beautiful Eyes in America." The venue was an upscale property in Denver called Cableland. There were ten named finalists (both men and women). I had been invited to serve on a panel of celebrity judges along with Denver's District Attorney Norm Early and three others. The attire for the judges was to be formal with tuxedo requested for the men. The function was widely attended by the "Who's Who" of Denver, and prior to the judging we were enjoying a beautiful buffet.

Suddenly, I got paged and requested to make an emergency response to a hostage situation ongoing at LAFB involving a civilian. Hastily expressing my regrets to the host, I made it to my Bureau vehicle and expedited, with the emergency equipment operating, to LAFB. Screeching to a stop at the gate, I asked the security police officer for directions to the incident. He responded and then, as he looked at my tuxedo, I'll never forget his next comment – "Wow, I've always heard FBI Agents were the best dressed in law enforcement and now I know why." I couldn't tell for sure whether he was serious! At any rate, we were able to de-escalate the hostage situation and free the hostage with a peaceful arrest of the subject.

As some of the above stories illustrate, not only did the goals and mission of the FBI show many parallels with the military, but the bonds between the two were strong and real. Clearly, this relationship paid dividends in many respects, including the ability to work together well in actual criminal investigations.

In North Carolina around March 1982, the US Army Criminal Investigative Division at Fort Bragg furnished us information that certain civilians were selling new military products at very low prices through surplus stores in Fayetteville, Wilmington, and Asheboro. This led to the first civilian and military Undercover Operation (UCO) in North Carolina history, and ultimately involved property worth millions of dollars, including C-rations, uniforms, gas masks, furniture, blankets, tools, canteens, batteries, auto parts, and even heavy equipment (a front end loader).

Among others, it involved a scheme to manipulate the military direct exchange program, which allowed criminal subjects to purchase old and worthless military articles, store them in warehouses, and then utilize a corrupt military supply sergeant to direct exchange the worthless goods for brand-new ones, which the fraudsters would then sell.

We used a Charlotte FO SA to act as our Undercover Agent posing as a military supply sergeant. Starting at Fort Bragg, the UCO-dubbed

STOMP, for Stop Theft of Military Property, spread to the Camp Lejeune Marine base, Marine Corps Station Cherry Point, and Marine Corps Station New River (all in the Jacksonville, North Carolina, area). It was worked jointly with the Army Criminal Investigation Division and the Naval Criminal Investigative Service (NCIS).

The investigation was high risk since one of the principal fugitive subjects was a former US Marine captain, formerly assigned at Camp Lejeune, who carried live hand grenades and vowed never to surrender. A search of his residence ultimately recovered ammunition, grenades, and automatic weapons. Another search recovered a marked police car stolen from the Greenville, South Carolina, Police Department and buried underground. This subject was eventually arrested in November 1984 near Hendersonville in western North Carolina, after shooting the owner of a tractor he was attempting to steal. By September 1984, STOMP had resulted in its first twenty-six indictments, and by the time I prepared to depart North Carolina for my next assignment, the number of indictments, arrests, and convictions had exceeded forty and was still growing.

During my time in North Carolina, another interesting situation developed involving Fort Bragg. It seemed every year the base was visited by a traveling carnival that brought the usual variety of rides and games for the enjoyment of the base and area population. Fort Bragg command personnel contacted us and passed on a suspicion that some of the games of chance might be rigged, and wondered if we could check it out. As requested, we brought in one of the FBI gambling experts from the FBI Laboratory, and had him visit and try each of the games at the carnival. Based on his expertise and experience, each and every game attempted was rigged and virtually impossible to win.

Applying for and receiving a federal search warrant, we prepared a massive raid of the Fort Bragg carnival. We did not necessarily consider it a high risk raid, but we needed to use dozens of SAs merely due to the size and scope of the operation. With the numerous targets identified and assigned to specific raid teams located around the carnival perimeter, I instructed that the simultaneous searches would commence when they heard my vehicle siren.

I should have known better, but I soon realized that a police siren was no match for the sounds generated by the music, rides, and festive voices of hundreds at a large carnival. I could barely hear the siren myself and had to resort to announcing the raid over the FBI radio. We successfully searched and seized a large truckload of illegal rigged gaming devices for further examination and confirmation of fraud by the FBI Laboratory. I think it was the least we could have done to help prevent some of our troops and their families, who were serving our country, from being ripped off by thieving con artists.

On a much more serious note, we teamed up with NCIS in 1984 in the case of a US Marine stationed at Camp Lejeune, who was arrested in May of that year for supplying nuclear, biological, and chemical warfare defense information to Soviet and Eastern European spies. This was the first espionage arrest in North Carolina to be made public in many years, and the subject was tried by the military in a general court-martial.

Fast forward then to 1991, I was now in Denver and encountered a very regrettable situation at Fort Carson. We received information that a twenty-two-year-old US Army warrant officer first class helicopter pilot was soliciting a murder-for-hire contract. Sadly, his would-be target was his own father, a retired commercial airline pilot residing in Reno, Nevada. Apparently, the motive was money, since the father had received a lot of it recently upon settlement of his own father's estate. The subject planned that his father's death would have allowed the wealth to be passed along to him. Fortunately, we were successful in getting an undercover FBI SA into position to play the part of the contract killer. The killer was to pick up a gun from a car in Fort Collins, Colorado, and drive to Reno, Nevada, for the "hit." The victim was to be killed in a "quick, violent, and surprise combat maneuver." The car was located as described, and contained a 9mm semiautomatic Heckler and Koch assault rifle, along with two loaded thirty-round magazines. Based on the evidence, the contract murder was aborted, and the warrant officer was arrested and charged.

All in all, when I look back through my years with the FBI, and the incredible relations I've had with all branches of the military and all the events and experiences we've shared, I sense a great irony. That is, if I had made the choice to stay and pursue a career in the military, there is every probability that I would never have had the opportunities, relationships, experiences, and highest level contacts I have enjoyed with the military as an FBI SA. I truly appreciate the irony and feel very confident that I made the right choice.

CHAPTER 20

What Does It Take to Become an FBI Agent?

"HOW DO YOU BECOME an FBI Agent?" is probably the most frequently asked question I've encountered, both during my years in the Bureau and on into retirement. To provide the most complete answer, I have condensed details from several of the FBI's recruiting brochures and am dedicating a separate chapter to the response:

- Age twenty-three to thirty-six (SAs' mandatory retirement age is fifty-seven, and they must have twenty years' service to retire)
- Be a US citizen
- Possess a valid driver's license
- Possess a college bachelor's degree plus two years of professional work experience (one year with a master's degree)
- Pass the FBI physical fitness test
  - Maximum number of continuous sit-ups in one minute
  - A timed three hundred-meter sprint
  - Maximum number of continuous push-ups (untimed)
  - A timed 1.5-mile run
- Pass an FBI drug test
- Drug policy:
  - Any use of marijuana within the past three years
  - Use of any other drug in the past ten years
  - Selling, distributing, manufacturing, or transporting any illegal drugs
  - Use of prescription drugs or a legally obtainable substance in a manner for which it was not intended within the last three years
- Ability to pass rigorous background investigation to obtain a top secret clearance
- Commit to serving as a Special Agent for a minimum of three years
- Available for assignment on temporary or long-term basis worldwide
- Carry a firearm and be able to participate in arrests, execution of search warrants, raids, and other dangerous assignments

- Entrance salary for SA: approximately $80,000 annually (including all benefits)
- Training period at FBI Academy, Quantico, Virginia, for successful candidate for twenty-one weeks
- The preferred backgrounds include the following five programs:
  1. Attorney
  2. Certified Public Accountant
  3. Cyber expert (information technology, science, or engineering)
  4. Expert in foreign language (Spanish, Russian, Chinese, Arabic, etc.)
  5. Diversified – military, law enforcement, intelligence agency, behavioral sciences, etc.

In addition, the FBI has an honors intern program and also recognizes a military veterans preference.

- Also important are the nonstarter, automatic disqualifiers:
  1. Conviction of a felony
  2. Violation of FBI drug policy or failure of an FBI-administered drug test
  3. Default on a student loan insured by the US government
  4. Failure to register with the Selective Service System, if a male
  5. Failure to file income tax returns
  6 Failure to pay court-ordered child support
  7. Knowingly or willfully engaging in acts or activities designed to overthrow the US government by force

Please note that the information above is effective as of November 2019, but interested candidates can visit the website www.fbijobs.gov at any time for additional information, as the qualifications do change occasionally due to the changing needs of the FBI.

As this is being written, the current Bureau recruiting brochure is entitled *The FBI, A Career Like No Other*. I couldn't agree more with that description, and would seriously recommend an FBI career to any qualifying American. True, competition for FBI SA positions is tough and demanding, but successful candidates would be part of a best of breed workforce with a most challenging mission. Moreover, you would be giving back to your country, through the honor and responsibility of enforcing its laws.

CHAPTER 21

After the FBI

Juvenile Justice, a Portion of the Passion

HOPEFULLY, BOTH THE DECISIONS in my life and my career moves have adequately demonstrated that my burning passion since early youth has been public safety. Whether that meant wearing a military uniform or carrying a badge and a gun, my life has vectored in that direction. So in 1992, as my retirement from the FBI approached, I knew that some new decisions would be coming. As the news of my retirement became public, along with my intention to remain in Colorado, I was contacted by a member of the Colorado governor's staff and asked if I would consider an appointment to one of the boards or councils that assist the Governor in serving the people of Colorado. I agreed to review a listing to determine if there was a spot where I might be able to contribute and also maintain my lifelong passion.

After a quick perusal of the organizations and their missions, one particular council caught my attention – the Colorado Juvenile Justice and Delinquency Prevention Council (JJDP Council). Working so long on the enforcement side, I had become interested and a believer in the value of prevention. Furthermore, at what better level could there be to get involved than with juveniles before they could become hardened criminals. I especially looked forward to applying some effort on the softer side of criminal justice to help make a difference for public safety. What I never expected was that my commitment would involve literally hundreds of hours, strictly as a volunteer, and that along with many thousands of air miles.

The Governor appointed me to the JJDP Council, and at the next scheduled meeting I began to learn more about the council and meet with the other members. It was staffed by members of the Division of Criminal Justice, which is a part of the Colorado Department of Public Safety. There were as many as thirty and sometimes more members, who represented nearly every possible organization or agency that might deal with criminal justice as it applies to juveniles. For example, we had prosecutors, members of the defense bar, juvenile court judges, college educators, law enforcement, social services representatives, youth representatives, Native American tribe representatives, youth corrections officials, and even representatives of the Colorado state legislature, just to name some of the groups. I also found it interesting that among the membership was Colorado's first permanent executive director of the American Civil Liberties Union, Jim Joy, who represented an agency whose policies and practices were sometimes at odds with the activities of law enforcement agencies. All in all, I surmised quickly that this would be an interesting and most appropriate group to address Juvenile Justice .

Unaware initially, I became aware early on that this council was born of a federal law called the Juvenile Justice and Delinquency Prevention Act (JJDPA), passed by Congress in 1974 to improve the effectiveness of the Juvenile Justice system. The act authorized State Advisory Groups (SAGs), with all members appointed by their state governors, to act in coordination with a federal office called the Office of Juvenile Justice and Delinquency Prevention (OJJDP). OJJDP is part of the Office of Justice Programs, which in turn is a component of the US Department of Justice (DOJ). It was not lost on me that I had just retired from an agency of the DOJ where I got paid, and was now a member of a council that was tied to the DOJ, and for which I was an unpaid volunteer.

In effect, my Colorado JJDP Council was actually the Colorado SAG, to be under the general supervision of OJJDP in Washington, D.C. Using a series of grants from OJJDP, the SAG was to award funding to state agencies and organizations that developed the best programs to help local communities address issues such as prevention of violence, drug and alcohol abuse, and youth gangs. In addition to awarding the OJJDP grants, the SAG was also responsible for coordinating the grants with other types of available state and federal funding to ensure all resources provided the most effective community solutions to juvenile crime and delinquency.

The JJDPA has been reauthorized a number of times, the last in 2018, and has consistently been anchored to four specific core requirements. They are:

1. Deinstitutionalization of status offenders, meaning that juveniles should not be locked up for situations that would not be criminal

if committed by an adult (e.g., runaways, truancy, curfew violations, etc.);

2. Removal of juveniles from adult jails or lockups;
3. Sight and sound separation of juveniles from adult offenders;
4. Disproportionate Minority Confinement (DMC), which changed
   to Disproportionate Minority Contact (DMC) and was related to
   racial and ethnic disparate treatment of juveniles.

SAGs of all fifty states, as well as US possessions and territories and
the District of Columbia, are constantly monitored for how well they
comply with those four core requirements. Grant funding itself, as well
as other funding from OJJDP, can be withheld from the SAG that slips
out of compliance with one or more of those requirements. The first
three requirements are reasonably easy to identify and measure. They
deal with the possible harmful effects that can result from nonviolent
juveniles' contact with dangerous and violent adult criminals. The
fourth has been an effort to deal with the statistical overrepresentation
of minority youth in the Juvenile Justice system.

Frankly, most will agree the DMC requirement has been the most
difficult, not just to quantify, but to deal with and resolve. Studies have
been exhaustive, special conferences held, and sincere programs initiated – yet the complete successful solution seems to be evasive. During
my tenure on the Colorado SAG, in conversation after conversation
with police chiefs and sheriffs, the topic would come up, and almost
without exception the response would be the same. According to them,
there was absolutely no targeting of minority youth per se. They were
either being contacted in connection with law enforcement activities
in specially designated high crime areas, or as a result of specific calls
for service from victims in high crime areas.

In a somewhat related context, I can recall several occasions while
serving on the Colorado SAG during which I would meet with small
groups of incarcerated youths in juvenile facilities. One hypothetical
question I sometimes asked both white and minority juvenile inmates
was along the lines of, "What would you do if out walking alone late
at night minding your own business and a passing police car slows
down and pulls over toward you?" Usually the white youth explained
he would stop and speak with the police officer, explaining he had been

studying with a classmate and was heading home, or would just calmly make up a lie about his activities. Curiously, the minority youth would frequently tell me he would probably take off running as the police approached. I believe it would be easy to understand how that action would probably initiate an unwanted police contact. Well, whatever the reality, the DMC core requirement has been very difficult to satisfy.

Attendance on the SAG meant many meetings of the entire group, supplemented by meetings of subcommittees formed to discuss activities surrounding each of the core requirements of the JJDPA. It also included attendance at related conferences and trainings, both inside and outside of Colorado. Probably the most important mission and work of the SAG involved review and ratings of large numbers of applications for the various grants available from OJJDP and other sources. After review of the lengthy applications, the SAG would meet to review the results and make awards. Frequently, meetings would also include presentations from and evaluations of programs striving to become best practices in the Juvenile Justice and violence prevention areas.

It was apparent to me that the mission and work of the SAG had considerable merit, and after serving for several months I agreed to honor a request from state officials to assume the position of chair. Then, after presiding over the Colorado SAG for an additional period of months, I was honored to be elected chair of the Western Region of the SAGs. The United States and its territories and possessions are divided into four regions, of which the Western Region represents the largest area, comprising sixteen states and the US territories of American Samoa, Guam, and the Northern Mariana Islands. The region also includes the distant states of Alaska and Hawaii. Meetings, correspondence, and travel to handle matters of the region understandably added an increased demand on my time, attention, and effort.

Into the future, after several additional months, I was truly honored to be elected vice chair of the national Coalition for Juvenile Justice (CJJ), headquartered in Washington, D.C., which is responsible for overseeing the organization, strategy, mission, and goals of all SAGs in the four regions – (1) New England Region with eleven states, (2) Virgin Islands and the District of Columbia (3) Southern Region with twelve states and Puerto Rico, and (4) the Midwestern Region with eleven states, in addition to my own Western Region.

My year as CJJ vice chair was spent to support the efforts of the national chair, an incredibly gifted and dedicated advocate for children from North Carolina named Linda Hayes. She would go on to be appointed by the governor of her state to the cabinet position of secretary of the Department of Juvenile Justice and Delinquency Prevention. That year ramped up to the year 2000, during which I represented CJJ as national chair into the new millennium, with support from the newly-elected vice chair, Judge B. Thomas Leahy, judge of the Superior Court of New Jersey. As expected, life during that year required

a tremendous amount of air travel, presentations, and presiding at meetings and conferences. It also meant frequent contacts with CJJ Headquarters, as well as OJJDP, in Washington, D.C. On one occasion, the contacts reached the level of the Attorney General of the United States. I reflected occasionally that my desire to play an expected minor role in Juvenile Justice had landed me in a virtually full-time volunteer position in its arena.

Meeting with US Attorney General Janet Reno regarding juvenile justice matters

Aside from the many lessons learned and lasting friendships from my year as national chair of the CJJ, one benefit of the position stands out and was clearly significant. I was able to decide on the theme and thrust of the 2000 annual report, which we prepared for the President, the Congress, OJJDP, and the American public. The topic was one that concerned me then and continues to haunt me to this day – the immense problem of mental health disorders among our youth. The title of the 2000 annual report was *Handle with Care: Serving the Mental Health Needs of Young Offenders*. We hired professional consultants and writers to conduct, and report the results for, a yearlong investigation into the shortcomings and successes of mental health services in the Juvenile Justice system. As we all had hoped, writers John Hubner and Jill Wolfson labored to produce a product of which I was immensely proud.

Worthy of sharing, some of the findings were:

- More than 50 percent and up to 75 percent of incarcerated youth had a diagnosable mental illness or disorder.
- Nearly 20 percent of youth in the Juvenile Justice system show warning signs of suicide, and youth suicide in corrections facilities occurs four times more often for youth than in the general public.
- Minority male youths are frequently misdiagnosed or not diagnosed at all due to behavior descriptions such as aggressive or threatening, but unknown as to whether directly connected to mental disorders.
- In many instances due to poverty or other circumstances, juveniles with mental illness end up being arrested, or otherwise given up to juvenile court and entering the Juvenile Justice system, merely in order to get treatment. However, many of the short-term detention centers are not designed or equipped to be mental health centers, especially in the area of suicide prevention.
- A significant percentage of youths with untreated mental illness will attempt to self-medicate with drugs and alcohol, exacerbating their existing situation with an additional substance abuse problem.
- The practice of early screening often made it possible to divert the troubled youth into a safer and more appropriate mental health setting, thus avoiding the stigma of being entered in the Juvenile Justice system.

In addition to the numerous findings, the report was able to identify some proven and other promising treatment models existing in our country. For example, specific focus was given to a private, nonprofit organization named Youth Villages in Memphis, Tennessee, which provided an impressive range of services, including residential treatment, group homes, home-based counseling, outpatient psychiatric services, an alternative school, and an emergency shelter for homeless and runaway teens, just to name a few. As with Youth Villages and the other positive treatment models, they recognized how prevalent mental illness is among the youth and how important it is to recognize it early, since it plays such an important role in potentially serious criminal behavior if left untreated. It can also effectively jam up the Juvenile Justice system at every point – detention centers, courts, and corrections facilities.

Finally, with regard to the *Handle with Care* report, it allowed CJJ to outline and make as many as fifty specific recommendations to the President, Congress, Juvenile Justice practitioners, and even stakeholders among the American public regarding the urgency of dealing with the mental health needs of young offenders. For example, the President was urged to use the visibility and power of his office to establish a national agenda, acknowledging the seriousness and pervasive nature of mental illness. Congress was requested to appropriate federal funding and more resources "upstream" to the early stages of prevention and intervention, rather than "downstream" for apprehension and incarceration of offending and violent youths. The American people were urged not to give up on youth ensnared in the Juvenile Justice system but rather to understand many are troubled with mental health issues, and with meaningful interventions can become productive and respected citizens.

As stated earlier, I was especially appreciative of the work done on the annual report by the writers and also by the CJJ Board and CJJ members who approved it for publication. Hopefully, at least some of the recommendations have since been implemented. While on the topic of CJJ annual reports, I want to mention another report that had particular meaning for me, and carried a message as true today as it was when it was written in 1995.

CJJ's 1995 annual report was titled *Youth Violence Prevention: A Fence or an Ambulance*, and it was written by the late Robert E. Shepherd, Jr., professor of law at the University of Richmond School of Law, Richmond, Virginia, and a strong, dearly loved juvenile advocate. The title was borrowed from a poem with the same title – "A Fence or an Ambulance" by Joseph Malin and published in 1936. It dealt with a hypothetical steep cliff overlooking a deep valley into which the "Duke and many a peasant" were falling, after slipping over the steep edge of the cliff. The village debated whether to build a fence around the cliff to prevent falling or buy an ambulance to rescue the fallen. The poem ends with a resolution that it would be better to prevent people from falling with a strong fence than to place an ambulance down in the valley to keep trying to rescue them after the fall. In other words, the metaphor advocated that prevention makes more sense and is better than waiting for a treatment or other consequences.

I think the same metaphor fits appropriately the situation with Juvenile Justice today. Picture the top of the cliff where the vulnerable youth reside with all their known risk factors (poverty, mental illness, one or both parents unavailable, exposure to drugs and alcohol, bullying, gangs, domestic violence, etc.). At the same time, picture the knowledge of the protective factors, the continuum of care services, and programs and risk-focused strategies that are now identified to represent the hypothetical fence to prevent them from falling off the cliff. Without the fence, the ambulance would be waiting for them as they come crashing to the valley below.

In the real world, the ambulance would represent law enforcement, arrests in response to delinquency and violence, juvenile or adult courts, prison, or very expensive correctional programs. The point was (and is) that we should consider committing our money and resources for better youth and society outcomes on the front end (prevention), rather than facing the costs of crime, violence, and expensive corrections programs (consequences) on the back end. At a CJJ conference in 1994, juvenile court judge James Farris, in Beaumont, Texas, put it another way and captured the essence well when he urged that resources be allocated to the "playpen" rather than the "state pen," and that we should build fences rather than buy ambulances.

Having been in a position to observe the reactions of practitioners on both sides of Juvenile Justice, I can honestly appreciate the sometimes colder, and frequently more hostile, view held by police officers as opposed to the caregivers who are working on the prevention side. For example, while still with the FBI, I recall visiting an area station of the Los Angeles Police Department. In a temporary holding cell, I observed a juvenile literally hanging off the bars, high on drugs or something, screaming threats and ugly obscenities. I remembered it was a scary sight, but was probably fairly typical of what law enforcement officers experience from some juveniles at violent crime scenes and during arrests. I think it is very important for both the soft and hard sides of Juvenile Justice to keep in mind the different pictures of juveniles frequently presented to law enforcement as opposed to the appearance presented later to a judge, probation officer, or other recovery specialist further down the Juvenile Justice pipeline.

While still a member of the Colorado SAG from 2007 to 2010, I was honored to represent Colorado as one of the members of the Federal Advisory Committee on Juvenile Justice. This committee was organized in 2004 and charged with annually providing advice to the President and Congress regarding state perspectives on legislation pertaining to Juvenile Justice and delinquency prevention. The membership of one representative and one alternate from each state, territory, and the District of Columbia, also provided advice on the operation of the OJJDP. In 2012, my formal connection to Juvenile Justice matters concluded as a newly-elected governor had taken office in Colorado and term-limited all current members of boards and councils. At that time, I became officially retired from the SAG.

After nearly twenty years, my close connection with Juvenile Justice matters allowed many takeaways, some of which I will gladly share:

- It seemed that vulnerable, at-risk youth had a better chance of escaping gang life and violence when one or more of the following factors occurred:
    1. They found a job;
    2. They found a wife, girlfriend, or significant other;
    3. They finished high school;
    4. They were still alive at twenty years of age;
- Law enforcement for the most part sees troubled juveniles in a much different light from program and service providers. It might be worthwhile to improve efforts to have each side better understand the work and experiences of the other. A hopeful sign appeared in the September 2018 issue of *The Police Chief* magazine, in which an article encouraged chiefs to understand and support the 2018 reauthorization of the JJDPA with its four core requirements. It also announced support for reauthorization of the JJDPA by the International Association of Chiefs of Police (IACP).
- Finding diagnosable mental illness in more than 50 percent of incarcerated juveniles should have been a siren call for all

Americans, and a critical issue to be addressed without delay. The red flag it raised for a possible similar situation among adult offenders, and possible future impact for public safety, should have been of serious concern.

- The "fence" versus the "ambulance" metaphor struck home for me and still has much merit. It makes sense to move resources up-front, using evidence-based programs to prevent problems with troubled youth rather than wait for difficult, costly, and sometimes unsuccessful cures.

- Thinking of the fence adds to the credibility of the old adage "an ounce of prevention is worth a pound of cure." However, we need to add a few words at the end: "but requires a ton of work."

- One of the most significant findings during my time in Juvenile Justice was development of the scientific proof that the adolescent mind is not sufficiently developed during adolescence for the youth to make decisions expected of an adult. For killers of minor age, this finding had definite ramifications for those convicted for first-degree murders and sentenced to life in prison without the possibility of parole. The courts agreed with the scientific proof and paved the way for some sentences to be changed, to allow parole and a second chance for some of the youthful offenders serving life terms for murder committed while they were a minor.

- In order for communities to avoid having to reinvent the wheel, in the late 1990s, the Center for the Study and Prevention of Violence at the University of Colorado in Boulder sifted through hundreds of juvenile prevention and intervention programs around the United States. After exhaustive review and evaluation, the center produced ten evidence-based programs that were called Blueprints for Violence Prevention. The Blueprints included such programs as Big Brothers, Big Sisters of America, a mentoring program; and Prenatal and Infancy Home Visitation by Nurses, a program designed to serve low-income, at-risk pregnant women bearing their first child, with home visits from qualified nurses. Our Colorado SAG fully supported the Blueprints effort, as did the OJJDP, which funded some training and technical assistance to communities that desired to replicate one or more of the Blue-print programs.

- The memory I cherish most about my Juvenile Justice years relates to the people who made up the practitioners in the myriad roles involved. From the Colorado SAG members to other program administrators, corrections executives, judges, prosecutors, and hundreds of CJJ members throughout the United States and its territories, I could not have been associated with a more dedicated, caring, unyielding to frustration, and professional group. There comes no higher calling than to work either on the prevention or rescue side of helping our troubled youth.

Whether we like it or not, the kids of the present will become the essential fabric of tomorrow's society. Today they include huge numbers who are economically, mentally, and morally challenged and desperately need a second chance. I believe my activities in Juvenile Justice definitely made me a better person, and the relationships brought many lasting friendships.

As a postscript, even after separation from the SAG in 2012, I was able to retain some of the passion for the prevention piece of Juvenile Justice and, hopefully, also some measure of public safety preservation, through membership on some Colorado youth boards, including the Denver Police Activities League Board, which serves nearly seven thousand Denver inner-city youth, and the Open Door Youth Gang Alternatives Board, for the organization run by Reverend Leon Kelly, which works predominantly with elementary school children in Denver.

That wraps up my post-FBI volunteer career – now on to a few tales from my post-FBI day job activities.

CHAPTER 22

Life after the FBI?
Absolutely!

AS WITH MOST FBI SAs approaching eligibility, with the minimum requirements, for retirement at age fifty and with twenty years of service, they usually start thinking about what is available to them outside the Bureau, and what lies ahead for them. Unlike the more common experience in today's world, which finds American professionals trying more than one job or profession in their career, FBI Special Agents (SAs) in my day normally remained in the FBI for an entire career. It should come as no surprise that the FBI, as with other law enforcement careers, demands many personal sacrifices, and can result in a lifetime of accumulated stress. For some SAs, a retirement of travel, golf, gardening, and leisure was all they desired. Others looked to stay in the game, so to speak, and wondered if their experiences in the Bureau had prepared them for other positions in law enforcement, private or corporate security, or even other business pursuits.

For sure, the same thoughts and questions started to clutter my mind, as completion of my thirtieth year in the FBI got closer in 1992. With the decision to retire made, the decision to remain in Colorado was easy, since the family had fallen in love with the western lifestyle. Separation from the early commuting, extremely long hours in the office, and the nonstop phone calls at home from the office, at all hours of too many nights, were all treats to eagerly anticipate. However, since the Bureau was not just a job but also a life of its own, it took literally months to escape dreams involving FBI issues and nerves jumping with every ring of the home phone.

In retirement, my ultimate passion to support public safety never really lessened. As I've already written, my volunteer activities in the Juvenile Justice area commenced immediately, with my appointment to the Colorado Juvenile Justice and Delinquency Prevention Council, and service on several independent youth serving boards. My "day job" work started as an independent security consultant and eventually flourished in a number of directions. Still, at the beginning, I admit feeling plagued by those same questions as my retiring associates, as to whether my experiences were of value in the private security field. So, with those concerns, I cautiously and a bit reluctantly agreed to accept a request from a corporate friend to handle a security assessment of a major Denver area country club and golf course.

Working alone, I spent more than one hundred hours during a two-week period, on-site both days and some nights, with personnel interviews, review of records, and physical observations. My completed report contained about forty recommendations for improving security. I thought some of the recommendations were fairly obvious and logical; for example, replacing the outside hinges with inside hinges on the door to an area housing extremely valuable equipment, and refocusing certain surveillance cameras for specific stated reasons. Obviously, I was pleased with the overall approval of the report and recommendations. It was a confidence builder for me, as at least, a positive contribution with some basic public safety steps.

I recall, with an appreciative smile, discussing my report with one of my trusted professional associates, already in the private security business. Hearing that it was my first attempt at an assessment, and that I had received a few hundred dollars for the effort, he shook his head and counseled me, "Bob, in the private security business, this project and the report you prepared were worth about $35,000." With that, I considered raising the expenses bar a bit!

On a strictly referral basis, I enjoyed the diversity of projects that came my way in the consulting area. From handling assessments for the hiring of police chiefs, to sitting on promotion and assessment boards for other law enforcement and corrections agencies, I experienced a mix of interesting assignments.

Outside of Colorado, I was invited to join some talented colleagues as faculty members for executive training seminars for large US corporations, organized by an organization in Washington, D.C., called the Center for International Leadership. Back in Colorado, on the local government front, I was requested and then contracted to troubleshoot and resolve a number of sensitive personnel issues in different local agencies around the state.

Despite my best intentions and repeated promises to myself, my love of golf got trumped by the heavy volunteering schedule, increasing consulting contracts, and a growing number of speaking commitments. I had prepared a trifold brochure with a menu of speech topics that I felt comfortable in offering. This combined with a membership, for a time, in the National Speakers Association and the International Speakers Network provided a springboard for a number of speaking opportunities.

What I always appreciated most from the speeches was later feedback from an audience member that something I said had resonated and, possibly, saved him or her from becoming a victim. For example, one of the speech topics was entitled "Pence's Personal Protection Principles (PPPP)," and it was formatted to stimulate thoughts and ideas for personal safety, initiated or suggested by each letter of the word "security." The letter "s" (which is one of the most important) stands for "always be aware of your SURROUNDINGS."

After one presentation of this particular speech, I was contacted a few days later by a gentleman who had been in the audience. He proceeded to explain that the night before, he had picked up his wife at the airport after a late flight and intended to stop for a late snack on the way home. As he turned into the parking lot of a local Burger King, he noticed a male wearing a stocking cap and dark coat standing at the entrance. As he pulled into a parking spot, he noticed the same man starting to walk toward his car, and in the rearview mirror he observed another young, dark-clad male approaching from another direction. Then, he noticed one of the restaurant windows, where yet another male was staring out. Without exiting his vehicle, he immediately locked all doors, restarted the vehicle, backed out and left the restaurant parking lot. As he pulled away, he couldn't help noticing both of the approaching males turn and walk away. He wanted to thank me, and told me that without hearing the PPPP speech, he would definitely not have paid any attention whatsoever to the actions of the young men the night before. He felt confident that he and his wife had probably avoided the carjacking, in the same area, that he was reading about in the morning newspaper.

My contacts with the Denver news media, primarily TV stations, carried over into retirement from the FBI. They honored me with continued contacts to seek advice and offered opportunities to air my comments on general law enforcement and public safety policies and procedures. These contacts, in time, led to requests for other interviews from cable TV networks, mainly Fox News and MSNBC, and opportunities to air my comments regarding major investigations and incidents. Unfortunately, ever-increasing travel outside the state made me unavailable to handle several requests from local TV stations; however, the networks could contact me nearly anywhere in the country and arrange interviews through their local affiliate stations in the nearest city.

Shortly after retirement, I made what I considered a strategic decision to broaden my knowledge beyond the law enforcement side of public safety. The American Society for Industrial Security International (ASIS) is the professional organization of corporate security executives and principals, numbering more than thirty-five thousand worldwide. By applying for and being accepted into membership, I hoped to complement my law enforcement experience with a better understanding of the challenges facing corporate management, both in the United States and around the world and more importantly, the best practices in corporate security for meeting those challenges.

Afterward, I considered joining ASIS a very smart decision, since methods of operation and ultimate mission goals differ significantly in the corporate security landscape from law enforcement. It became clear to me that a blending of the skills required for each sector would be valuable and a real plus for public safety. As I saw it, prevention is one of the paramount goals of corporate security, while law enforcement, more frequently, is called upon to intervene in a criminal situation, or solve a crime and make an arrest, after the fact. Clearly, both goals are essential and targeted in the search for good public safety.

Inside the overall membership of ASIS are a number of smaller councils, made up of ASIS members with skills or interests in a particular area. With my background and interest in public safety, I was fortunate to be accepted as a member of the Law Enforcement Liaison Council (LELC). The LELC was (and is) one of the most active councils, numbering around thirty subject matter experts from both current and former law enforcement careers, as well as current leaders in corporate security, both in the United States and abroad. In addition to hosting a stable of subject matter experts ready and willing to assist other ASIS members anywhere in the world with specific questions or challenges, the LELC is all about promoting, recognizing, and supporting public-private partnerships (P3s). For example, back in 2009, the efforts of ASIS, working with the IACP, had already been successful in crafting a memorandum of understanding, bringing the two major organizations together in working to promote cooperation and P3s.

With that partnership, the eyes of eighteen thousand federal, state, and local law enforcement agencies, with sworn officers numbering up to approximately eight hundred thousand, were immediately supplemented by more than one million private security guards, with all eyes now alert for suspicious activities and the ability to respond to criminal incidents.

After joining the LELC, and already a member of the IACP, I was able to conduct P3 seminars at the national conferences for both the ASIS and the IACP, in the following few years. Together with guests I invited from successful P3s around the country, we endeavored to convince more participation from police chiefs and corporate security executives to consider starting their own P3. After a few years of our P3 seminars for the ASIS and the IACP, I noticed an interesting phenomenon. A perusal of the complete program agenda booklets for each of the annual conferences began to show an impressive increase in the number of presentations from individuals, groups, and other organizations, which actually included a P3. P3s had caught on, big time, and not just in public safety but in various government agencies working together with corporate entities for a better product or service.

Meanwhile, we were proud of our efforts in the LELC, and continued forging relations between ASIS and other public safety agencies, such as the National Center for Missing and Exploited Children; the National Sheriffs' Association; the Bureau of Alcohol, Tobacco, Firearms and Explosives; and the FBI. Another memorandum of understanding was successfully completed and signed between the ASIS and the BATF in 2018.

As the years in my post-FBI career passed, I found myself involved in longer-term arrangements and contracts with large corporations, including IBM, serving a variety of roles, which included speech presentations, law enforcement liaison, consulting, and troubleshooting. A number of projects involved assisting with the introduction of emerging technology products to corporate security and law enforcement contacts throughout the United States and the world. My personal criteria for agreeing to assist on any project were always conditional on one of two questions: one, would it help solve or prevent a crime? or two, could it help save a life? As expected, each and every project normally involved extensive air travel, both domestic and foreign. Despite long hours in airports and airplane seats, the conferences and meetings with law enforcement and corporate security across the globe increased exponentially my understanding of different public safety challenges and police practices in many states and nations. However, for one who loves good food and drink, appreciates history and a variety of different cultures, the experiences have been both incredibly enlightening and forever memorable to me. Hopefully, you will find some of the travel adventures both informative, and worth my sharing, in the pages that follow.

However, before we depart the lower forty-eight and head off to distant shores, including Alaska and Hawaii, I would like to focus on a very important personal priority in conjunction with my frequent domestic travels. I have always had an especially keen interest in American history – how it developed, where, and when. If at all possible and time permitting, I would make a special effort in my US travels to visit, at least briefly, the historic sites in my itinerary's path.

In conjunction with police meetings in New England states, I made it to Plymouth Rock in Massachusetts, the popularly reported first landing of the English Pilgrims in 1620, but I also made it further on to Provincetown, Massachusetts, where a monument reports the actual first landing of the pilgrims, before moving on to Plymouth.

In Boston, walking the 2.5-mile Freedom Trail, I visited the sixteen historic stopping points, many of which tell the story of our involvement in the Revolutionary War. The Bunker Hill monument memorializes the first battle against the invading British in 1775. The historic ride of Paul Revere, and the signals in the steeple of the Old North Church, warned of the arrival and approach of British troops. Also included is the Old South Meeting House, where colonists debated and decided on dumping British tea at the Boston Tea Party. Downtown and close to the trail's starting point sits the famous Boston Common, where public debates and protests were famously carried on. En route from downtown toward Bunker Hill, along the water stands Old Ironsides, or the USS Constitution, named by George Washington and launched in 1797. It is reportedly the oldest commissioned naval vessel still afloat in the world.

As a member of the Florida Police Chiefs' Association, several trips to the southeast part of the country introduced me to the start of American history there. Founded in 1565 by the Spanish, St. Augustine, south of Jacksonville, still claims the title of the oldest continuously occupied settlement by Europeans in the continental United States. The Oldest House Museum in downtown St. Augustine was built as a residence for Spanish families in the 1600s, and then in the mid-1700s was remodeled and occupied by American families until it became a museum. It is believed to be the oldest house currently in St. Augustine.

Along the middle Eastern Seaboard of the country sits the veritable cradle of American history – the city of Philadelphia. Probably most of the major historic sites there are already known; however, on frequent visits, there are a couple of repeat stops that I always try to make. I visit Christ Church, the Episcopal landmark built in 1727, and the worship home of General George Washington, Betsy Ross, and an assortment of signers of the Declaration of Independence. Not far away at Christ Church cemetery, located at the corner of Arch and Fifth Streets, I join passersby as they throw pennies onto the large, flat gravestone of Benjamin Franklin, who passed away in 1790 at the age of eighty-four. The pennies are meant to honor Ben, who had coined the phrase "a penny saved is a penny earned." The Christ Church Foundation reports that the "penny offerings" amount to about $5,000 per year. By the way, Benjamin Rush, the founder of my college alma mater, Dickinson College in Carlisle, Pennsylvania, was a signer of the Declaration of Independence and is buried in that cemetery.

Not far from Philadelphia, other business allowed a side trip to Valley Forge, Pennsylvania, where General George Washington wintered during the Revolutionary War in 1777–1778, and also to the point where his beleaguered troops actually crossed the Delaware River to surprise and defeat a Hessian contingent in Trenton, New Jersey. This historic crossing occurred on Christmas Day in 1776, and changed the course of the American Revolution.

In the same general area, a trip to the Inner Harbor of Baltimore, Maryland, always affords me a short visit with the *USS Constellation*. Launched in 1854, it was the last sail-only warship in the US Navy, and was not decommissioned until 1954, after which it was anchored at Baltimore for all the public to enjoy.

While assigned to FBI Headquarters in Washington, D.C., conferences and meetings in neighboring Virginia allowed perfect opportunities for me to examine life as it was in the 1700s, through visits to Colonial Williamsburg and its historic environs, and the home of President and General George Washington at Mount Vernon. Also, a period of training at the Federal Executive Institute in Charlottesville, Virginia, allowed a weekend visit to Monticello, the home of President Thomas Jefferson.

Although there were numerous other visits and trips, both while in the FBI and post-FBI, that helped feed my interest in American history, I gladly admit that one of my all-time heroes has been President Abraham Lincoln. I sincerely respected his accomplishments in the face of so many personal losses and political setbacks. In the true American spirit, as we know it, he kept up the fight and never gave up in the face of some of our darkest hours and gravest challenges. I try to read all I can about Lincoln as I encounter it and depending on my available time. Fortunately, both while in the Bureau and afterward, opportunities popped up to deepen my knowledge of Lincoln.

While assigned as Assistant Special Agent in Charge in Kentucky, I had the opportunity to visit Lincoln's rural birthplace near Hodgenville. During assignments at FBI Headquarters, I made numerous visits during lunch hours to the Ford Theatre, just across the street, where he was assassinated. Most of that time was spent in the basement museum dedicated to Lincoln and the shooting, where I studied and examined most of the exhibits. A few other lunch-hour visits took me across the street from Ford Theatre to the house where Lincoln was carried after the shooting, and soon thereafter passed away.

At one point, I committed to memory his entire Gettysburg Address from November 19, 1863, after the Civil War battle at Gettysburg, Pennsylvania. I included portions, or all of it, frequently in some of my speech presentations.

During visits to Illinois State Police Headquarters in Springfield, I would visit Lincoln's former residence there, where he lived from 1844 until 1861, when he moved to Washington, D.C., as President. The entire neighborhood in Springfield is part of a national park, which includes the buildings and businesses that he undoubtedly visited and patronized. Although he had moved a number of times, the house in Springfield was the only house he ever owned.

Finally, I have visited the massive memorial and tall, obelisk-dominated tomb of Lincoln and most of his family in Springfield at the Oak Ridge Cemetery. Yes, I have also rubbed the nose of the bronze face statue of Lincoln placed in front of his memorial. Wishing for the promised good luck, so many visitors have done the same that the dull bronze face now has a nose that shines like gold.

Now, it is time to move on from recollections of American history, and take off on some of the "long-haul" trips that opened my eyes to some of the most fascinating and distant stops throughout our wonderful world.

Abraham Lincoln grave and memorial in Springfield, Illinois. The inset photo shows how the nose on the bronze sculpture of Lincoln's face has been polished to a bright gold by visitors rubbing it for good luck.

CHAPTER 23

Up, Up, and Away!

NOW, AS CROONER Frank Sinatra sang in his hit song of 1958 – "Come Fly With Me."

For the next several years after retirement, I regretted the frequency and length of the trips away from Denver and family. The international flights of sometimes more than twenty hours were always exhausting and uncomfortable, but the trade-offs were visits to world-class cities from Europe to East Asia and beyond, rich with cultural treasures, and many different public safety experiences.

However, before I launch readers into what appears to be a world vacation tour or travelogue, let me hasten to explain my reasoning and possible benefits. First, all travel had, as its genesis, a business purpose, whether for conferences, meetings, speeches, or participation on projects. Understandably, based on security and proprietary restrictions additional details, relevant to the primary purpose of travel, cannot be discussed or reported. However, what might be of interest would involve the nonsensitive and unclassified activities away from classrooms and meeting rooms, including dining, entertainment, and sightseeing. Some of these would occur during lunch, dinner, or weekends and after-hours. In some cases, events occurred during a few extra days taken after the business event terminated.

Certainly, the main reason for providing the narratives here is not to describe the locations themselves, which, of course, are available to tourists worldwide. The "secret sauce," so to speak, for reader value and interest in my narratives has everything to do with the source of the recommendations for the events and activities.

Uniquely, each and every trip mentioned was hosted by, or included contacts with, law enforcement or corporate security executives from the countries listed. That said and noted, I couldn't imagine more authoritative sources for recommendations as to where to visit (or not to visit) for sightseeing, when and where to dine (or not to dine) and of course, places to avoid for personal safety. In a broader vein, narratives also serve to offer a few insights and details concerning some of the agencies that actually provide the public safety in their countries and cities.

Thumbnail narratives and a few personal highlights from some of the travels include the following.

France
Paris

Arriving before dawn at one of the many farmers markets in the middle of Paris, I enjoyed a bowl of probably the best French onion soup of my life, as I sat with some of the farmers arriving from all over France to bring their products to market. The soup was piping hot with super-thick melted gruyere cheese drooping over the large crock. I was seated upstairs at an outdoor picnic-like table and devoured every spoonful of the delicious soup. By the way, the experience also came with a number of cats sitting on either side of me and one more perched on my lap.

England
London

Reportedly rebuilt in 1667, after the Great Fire of London in 1666, one of London's earliest pubs at 145 Fleet Street, in the downtown area, hosted me on more than one occasion. Serving local beers and typical English fare, Ye Olde Cheshire Cheese is almost a must for visitors to the city. I've enjoyed the Yorkshire Pudding, steak and ale pie, fish and chips, and other dishes, while other visitors sometimes apparently have not, since the food frankly used to get mixed reviews. However, with the dark rooms and open fireplaces situated off of stairs reaching different levels, the atmosphere and history draw huge numbers of visitors. Regular patrons in their day included literary notables Mark Twain, Charles Dickens, Sir Arthur Conan Doyle, and certainly Samuel Johnson, who lived nearby. Johnson was a poet, essayist, biographer, and writer credited with producing a well-known work called *A Dictionary of the English Language.* Some described Johnson as the most distinguished man of letters in English history. On one of my visits to the pub, there was a chair roped off at a table on one of the floors, reportedly used by Johnson as a regular at the establishment.

On one American Society for Industrial Security (ASIS) visit to London, organized by the United Kingdom chapter, corporate security executives were hosted at a security briefing and enjoyable reception at the world-famous British Museum. A massive organization of ninety-four separate galleries, we met in Room 4 of the Egyptian Gallery, which houses Egyptian mummies and sculptures, which are some of the most valuable artifacts in the entire museum. In fact, the centerpiece of the long gallery was none other than the Rosetta Stone, by far one of the most celebrated, popular, and certainly priceless possessions of the entire museum. The Rosetta Stone was discovered in Egypt in 1799. It is a granite stone inscribed in 196 BC, and contains the same decree by a council of priests, essentially in three different languages (ancient hieroglyphics, common script of the day, and Greek). Our host, the security director (former Metropolitan London Police) explained it is one of the most important ancient Egyptian objects ever found, and the key to deciphering ancient Egyptian hieroglyphics. He explained it has been in the British Museum since 1802, and is probably the most

visited object. In fact, according to the security director, thousands of visitors will arrive at the museum, with its multitude of separate galleries, and rush to the Egyptian Gallery, Room 4, just to see the Rosetta Stone and then hurry off to other tourist sites. Interestingly, almost acting as an ancient jealous guard, a massive imposing stone bust of the great Pharaoh Ramesses II looks down from an elevated position nearby, as if to protect the stone.

On that particular London trip, the delightful surprises just kept coming! The security executives attending the conference were invited one evening to observe security at the British Parliament and meet some of the officials responsible. From the regular police with their "bobby" helmets outside at the street level, to tactical officers with body armor and heavy weapons as you access the building complex, we attended a briefing and reception hosted by a member of the House of Lords. Baroness Harris of Richmond DL, who personally addressed our group, was incredibly friendly and witty, and delighted us with her explanation of Parliament's workings, and especially her house's relationship with the House of Commons. The room for the reception had an impressive location, as a doorway on one side led out to a walkway directly over the River Thames. A walk out the door and quick glance to the left along the Thames, and the

Outside the House of Lords with the London Eye in the background.

storied Elizabeth Tower, which is the Big Ben clock tower, was clearly visible, as was the Westminster Bridge. The food, drink, location, and atmosphere were the makings of lifelong memories.

Italy and Greece
Rome and Athens

It would seem absurd for any American to attend meetings (in this case corporate security meetings) in Rome or Athens and not take the opportunity to visit some of the wildly popular and well-publicized historic treasures. From the ancient Forum, Coliseum, Catacombs, and so much more in Rome, to the Acropolis, topped off by the Parthenon in Athens, these cities present tourists more of the world's scenic and historic culture than can be seen and appreciated in even several days, in either place, or easily summarized here. So I will just offer a few personal observations.

Either standing in front of the Parthenon atop the hill hosting the Acropolis, or sitting in a small boat wending its way through the Corinth Canal to the Gulf of Corinth, just outside of Athens, and looking skyward, prepare to be amazed. The sky in this part of Greece was the brightest and most striking shade of blue I had ever experienced.

In Rome, for a devoted fan of great Italian food, a special surprise awaited. On one trip to Rome, I was accompanied by my wife, Irmgard, who was very familiar with the city from her flying days as a stewardess (now called a flight attendant), with Pan American World

Airways. Knowing my passion for Italian food, she suggested a special restaurant that served one of my favorites – Fettuccine Alfredo, and more special because it was run by the family of Alfredo di Lelio, who actually created the dish.

It's interesting that Fettuccine Alfredo probably finds itself on nearly every Italian restaurant menu in the United States and elsewhere around the world, but, undoubtedly, very few fans or customers have any idea how it got that name. Well, according to its history, Alfredo created the dish in 1914, at his restaurant called Alfredo alla Scrofa. That restaurant was sold in 1943, and in 1950, Alfredo and his son, Armando, opened a new restaurant, II Vero Alfredo (translated as "the true Alfredo"). That is where Irmgard and I headed for dinner and a great experience, located at the Piazza Augusto Imperatore.

Seated by the maître d', we were attended by the head waiter who provided drinks and bread, and who took our order for the famous Fettuccine Alfredo. After a short time, the waiter announced and introduced a

Having Fettuccine Alfredo with Irmgard in Rome.

gentleman in a business suit as Armando, the son of Alfredo (who had passed away in 1959). Armando was handed a large silver metal bowl, which had been filled with the fettuccine. Placing it on the table, he began to mix the luscious-looking contents with a large golden fork and spoon, supposedly donated to Alfredo in 1927 by silent movie film stars Douglas Fairbanks and Mary Pickford, who had enjoyed the fettuccine while on their honeymoon in Rome. To complete the ceremony, Armando dished out a portion of the fettuccine on a regular plate for me, and then proceeded to place the huge amount remaining in the metal bowl in front of my wife. After his "bon appetit" greeting, photo opportunity, and warm smile, Armando hurried off to greet another customer. I remember the experience every time I order Fettuccine Alfredo, and only wish I could replicate the incredible original taste.

United Arab Emirates
Dubai

On multiple visits to Dubai, United Arab Emirates, the first delay noted on each and every arrival was the huge crowd of visitors lining up for a lengthy and tedious wait to process through immigration, due to the large number of flights normally landing at the same time. Usually staying in the Festival City area near the airport, I was always captivated by the Dubai skyline directly across Dubai Creek, especially as the morning sun exploded into a blinding silver color off of the tower

of the Burj Khalifa. Truly, Dubai is a wealthy and beautiful city with its diverse and sparkling architecture, highlighted in the high-rise buildings that accent its skyline, but the Burj Khalifa, appearing

The Dubai skyline with the Burj Khalifa shining as it rises above the rest..

in the center of the skyline, cannot be missed.

It stands nearly twenty-eight hundred feet tall with more than one hundred and sixty stories. It is the tallest building in the world and the tallest freestanding structure. Having also the highest occupied floor in the world, the Burj Khalifa dwarfs everything around it. If you can imagine its size and height from just viewing it along the skyline, you can probably appreciate the view when you stand at its humongous base looking straight up. It was extremely interesting to discuss some operations of the high rise with its director of security.

Another not-to-miss spectacle in Dubai is the Gold Souk, located in the business section in downtown. Nowhere is the sheer wealth of Dubai demonstrated so clearly as in the Souk area. The streets there host three hundred and eighty jewelry businesses, of which about two hundred and fifty are gold stores. I am hardly exaggerating when I say that the brilliance of the gold displayed in the windows of the Souk shops can nearly strain the eyes.

In an area of such wealth, largely due to the oil-rich neighbors of the Middle East, it would not be a great leap to understand that Dubai law enforcement enjoys adequate funding and staffing. The Dubai Police have about fifteen thousand sworn officers and cover a population of nearly three million people. They are equipped with, and have a great interest in, all of the available high-tech emerging technology. For example, the police related that the city of Dubai has deployed an extensive network of surveillance cameras. If necessary, they explained that they can cover a visitor of interest from the time he or she arrives at the airport until departure, without any loss or break in coverage.

Turkey
Istanbul

Recalling the amazing experience of walking through the brilliant display in the Gold Souk of Dubai, another spectacle of equal glitter comes to mind. The Grand Bazaar, better known as the Gold Bazaar, in Istanbul, Turkey, is absolutely loaded with gold shops and stalls and has been the scene of gold trading since the 1400s. During a visit, I tried my hand at a small gold purchase and heeded advice from the police to definitely bargain and negotiate. To do otherwise, they warned, and pay the asking price, would disappoint and might even anger the merchant. It worked. I settled on a small gold medallion about the size of a quarter and embossed with the classic scale of justice, which I considered of excellent quality and very appropriate. I got it for about half of the asking price!

The Turkish Police first recommended that my visit to Istanbul would not be complete without a stop at the Topkapi Palace Museum. Indeed, if you are not interested in buying gold but wish to view an incredible display of wealth almost beyond belief, then head to the Topkapi. From the mid-1400s, for nearly four hundred years, sultans of the Ottoman Empire ruled from the Topkapi Palace, a maze of palatial structures divided into four courtyards, which now remain as a museum exhibiting the imperial art, culture, and treasures of the Ottoman Empire. If time is a factor, head right through the Gate of Felicity and into the third courtyard, which contained the private residence of the sultan. Now, as a museum, it houses the Pavilion of the Conqueror and contains the imperial jewels. The rooms of this treasury contain items of inestimable value and beauty, almost hard to comprehend or describe.

You can see the Spoonmaker's Diamond, one of the largest cut diamonds in the world, as well as the Topkapi Dagger, made of gold, emeralds, and numerous other jewels. In 1964, a Hollywood feature film titled *Topkapi* focused on a fictitious plot to steal this very dagger. Some of the rooms of collections are virtually packed with one treasured item after another, encrusted with gold, diamonds, and other examples of the most valuable jewels known. All told, Topkapi loudly attests to the incredible wealth of the Ottoman Empire.

Poland

Warsaw

At a law enforcement conference in Warsaw, Poland, in September 2014, the Polish National Police (Policja) hosted law enforcement agencies from throughout Europe, during which current topics of

Murals in Warsaw reflect the horror of Nazi occupation.

mutual concern were discussed. The Policja also provided opportunities for briefings regarding the Polish experience at the hands of the Nazis during World War II, including visits to museums and various sites throughout the city of Warsaw.

For me, the highlight was the personal appearance, at our conference, by Lech Walesa. Walesa, a stout gentleman with white hair and his trademark white handlebar mustache, was the labor leader and activist who cofounded Solidarity, an independent trade union during the period that Poland was controlled by the Soviet bloc. He is credited with rescuing Poland from communism, and won the coveted Nobel Peace Prize in 1983. Later, from 1990 to 1995, he was elected and served as the president of Poland.

With Nobel Peace Prize winner Lech Walesa

Walesa's remarks to our group were spirited, animated, and even fiery, as he railed against the feared current motives of his communist neighbor states. He spoke in Polish, with a female interpreter who frequently could not keep up with him, as he interrupted to rapidly continue his emotional message. Afterward, I enjoyed speaking with him briefly and having a photo opportunity.

The Netherlands
Amsterdam and The Hague

Travel to Amsterdam and The Hague, in the Netherlands, turned out to have its cultural as well as public safety benefits. With legalization of medical, and later recreational, marijuana becoming a reality for Colorado and other states, I spent some time in Amsterdam learning from law enforcement, and members of the public alike, their experiences with the recreational use of marijuana, after it had become legalized in 1976. Inquiries helped me better understand the current status, and how the experiences have changed through the intervening years in Holland.

In The Hague, I had the opportunity to visit the Organization for the Prohibition of Chemical Weapons (OPCW), which monitors adherence to the Chemical Weapons Convention and participates in the dangerous destruction of such weapons around the world. Prior to my visit, the OPCW had just won the 2013 Nobel Peace Prize for their work. After seeking permission, I couldn't resist the opportunity to have a photo opportunity with the actual framed and wall-mounted Nobel Peace Prize. Directly next door to OPCW is the headquarters of Europol, which is made up of twenty-seven European Union nations. My visit there included a briefing concerning their important work to help achieve a safer Europe by working against international crime and terrorism.

The big cultural revelation was the resplendent display of flowers and floral decorations throughout the streets and boulevards of The Hague. Even more spectacular were the millions of tulips and other flowers visible on the train ride between Amsterdam's Schiphol Airport and downtown The Hague. Fields of brilliant yellow, purple, red, and other colored flowers, resembling giant carpets stretching for acres and maybe miles, were planted right along the train route, visible on both sides and mesmerizingly beautiful.

Austria
Salzburg

Salzburg, Austria, was the home of the classical music legendary composer Wolfgang Amadeus Mozart, whose name and caricature are visible on signs, buildings, and even candy nearly everywhere in the city. In 2015, the Austrian Federal Police hosted more than three hundred FBI National Academy graduates from all over Europe for a conference. For me, there were many highlights, and I will mention just a couple that stand out in memory.

One evening the police hosted us in the old part of the city at a massive beer hall for dinner. The entertainment was an Elvis Presley tribute artist with the stage name of Rusty, who frankly was the best Elvis impersonator, considering voice and appearance, whom I have ever  experienced. Rusty had traveled the world, and for a number of years had his own show in Las Vegas, before returning to his native Austria.

He had known Elvis and reportedly had been given some of Elvis's personal stage outfits by his widow. Anyway, after his performance, Rusty approached me and said, "I understand you worked for J. Edgar Hoover." He turned out to be an FBI fan and was particularly fascinated by Director Hoover. He asked if we could meet somewhere later and talk about Mr. Hoover. Rusty arrived at my hotel later that evening to have a drink with some of the police executives, and we had a nice chat about the FBI under Mr. Hoover's leadership.

The other highlight involved my opportunity to partake of one of my favorite desserts in the whole world, which also happens to be the signature dessert of Salzburg. Salzburger Knockerl is a sweet soufflé dessert found on the menu of nearly every good restaurant in Salzburg. Its ingredients are egg yolks and egg whites, flour, sugar, and vanilla mixed into a thin dough. The mixture is formed into rows of dumplings appearing like the mountains that surround the city of Salzburg with their peaks. A sprinkling of powdered sugar over the dumplings even enhances the appearance to resemble the snow-covered Alps. It is a very large dish indeed, and I had learned from previous experience that there is more than enough for two persons.

Germany
Frankfurt and Dresden

In Germany, visits to Frankfurt (in the former West Germany) and Dresden (in the former East Germany) provided very interesting and valuable information from law enforcement agencies regarding the policies and procedures for the purchase, maintenance, care, and protection of firearms, as well as the ability to use personal firearms legally. The very unique restrictions and regulations covering firearms in this country undoubtedly play a significant role in their much different experience in the use of firearms in committing crimes. However, while effective in limiting gun crimes within their own native populations, according to the authorities, it has not prevented the smuggling of weapons from less-regulated countries in central Europe by illegal immigrants and organized crime groups.

In Dresden, it was truly amazing to see the wonderful recovery and reconstruction of this major city, which was nearly leveled in the firestorm of allied bombing in February 1945, during World War II.

Australia

Gold Coast

In 2015, the Asia Pacific annual conference of police executives from that world region, who had received extensive training at the prestigious FBI National Academy at Quantico, Virginia, was held in Australia. After a long flight from Denver, I made it to the Surfer's Paradise section of the Gold Coast, located in the state of Queensland. As a member of the National Academy associates, I was invited to attend this conference hosted by the Queensland Police Service, to listen and learn of current law enforcement problems and concerns in the region.

Queensland lies along the northeast coast of Australia, with a coastline of nearly seven thousand kilometers (nearly forty-five hundred miles), and with Brisbane as its capital city. Queensland Police Service protects a population of nearly five million with approximately fifteen thousand police officers and staff. Their crime rate is comparatively mild when compared with crime in the United States, but as with most countries in the region, they are faced with the presence of youth gangs and considerable drug-related crime.

Unfortunately, I never made it to the seven miles of pristine beach that lay just a short walk from our hotel, but I did manage to claim one of my hoped-for firsts. I petted my first koala and was quickly corrected by a native for calling him a koala bear (a no-no). The darling little guy was clinging to a eucalyptus tree with his long sharp claws, and nonchalantly chewing the leaves. I was told they consume the equivalent of a few large garbage bags full of these leaves every day, which makes up nearly their entire daily diet. He looked just like a teddy bear with his squat, stout body, large head, round fluffy ears, and no tail. He was about thirty-six inches long and probably weighed about twenty-five to thirty pounds. Apparently, their choice of diet leads to a pretty drowsy day and nearly twenty hours of sleep. Their native home is limited to just a few states in the eastern part of Australia (including Queensland), and they number only in the thousands, with their numbers dwindling. As long as I did not interrupt his eating, the koala welcomed my touch in petting him without "cuddling" him. In some areas, it is illegal to pick up and cuddle a koala, since the practice apparently stresses them and makes them very uncomfortable. While meeting my first koala was a real treat, the fact my other wish was not granted was a real shocker – I never saw even one kangaroo. Even though I had been out and about, walking through the neighborhood, not one of the more than forty-five million estimated population of "roos" crossed my path. My local hosts were also amazed, since the kangaroos freely roam throughout the area and outnumber humans in Australia by about two to one.

Singapore

Singapore

Enduring a nearly twenty-four-hour flight from Denver (including a plane change in Tokyo's Narita Airport), I arrived at the Island city-state of Singapore in Southeast Asia. This was mostly on my corporate security business side, and included an ASIS Asia-Pacific Conference at the magnificent Marina Bay Sands Hotel. While the name might not be familiar, anyone who has seen tourist advertisements for Singapore has undoubtedly viewed this hotel – the one with three separate tall

towers in a row all connected at the top by a platform containing a large pool, gardens, and a restaurant.

In addition to my business commitment, I had one long-awaited wish I had hoped to satisfy, if ever I made it to Singapore. At various social occasions in my past life, I had the opportunity to sample a tasty and fruity cocktail called a Singapore Sling. I knew it originated at the iconic Raffles Hotel in Singapore, and there was no way I was not going to pay a visit there while in the city. One evening after dinner with some associates, I made my way alone over to the world-famous Raffles, with its white colonial facade, and up the one flight of stairs to the Long Bar.

There it was with its incredibly long teakwood bar, wicker chairs, and the traditional slow-spinning reed ceiling fans. As advertised, the floor was covered with shucked peanut (monkey) shells, just as it would have been decades earlier, with shells thrown down by famous earlier customers such as writers Ernest Hemingway, Somerset Maugham, and Rudyard Kipling. Finding an empty seat at the bar, I ordered my Singapore Sling, which had been invented by a bartender at the Raffles in 1913. Apparently, there have evolved a wide variety of recipes for the iconic pink-colored, gin-based cocktail, but the bartender assured me his sling contained the original ingredients – gin, cherry brandy, triple sec, Benedictine, pineapple juice, lime juice, cointreau, grenadine, a dash of angostura bitters, with a frothy top from shaking the mixture, and topped off with a slice of pineapple and a cherry. It was delicious, even more so after shucking a few monkey nuts and pitching a few shells on the floor. The "sling" part of the name supposedly comes from the German word *schlingen*, which means to swallow spirits diluted with water or tonic. To make the event complete, I stopped back downstairs at the gift shop, and left the Raffles a happy camper with my very own Singapore Sling glass (for another $25).

On the law enforcement side, the Singapore Police Force has an interesting organization structure to police the five to six million population in the city-state. With approximately ten thousand full-time sworn officers, they utilize a number of reserve officers, as well as security guards and other volunteers, which can swell their number, if necessary, to a sworn force of approximately forty-five thousand. Laws in Singapore are strict and no nonsense. Bad behaviors are not tolerated and violators are punished severely. This can be illustrated better by the fact that not only murder can bring a death penalty, as a capital offense, but so can some gun crimes and aggravated drug trafficking. Chewing gum and spitting on the sidewalk are just a few examples of other behaviors subject to fines and criminal sanctions. There are several others!

Hong Kong and Macau

While still in the FBI and working Chinese cases at FBI Head-quarters, our Legat Office in Hong Kong was very important to me. The Legat was my very good friend and a tremendous FBI Special Agent named Dan Grove. His excellent relations and work with the Royal Hong Kong Police (Hong Kong did not revert back from being a British Crown Colony to the People's Republic of China [PRC] until 1997) were key to some of our investigations, since Hong Kong was as close geographically to the PRC as we could get. When Dan retired, he moved back to the Washington, D.C., area with his wife, Tessie, and worked on security issues in the private sector. After a few years, in 2010, he and Tessie longed for the friendship and the surroundings back in Hong Kong, and moved back for his last years. As a private security executive, he joined and became very active in ASIS.

When I first visited Hong Kong, while still in the FBI, Dan hosted me and facilitated my ability to at least take a look into the Canton Province of the PRC, from the closest elevated security outpost. On that trip, I recall seeing many poor and homeless refugees in moun-tainside areas, living in cardboard or plywood shacks with only a corrugated tin piece as a roof, while others were jumbled together in old, and no longer seaworthy, junks in an area called Aberdeen.

In 2012, on my next trip to attend an ASIS Asia-Pacific Confer-ence, I did not notice the shacks on the mountainside and was told that the situation in Aberdeen had been cleaned up. What I did notice was a series of very thin and tall skyscraper-type buildings that actu-ally resembled a concrete forest. These buildings had apparently been constructed to house numbers of lower-income Chinese citizens. By this time my friend Dan Grove had passed away, but not surprisingly, his name and impressive reputation were discussed prominently at the ASIS conference. So respected was he, that the Hong Kong ASIS chapter had created an award in his name and memory. I was delighted to be able to meet and have dinner while there with Tessie, Dan's widow.

During my meetings, I learned from law enforcement officials how different policing can be in Hong Kong as opposed to major US cities like New York. For example, in 2017, the New York Police Department (NYPD) with a sworn force of more than thirty-seven thousand officers policed a population of about 8.5 million Americans. Hong Kong Police, with a force of approximately thirty-three thousand officers, served a population of approximately 7.4 million. During that year, NYPD investigated ninety-five thousand felonies, including more than two hundred and ninety murders, most of which involved firearms. In Hong Kong, the police had about nine thousand felonies, including twenty-four murders, which involved strangulation, stabbing, and falling (presumably, some victims being pushed off those concrete skyscrapers) and zero as a result of a firearm shooting. It is extremely difficult to purchase a firearm in Hong Kong. Hong Kong Police advised their crime rate mostly involved property crime.

My next visit to Hong Kong came the following year in 2013, and was very short, since my main purpose was to travel on, by ferry, to nearby Macau for security meetings. Portuguese Macau, nicknamed "Las Vegas of Asia," reverted back to China in 1999 to become a Special Administrative Region of the PRC. Its main function, as the nickname indicates, is gambling. While Las Vegas can appear loud and glitzy, I found Macau to be much more reserved and sophisticated. This trip was around the Christmas season, and while some of the buildings have a resemblance to Las Vegas (for example, the Venetian with its replica Doge's Palace and other buildings familiar in Venice), the decorative furniture and other appointments inside and outside the casinos are beautiful, and appear more "artsy" than most in the United States. However, there is another difference between Macau and Las Vegas, a big one – the money!

In 2017, the gross gambling revenue in Macau reportedly beat Las Vegas by thirty-three billion dollars to 3.64 billion dollars, and apparently that trend had existed for several years. Although the slot machine take in Las Vegas beat that in Macau, the take from table games in Macau, especially the high stakes Baccarat, swamped the table earnings in Las Vegas. In terms of numbers, there are sixty casinos in Las

Vegas compared to forty in Macau, and in 2017, Las Vegas had 42.2 million visitors compared to 32.6 million for Macau. Some of the reasons for the big money disparity in gambling revenue is probably the decision by Las Vegas to accept limiting the revenue from gambling to add to the revenue from food, hotels, and entertainment, while Macau focuses strictly on income from the gambling.

The law enforcement picture finds the Public Security Police numbering about forty-one hundred sworn officers to police a population of approximately six hundred and twenty-five thousand. Although they share with Hong Kong the benefit of very few firearms problems, they are fighting the expected violations that come with the presence of big stakes gambling. Their cases involve some gang activities from the Triad Chinese organized crime groups, money laundering, human trafficking, and lots of pickpockets and property thefts.

China

Shanghai

Considering a year of my life spent learning the Chinese language, and years afterward working FBI cases involving possible Chinese espionage activities, it would not be a huge surprise to assume I had developed a great interest in China. I learned to love their food and culture, and developed a great respect for the people and their history.

However, during the years of my FBI career, Mainland China, with few exceptions, was closed under the rule of the government of the PRC. One of my career goals was always to make a personal visit to Mainland China, but I never made it beyond Hong Kong.

After retirement, travel restrictions had eased, and it became possible for Westerners to have easier access. In fact, in 2013, I was invited to

The famous Shanghai skyline.

visit Mainland China to assist some police departments in a consulting project. I obtained my Chinese visa (a lengthy and rather expensive procedure), but the project was postponed to a later time. Then, in 2016, it finally happened and one of my longtime goals was realized. The ASIS Asia-Pacific International Security Conference was held in Shanghai, and I attended.

Shanghai is a city of nearly twenty-seven million people, in an area that approximates twenty-five hundred square miles. The food was outstanding, as I expected, and the people were warm and friendly, but with very little English spoken. Chinese culture, and the majestic architecture and unique buildings, at every turn, proved to be one photo opportunity after another. Conference meetings were informative and dealt with the highest corporate security challenges in East Asia. Incidentally, every meeting was monitored by an individual presumed to be a PRC officer. The mood of the Chinese meeting attendees, as well as citizens on the street, seemed very light and happy, with no real stress or tension noted.

During my visit, China's reputation for smog and pollution was not really in evidence, but the fact that my hotel room (and presumably all other rooms) was provided with two mask kits for use in air pollution emergencies, certainly highlighted the risks and possibilities.

For an American familiar with the challenges of New York as our largest city with 8.6 million population, it is difficult to comprehend the challenges of a city with nearly twenty-seven million people. Shanghai goes on for miles in every direction, with tall skyscrapers (some built but apparently not occupied) as far as the eye can see in every direction. Also noted was a seemingly unending parade of high-rise building cranes, which appeared to be sitting idle all around the city. Traffic was truly a nightmare, with some highways and streets limited for use only by citizens of Shanghai itself. Throngs of pedestrians were everywhere, and one official advised me that there are customarily a significant number of pedestrians killed daily, just trying to cross the streets in intersections around the city. All in all, considering the incredible size and challenges confronting such a huge population, you can almost feel the vibes of a great city. It was a magnificent cultural experience, one that, for me, was well worth the wait.

Chile, Argentina, and Panama
Santiago, Buenos Aires, Panama City

Trips to South America involved meetings, presentations, and conferences that provided valuable information as to law enforcement problems and challenges in various countries, and how they are being addressed. For example, in Santiago, Chile, my group learned that law enforcement in Chile is provided by two main organizations: one, the Carabiniers (Chilean National Police) who are a military-uniformed force of about eighty thousand and provide general public safety, including highway patrols countrywide, and two, the Investigations Police of Chile (PDI), numbering about twelve thousand investigators, who have immigration and border security and conduct investigations all throughout the country.

Demonstrations and information discussed at both of their training academies in Santiago were supplemented by cultural visits and social events. It was at these events that I was introduced to the Chilean national cocktail called the Pisco Sour, which I thoroughly relished and enjoyed on a number of occasions while in the country.

The Pisco Sour is also claimed as the national drink of Peru, where documented evidence seems to prove it was originally invented, but made differently. The Chilean version has it made with Chilean grape brandy, called Pisco, and blended with lemon (some say lime) juice, powdered sugar, and ice cubes – shaken but served straight up without ice. It has a light green appearance, and a smooth, sweet, and wonderful taste.

A separate conference in Buenos Aires, Argentina, hosted by the Argentine Federal Police, on the business side, explained how law enforcement is organized and deployed, as well as the challenges faced in Argentina. On the cultural side, without a doubt my most memorable and enjoyable events were: one, beef, and two, tango dancing (watching, not doing!). Argentine beef lived up to its worldwide reputation. Although an admitted seafood fanatic, I couldn't get enough of the thick juicy steaks eaten during opportunities made available by our hosts, and usually located at entertainment venues, where we could also enjoy the finest and most talented local tango dancers. For both learning and enjoying national cultural treasures and highlights, the trips to South America were exceptional.

One other trip in early 2018, not quite to South America, but about one-half the way there from Denver, I checked another item off my wish list, with a conference in Panama City. The Panama National Police hosted the conference, and much to my delight, organized a field trip from Panama City to allow the law enforcement participants to ride a vessel through several locks of the Panama Canal. During the trip, law enforcement topics were discussed and training provided, along with highlights of the history and operation of the canal. I had hoped to get through the Panama Canal at some time in my life, and the Panama National Police conjured up a first for a lot of us –combining training and culture at the same time and same place.

Finland
Helsinki

In September 2018, the Annual European Conference of the FBI National Academy Associates was held in Helsinki, hosted by the Finnish National Police (Poliisi). For me, beyond the culture of a wonderful city, there was one very significant law enforcement takeaway. It was especially surprising to me the extent to which countries like Finland have become interested in drone technology. Based on the discussions and demonstrations, the Poliisi have dozens of officers trained for drone operations, and a number of drones ready for action, twenty-four hours per day. They are used almost daily, covering public events, security operations, lost person searches, and support for crime scene coverage. One officer told me that they hope to have even more officers trained soon, so that immediate reactive situations will allow for using a drone in fast-breaking incidents, such as using one to follow a fleeing vehicle in order to avoid a risky and dangerous high-speed chase. It appeared clear that countries like Finland are far ahead of most parts of the United States in employing the drone technology to fight crime.

Alaska

From multiple business trips to Alaska, the one reality I have come to appreciate is the tremendous challenge and responsibility on the shoulders of the Alaska State Troopers (AST) to provide law enforcement in the state with the largest land area. With the exception of a limited number of medium-size metropolitan areas, including

Anchorage, Fairbanks, and Juneau, the AST, with sworn officers numbering about the same as the Anchorage Police Department at around five hundred, is the law enforcement for the state's rural towns, villages, and highways. Bear in mind that every household has a gun (or more), and Alaska annually seems to rank on the upper end of those states experiencing high violent crime and homicide rates. Of course, this is on a per capita basis and not by sheer numbers, since Alaska's population is just over seven hundred thousand. However, add to that the same mental health issues, substance abuse of alcohol and drugs, and domestic abuse situations experienced by other states, and you have a huge red flag, meaning very high risk situations for AST first responders. When you factor in the small number of troopers required to cover the vast distances and remote areas between the villages, you get the picture that any backup would probably not get to a trooper anytime soon. True, this situation is not limited to Alaska or to the AST, but with them it is certainly acute and exacerbated.

Culturally, especially for the outdoors fanatics, Alaska is the best of all worlds and one of my favorite states to visit. Covering nearly three thousand square miles, Alaska's capital, Juneau, is reportedly the second-largest city in the United States by land mass, but only has a population of about thirty-two thousand. The city has no roads in or out, accessed only by ferry or plane; however, you can drive the twelve miles to the scenic Mendenhall Glacier.

In Ketchikan, a city on the Inside Passage of approximately eight thousand population, you can stand on a bridge over Ketchikan Creek and watch what looks like a dark carpet moving upstream in the water below. During the fall spawning season, this would be a dark mass of thousands upon thousands of salmon fighting their way up to spawn, even through the intricate human-made concrete ladders, allowing them to gain elevation. Their eggs secured in the gravel bed where they themselves were originally hatched, they have now stopped feeding, and some will make it back downstream turning a dark red, meaning their days are numbered. Too exhausted to make it back to the Pacific Ocean, they prepare to die.

You would probably need an umbrella to shop on historic Creek Street in Ketchikan, since this city takes on about 12.5 feet of rain annually, and brags that it is the rainiest city in America (a claim that other cities relish to dispute). Ketchikan is also a mecca for visiting cruise ships, whose harbor is always lined with them, as a popular stop on the Inside Passage tours. In addition to the salmon, tourists like to watch Alaska Natives carve totem poles, and peruse dozens of beautiful totems displayed all over town.

When in Anchorage, I always save one evening for a special seafood dinner at Simon and Seafort's Saloon and Grill. The king crab legs droop over the edge of a full-size dinner plate, and the halibut is excellent. Simon's (as the locals know it) is in downtown Anchorage, and situated to provide a panoramic view of Cook's Inlet just below, and across the water to the picturesque mountains of the Alaska Range. Close by at street level, near a stairway leading down to the inlet, is a statue of Captain James Cook, the noted English explorer who visited the coast of Alaska in the late 1700s.

Hawaii

In a number of law-enforcement-related meetings and conferences in Honolulu, Maui, and Hilo on the Big Island, I have not only learned of the criminal justice problems, but have also enjoyed the culture and history of Hawaii. It was very meaningful to visit the USS Arizona Memorial by boat, off the harbor in Honolulu. In the Japanese surprise attack of December 7, 1941, bringing the United States into World War II, the battleship was sunk and nine hundred sailors entombed. It now lies in forty feet of water and serves as a memorial for the lives of nearly twenty-four hundred soldiers, sailors, marines, and civilians lost during the Pearl Harbor attack. It was also important to tour the bomb damage and bullet holes preserved around the billets and grounds of Hickam Air Force Base, as a result of the enemy strafing runs on that fateful day. They have been saved as a lasting memory and memorial for those lives lost there.

On the more pleasant food-and-drink side, one of the regular stops on each and every visit to Honolulu is Duke's Canoe Club in the Outrigger Waikiki Beach Resort on Kalakaua Avenue, which opens directly onto Waikiki Beach at the rear of the building. Hard to beat their tropical cocktails, and I particularly enjoy the original classic Mai Tai. Duke's gets its name from Hawaii's very own local hero, Duke Kahanamoku, who was a gold medalist in swimming in both the 1912 Olympics in Stockholm and the 1920 Olympics in Antwerp. He is also considered the father of modern surfing, for which he is immortalized by a prominent statue with Duke and his surfboard along Waikiki Beach.

After a meeting with the county police department on the Big Island at Hilo, I had one of my most interesting experiences ever. Driving the thirty or so miles from Hilo, I visited the Hawaii Volcanoes National Park, site of the amazing Kilauea shield volcano, which is one of the most active volcanoes in the world, and which has been erupting fairly continuously since 1983. As you drive closer, you can observe relief crevasses emitting steam and heat next to the highway, and smell the acrid sulfur-like smoke. Fortunately, the volcano was not active at the time of my visit, and I was actually able to walk directly up to the edge of the massive crater and look down into the smoldering and smoke-emitting center. Standing at the crater, the smell of sulfur and blast of hot gas push you back quickly after you have had a quick glimpse into the vast circular, cavernous hole, emitting a slight rumbling sound along with its hot, stinging gas. The large lava field surrounding the crater was covered with acres of black ash and billions of chunks of lava, which were still warm to hot underfoot. The area resembled what I would expect if reviewing the results of a nuclear blast in the area – no vegetation, just a few trunk stubs of what were incinerated trees.

For me, it was such a historic, fascinating, and other-worldly experience that I thought it important to memorialize it by scooping up a few of the small black ash chunks of lava from the billions surrounding me. Back at the hotel, I contacted my friend, Jay Kimura, who was the prosecuting attorney (same as the district attorney in the mainland states) in Hilo, for the county of Hawaii, to inform him about my wonderful experience visiting the volcano. When I told him about my small lava rocks, he gave me the bad news. The island legend has it that the goddess of fire, Pele, lives in the crater and is very jealous of anyone who purloins the materials she spews forth and takes away from Hawaii. She supposedly gets so angry that she issues a curse to bring the thief very bad luck.

Enough said. After hanging up the phone, I reluctantly, but without hesitation, took my few small specimens out to a nearby beach and returned them to Pele. Jay told me later that it is a common practice for many past visitors to Hawaii, who challenged Pele's curse and were apparently having some bad luck, to eventually mail their packages of treasured lava back to Hawaii.

Jordan

The last international trip I will mention was undeniably, for me, the most interesting and important for several reasons, and helped me tick a few more items off my bucket list. In 2014, the Jordanian National Police (JNP) hosted a conference of the FBI-trained law enforcement executives from Africa and the Middle East, and the level of their hospitality seemed to have no equal. Meeting attendees at the Amman Airport, the JNP transferred us to a resort directly on the Dead Sea for lodging and meetings.

On the business side of the visit, it was highly instructive to learn how the JNP, and other Middle East law enforcement agencies, were dealing with terrorism, espionage, and other crimes, especially in the face of surging refugee numbers relocating from war-torn Middle East countries, such as Syria. But, as if the topics weren't interesting enough by themselves, the cultural opportunities were unmatched.

First, right outside the hotel, dressed in swimsuits and rubber slippers, we had a chance to slather each other with a black mud and proceed directly into the Dead Sea. Rubber slippers were needed since the salt covering the rocks was sharp as glass. A few steps into the water, in which nothing can live, and you literally flip onto your stomach or back and float, since the intense salt content makes it impossible to stand or sink. After floating for a while and having the mud washed away by the water, we emerged from the Dead Sea feeling probably more relaxed and refreshed than we had in a long time. But life got even better!

The next day, one of the JNP officials asked us if we would like to have an interesting experience over the lunch hour, and of course, we all voted "yes." After loading into buses, we traveled through the countryside where camels roamed freely, and nomadic shepherds, with massive tents pitched, guided herds of hundreds of sheep on and off roads, while we waited until the road was clear in order to proceed. It appeared that if we were not on a paved road with auto traffic, the scene could have been one straight out of biblical times. Eventually, the road started to wind upward and upward around a mountain, and at the top a sign suddenly appeared that, for a Christian, seemed surreal – it said "Mount Nebo." Off the buses, one of the JNP officers led us up a path, amid many religious signs and memorials, to a point where he stopped. It was a point that allowed a panoramic view of a great valley, a body of water, and the land beyond. It's hard to forget what he said next: "As far as we can tell, you are at the exact spot where Moses stood and viewed the Promised Land." Sure enough, that body of water was the Dead Sea, and the land beyond was Israel.

The next day after our meetings, the JNP official asked us, "Would you like to visit another interesting place today?" The "yeses" came quickly. The buses went in another direction through similar biblical-seeming country and stopped at a relatively flat area of arid land, with some meager brush and small trees. We were led several hundred yards into the desert-like land until we came to a depression in the ground, with a few steps by ladder leading down into it. Again, memorials and religious-appearing symbols were noticed around the area, as our guide announced: "This is the spot where Jesus was baptized by John the Baptist." When someone asked the inevitable question about the baptism, which supposedly occurred in the Jordan River and not in the desert, our guide indicated "follow me" and started walking.

The exact flow of the Jordan River was changed through the ages, but a short walk brought us to its current location at a very narrow point, where Jewish visitors and pilgrims were observed directly across from us, on the Israeli bank of the river.

Much more could be written about this particular trip, but, rest assured, all the hours and details of the happenings will be etched in my memory for all my remaining days. The hospitality of the JNP will never be forgotten.

As others also probably do, I occasionally reflect and try to measure my life experiences actually lived against my hopes, dreams, and plans at my early beginnings. Although I decided to leave the military, which I respected immensely, the relationships I would go on to experience with officers and representatives of all branches were unforgettable and will always be cherished. Although never a cowboy, I got to dress like one, saddle up a horse, and socialize with real cowboys several times in Wyoming.

Okay, you might ask, but what about your dream to become a Canadian Mountie? Well, while I never had the opportunity to wear the classic scarlet Red Serge uniform of the Royal Canadian Mounted Police (RCMP), I lucked into the next best opportunity. In 1988, I was selected and honored to join the FBI National Executive Institute, an organization of executives who lead the largest law enforcement agencies in the free world. During the training, my classmate and a new friend was none other than the RCMP Commissioner N. D. (Norm) Inkster, who was in command of the more than twenty thousand Mounties in Canada. So I never got the uniform, but I still enjoy wearing his gift of an official belt with the gold-embossed RCMP logo buckle. Subsequent speaking engagements in Canada afforded additional opportunities to meet and socialize with other RCMP command officers. All in all, I can honestly feel, in one respect or another, all my early dreams and goals were satisfied, a trifecta, or better, so to speak!

Finally, in sum, after a long career with a wealth of experience in the FBI, I honestly consider myself doubly blessed and eternally grateful to be able to continue enjoying great and meaningful experiences after retirement. So for those inside or outside the FBI asking whether there is life after an FBI career, the answer is a resounding – absolutely! I remain grateful to the FBI, principally because I strongly believe that my post-FBI activities would most probably never have been possible, except for my original decision to become a Special Agent of the FBI.

CHAPTER 24

Violence

A Sad and Shameful American Tradition

LIKE SO MANY OF MY ASSOCIATES who have given so much over so many years, some of them their very lives, to make America safer, I regret that, despite our best efforts, at least one area has seemingly and regrettably gotten worse – violence in America. As my personal story comes to a conclusion, I will take the liberty of offering a few thoughts and suggestions to focus on the problem, its causes, possible solutions, and my hope for America's future.

There are those who will point to statistics, over certain time periods, and then attempt to explain why crime rates go up or down for a particular category of property or personal crime. Granted, this might explain how the country's economy, after a period like the Great Depression, led to the prolific bank robbery gangs of the early 1930s, and resulted in a high crime rate. Likewise, an extended period of extremely cold weather could affect criminal activities on the streets, effectively lowering the crime rate. Interpretations and explanations of crime rates can be instructive and helpful. However, what should concern us even more, I believe, is how we can deal effectively with the ever upward-spiraling problem of deadly violence in the country. Sadly, the fact is that for the unfortunate victims of random and unexpected violence in their homes, schools, businesses, and streets of America today, the knowledge of any crime rate trend is probably irrelevant. What is relevant, however, is the understanding that violence, while apparently accelerating, is not new to the country.

Please check out the following quotes on this page and then turn the page to identify their sources:

1. "The murder and mayhem in our great city have reached epidemic proportions thanks to the numbers of English prisoners banished to our shore as punishment."

2. "And be sure to avoid Central Park after sundown because of the extreme risk of murder or violence. In fact, avoid the city generally at night except the busiest and best lighted streets."

3. "Human life was never as cheap and insecure in the US as it is at the present time and murder is decidedly more common in this country than in any other country of the world which makes the claim of being civilized."

4. "It is an age of fear – a stark, pervasive, gnawing, clawing, mind-numbing, gut-wrenching fear. Old men are robbed, then stomped to death a few feet from their front doors. Young girls are raped in crowded, well-lit suburban shopping malls. Shopkeepers are murdered for $20. The stick-up man, who once would have been satisfied with your money, now wants your life; the burglar, who once would have fled or frozen when detected, now ducks behind the nearest make-shift barricade, pistol in hand, ready to shoot. The boy down the street, who once would have ridden his bicycle to deliver newspapers, now pops pills and uses his bicycle chain to smash someone's face in for the sheer, delicious hell of it."

You might be surprised to identify the sources of the quotes on the previous page:

1. Benjamin Franklin, Philadelphia, 1785
2. *The City Guide to New York City*, 1872
3. *The Spectator* (national periodical, Dr. Frederick Hoffman), 1933
4. *The Los Angeles Times*, New Year's Eve edition, 1972

So given the fact or at least, the perception that violence has plagued our existence ever since the beginning of our nation, why would I and others have the justification to believe it has gotten more grievous and horrific in recent years? To answer that question, I like to use the illustration of a particular murder that some characterized for years as the "crime of the century."

On August 4, 1892, young Lizzie Borden allegedly murdered her father, Andrew Borden, and stepmother, Abby Borden, in Fall River, Massachusetts. She was tried and acquitted of the ax murders. The crime fascinated America for years, leading to legends, poems, and even a feature movie. Some folks still remember a poem that this criminal act generated, which started, "Lizzie Borden took an ax and gave her mother forty whacks, when she saw what she had done, she gave her father forty-one." Regardless of the true facts and merits of that case, the publicity generated worldwide at the time would probably be a one-day media headline among today's daily American bloodbaths.

Today, murders of that magnitude, and if possible, even more brutal, sadistic, and of a nature and intensity almost incomprehensible in regard to how one human being could treat others, are occurring almost daily. Domestic disputes result in one or the other parent killing their entire family in shootings, drownings, and other almost unbelievable incidents. Bizarre, horrible crimes include beheading and other dismemberment. Students show up at their schools to commit mass shootings of their fellow students and teachers. Active shooters return to their business locations and execute fellow employees and supervisors, while other mass shooters occupy an elevated position, with automatic weapons, to mow down unsuspecting pedestrians in public areas below. As we know, these types of violent acts can be preplanned or spontaneous, and can be drug or alcohol infused, or the result of mental health disorders, including post-traumatic stress disorder or other illness. Sadly, in some cases, the trigger or motive may never be known. Unfortunately, although the resulting violence in these cases can be explosive, unexpected, and deadly, these incidents represent only one of three violent threats to our public safety.

The second threat comes from the more traditional criminal activities of the dangerous, but "sane" or "normal" (if you will), actors who prey on our citizens for a specific purpose. This includes those who commit rapes, sexual assaults, hate crimes, robberies, home invasions, kidnappings, homicides, other physical assaults, and contract murders. Here we need to be more interested and aware of the reported ebbs and flows of personal crime rates in our personal areas of activity.

The third risk lies with those inside and outside the country who seek to bring America to its knees through insidious and destructive acts of terrorism. Subsequent to the unspeakable loss of human life and destruction at the New York Twin Trade Towers in the September 11, 2001, disaster, much has changed to protect the country from foreign-based international terrorists. Law enforcement agencies at every level have effectively come together in an attempt to "connect the dots" so that a repeat of anything like 9/11 will never happen again in the United States. Needless to say, the efforts of foreign-based terror groups and individuals have not died off, but the efforts of American defenders have thankfully thwarted and prevented further 9/11-type attacks so far.

What hasn't been entirely successful since 9/11 is dissuading some weaker-minded American citizens from becoming terrorist sympathizers and haters of their home country. Some have successfully traveled to Middle Eastern terrorist strongholds for training, and others have been recruited and brainwashed by a flood of social media, internet videos, and publications designed to poison their minds against their country. It appears the main message to the newly converted "homegrown" terrorists is that they do not have to travel to Syria, Iraq, Afghanistan, or anywhere in the Middle East for training. Indeed, the disaffected Americans, who are normally younger, are told not to leave the United States but instead just to get a gun, or get into their vehicles and go kill Americans.

Unfortunately, considering each of the three prongs of the violence pitchfork – mentally affected, traditional criminals, or terrorists – it is logical to expect that law enforcement and other first responders are certain to be among those suffering the heaviest casualties.

According to information and statistics reported as of April 2019 by the National Law Enforcement Officers Memorial Fund, the following facts should be of interest.

There are now more than nine hundred thousand sworn law enforcement officers serving in the United States, of whom about 12 percent are female. Since the first recorded police death in 1786, there have been more than twenty-one thousand law enforcement officers killed in the line of duty. Currently, there are 21,910 names engraved on the walls of the National Law Enforcement Officers Memorial. A total of 1,582 law enforcement officers died in the line of duty during the past ten years (reported as of 2019), which is an average of about one death every fifty-five hours, or an average of 158 per year. There were 158 law enforcement officers killed in the line of duty in 2018, including eleven female officers.

On average, during the last ten years, there have been nearly sixty thousand assaults against law enforcement each year, resulting in more than fifteen thousand injuries. The deadliest day in law enforcement history was September 11, 2001, when seventy-two police officers were killed while responding to terrorist attacks against our country. New York City has lost more police officers in the line of duty than any other department, with nearly nine hundred deaths. The state of Texas has lost more than seventeen hundred officers, more than any other state, while the state with the fewest deaths is Vermont, currently with twenty-four. There are 1,166 federal officers listed on the memorial, as well as 713 correctional officers and forty-three military law enforcement officers. Among those listed on the memorial are 348 female officers.

Refining some troubling data a bit further, the FBI Law Enforcement Officers Killed and Assaulted report for 2017, reports that for the ten-year period from 2008 to 2017, there were 496 officers killed in the line of duty, with 455 of them by firearms (majority by handguns – 323). Even more troubling, as the years passed, the period from 2013 to 2017 had 231 officers killed, with the majority by firearms and the largest number (forty-five) under the scariest circumstances possible – ambushed (they had a target on them simply because of their uniform).

Before we leave the statistics, I might mention an interesting aside. The period leading up to the financial depression of 1929, and the early 1930s thereafter, was a terribly costly period for the lives of law enforcement officers. An average of nearly two hundred and fifty died in the line of duty annually, and 1930 was the high-water mark, with 310 killed. In researching the cold-blooded, murderous activities of the bank robbery gangs of that period, including the likes of John Dillinger, Machine Gun Kelly, Baby Face Nelson, the Barker Family, and Bonnie and Clyde, some surprising facts appeared. These gangs were heavily armed with machine guns, semiautomatic rifles and pistols, and for years, outgunned law enforcement and showed no reluctance or hesitation to gun down officers and even innocent citizens (simply as collateral damage, if they got in the way). Although it becomes a small and relatively irrelevant victory when weighed against the felonious death of a police officer, at least today we can find some comfort in the fact that the bad guys' automatic weapons have mostly given way to handguns, rifles, and shotguns.

As the above statistics clearly demonstrate, a large percentage of the violence in society involves a bullet, exploding out of the barrel of one of the millions of firearms maintained in the United States. Many Americans hold that the number of guns, and their easy availability, are excessive. Too often they fall into the hands of juveniles, and therein lies one of our huge problems, since science has now proven that the juvenile brain is not sufficiently developed to allow the rational thinking and decision-making expected of a more mature adult.

So, when you think about the combination of a young shooter in possession of a deadly weapon, you can realize the potentially dire consequences that are immediately evident. Bear in mind, the gun is an extremely disciplined tool that lies quietly in wait for a command to function. When the order is given (trigger pulled), it acts without hesitation. Obviously, all the thinking, reasoning, and decision-making must occur in the mind of the "commander" before the command is given. Surely, we should not be surprised at the result, when the commander is an immature and irrational juvenile.

Ironically, on the very day that my thoughts were on this issue, my attention was drawn to the April 28, 2019, issue of the *Denver Post* and an article borrowed from the *Washington Post*, which I believe illustrates my previous point perfectly. In Albuquerque, New Mexico, a US Postal Service mail carrier (a US Army veteran) named Jose Hernandez, had just been murdered along his route in a residential neighborhood. He encountered and was attempting to break up a fight between a mother and her teenage son outside their home. The seventeen-year-old son became aggressive and retreated inside the house, only to emerge with a gun, which he used to shoot and kill Mr. Hernandez.

Where Do We Stand Today?

One needs to look no further than the caseloads of FBI Field Offices, and the myriad other law enforcement agencies, to know that the United States is in trouble. Consider the violence to victims of human-trafficking organizations that ensnare innocent human beings for prostitution and other illegal purposes. How about our soaring homicide rates that steal the future of so many of our young, particularly due to youth gang violence? Then, there is the explosion of horrendous domestic violence cases, tearing apart so many families.

Other examples include the mass shooters and active shooters in and around our schools and businesses. If these concerns weren't enough, we live under constant fear of a foreign-conducted or home-grown terrorist attack against our citizens and institutions. Then, not finally, but in addition, we have deadly attacks from those whose motives are simply hatred for racial, religious, or gender reasons. Unfortunately, sometimes it seems that part of the icing on the cake, so to speak, of problems in the republic, with all our freedoms and our major two-party political system, is that both parties are fighting each other rather than working together to solve our problems.

My belief is that this great country is made up of three major groups of people:

Group A – First of all, I have faith that the majority are good, honest, and hardworking. They might be silent and preoccupied with their own lives and interests but are solid Americans who will obey the laws and are capable, if energized, to continue doing the right thing.

Group B – I see a second surprisingly large group of "residents" who are vulnerable to an overwhelming tide of drugs, alcohol, gangs, corruption, mental illness, and other moral, ethical, and legal dilemmas. Their difficulties have either immersed or swamped them, or have them at risk of sinking into troubled waters. These individuals can be citizens, as well as legal or illegal immigrants. They can be homeless, rich, poor, or incarcerated. The important point is that this admittedly massive group, given time and the appropriate help or corrective action, can be returned to the "good" Group A (hopefully, at least many of them).

from England. They participated willingly, along with their appointed official protectors, as part of the "Watch," helping to patrol along the streets, or serving on a mounted posse to assist the sheriff.

Through the years, much has changed in the relationship as our population has increased and the police agencies have grown large and more formally organized. Some observers would proffer that one forever change occurred when officers left the street patrols and close contact with the community. These observers would argue that police officers became invisible and aloof by climbing into their vehicles and rolling up their windows to complete a separation from the citizens they serve.

Trying to definitively determine how a sometimes vicious anti-law-enforcement movement has developed is not an easy task. Whether it was a pattern of behavior by law enforcement, generating a lack of respect from segments of the population, or erratic and frequently violent reactions from those contacted by the police that has engendered an attitude of mutual distrust, is unclear. In fact, it is somewhat like trying to address the age-old question of "which came first, the chicken or the egg?"

Regardless of the theories or even the reality of why and how it happened, and the arguable "chicken or the egg" cause, the situation seems to have evolved into an "us versus them" status between law enforcement and various communities. There definitely is a problem, and it cries out for a solution.

Cries and protests are loud that police are using excessive force and needlessly shooting innocent residents. It appears true that there are some widely publicized, but very limited few, law enforcement officers who have lost control, usually under very stressful circumstances, and crossed the line into unwarranted excessive force. However, I truly believe the vast majority of America's law enforcement officers have no intent to use deadly force, absent a genuine concern and real fear that their life is in danger. Widespread events have been occurring in the United States throughout the current millennium, that find officers being ambushed and assassinated without any provocation, officers being shot or assaulted merely for stopping a suspicious vehicle, individuals drawing a weapon on an officer in order to initiate a "suicide by cop," and myriad other situations in which a lawful order from an officer is met with a weapon being pulled, or a blatant refusal to obey.

I have been able to review a number of body camera or vehicle dashcam videos of car stops and street stops, which start with a reasonable request, or direction, for a subject to stop or exit the vehicle, keeping the hands visible. There follows then, far too often, a refusal to willingly cooperate with the request or order, leading to various scenarios – whether a verbal argument, reaching or appearing to reach for a weapon, or other physical attack or threat. Officers understand that contact with individuals under the influence of alcohol or drugs (or both), or a wanted felon, will be difficult and potentially dangerous, but disrespect from others is difficult to understand, and frankly inexcusable. These incidents then frequently escalate and deteriorate into a foot chase or a high-speed vehicle chase, endangering the officer, the subject, and too often, other innocent citizens.

With a degree of sadness, I recall a portion of the address I delivered to the graduating class of North Carolina State Highway Patrol troopers at their academy in Raleigh, North Carolina, in May 1985. I remember it because the address was covered by the press, and a portion appeared in the Raleigh newspaper the next day. The quote stated, "You will be respected because of the uniform you wear. You can't buy that respect, but the people are going to give it to you for free." It seems so convoluted and strangely ironic, that if I were speaking to them today, I would have to warn them to be careful, since that uniform they wear might put a target on their backs. It seems a bit like our world has been turned upside down.

Although it still remains difficult to totally understand how the distrust of American law enforcement has developed, there is one possibility that might have contributed to it. In the last several years, our population has seen the arrival of large numbers of both legal and illegal immigrants from countries well known to have police and law enforcement agencies that are poorly paid and subject to high levels of corruption. It is certainly possible that the immigrants have brought the dislike, distrust, and fear of corrupt police with them, and assume that the same level of corruption exists here. That is not to say there is no corruption in American law enforcement, but the number of instances pales in comparison to reports that exist involving corruption in many other countries.

Whatever the reasons, the existing malaise of distrust is having its deleterious effect on law enforcement. Suicide rates are significant, agencies are finding some difficulty in hiring and retaining officers, and many officers are essentially experiencing the feeling that "enough is enough." Facing the lack of respect, it's possible that a few officers might elect to avoid a personal life-risking situation and emergency response in which they might have to use excessive force and be criticized for it. A few others might regrettably get involved in a critical situation, which would actually require deadly force, and hesitate to use it, potentially sacrificing their own life. It is probably fair to say that a majority of officers facing life-and-death situations, with adrenaline pumping and heart pounding, are struggling with the ability to remain calm, and some possibly take premature, and sometimes lethal, action to defend themselves. I have heard officers voice the expression, "Better to be judged by twelve (jurors) than carried by six (pallbearers)."

As a result of the anti-law-enforcement actions, including assault and deadly ambush of officers, we have noted some cases of a regrettable, yet understandable, trend. Some officers responding to potentially dangerous situations are hesitating less than in the past to use deadly force. In today's explosive environment, any number of irresponsible and foolish failures to obey a command or request could trigger deadly force, and might include failure to obey a command for a person to drop a knife, failure to stop reaching into a pants pocket (when it contains a cell phone only), encountering a youth aiming at the officer with a toy weapon (which from a distance appears real), or observing a suspicious movement of a driver to reach down inside the car for anything. Although sad, even heartbreaking, some of the incidents turn out that the person was not actually reaching for a weapon. Prosecutors will carefully review the incidents and determine that, in most cases, officers acted out of a genuine belief that his or her life was in danger. These shootings are normally going to be brutally unfortunate, but are determined by prosecutors to be legal "good shoots," so to speak, leaving the officers frequently traumatized, and the subject dead, both victims of an incident involving a simple failure to comply with a legal order.

All that said, I feel comfortable in the knowledge, faith, and belief that the overwhelming majority of our law enforcement officers, despite all the current stresses, are now, and will continue to be, running toward the active shooter and into the bombed and burning buildings, while the protected citizens are fleeing in the opposite direction.

Looking beyond law enforcement briefly, loss of the LCR factor can easily be detected among the general population, where too many Americans are showing none of it to each other. Families are torn apart from domestic violence situations that, too frequently, end with one or both parents dead along with their children. Hit-and-run vehicle encounters are rampant. Property theft shows how little respect we have for the property of others. Revered institutions, including businesses and banks, have fallen into fraudulent practices even at the highest corporate levels. For example, on May 16, 2019, the *Washington Post* reported that of the eighty-nine chief executive officers ousted from their positions in 2018, 39 percent of them were removed for ethical misconduct. This involved acts that included fraud, bribery, insider trading, environmental disasters, inflated résumés, or sexual indiscretions.

As mentioned elsewhere in this book, we have identified severe mental illness as a major problem in our country, which often manifests itself in acts of unspeakable human disaster and destruction. Yet for too long as a nation, we have shown very little concern and respect for those affected and seriously suffering. We need to realize that a bit of that concern and care just might have prevented the resulting incidents that we are now encountering. Finally, too many of us have lost respect for ourselves and our very life itself, pushing suicide rates to the highest levels ever.

What About the Gun Issue?

It would be no surprise to any American that the use of firearms looms large in the problem of violence that besets the country. However, just as large is the political divide, almost a firestorm, which debates what to do about the problem. Passionate arguments come from those who fervently support some form of gun control to attack and lessen the violence. Loud and persistent arguments from an opposing segment of the population advocate that guns are not the problem but rather the people who are misusing them to create the violence. Their position appears to hold that gun control, in any form, would be unconstitutional in as much as the Second Amendment of the US Constitution reads, in part, "The right of the people to keep and bear arms shall not be infringed."

As thorny and difficult as the gun issue may be, I always refer back to my belief in the Carl Sandburg quote as to the failure of a nation "when they lose sight of what brought them along." Unlike the loss of the LCR factor, nobody could honestly assert that the bearing of arms had no part to play in literally every stage of the development of the United States. Guns in America, one might argue, are "as American as apple pie." We have borne arms for hunting, sport, and protection, and in a larger sense, to protect the country in a litany of wars and physical struggles. Ironically, one could argue that arms have actually "brought us along," and we have not forgotten or lost sight of that fact.

Rather than violate or alter the Second Amendment to the Constitution, it would be great if cool and wise minds, on both sides of this critical national gun violence issue, could work together and solve it. Answers need to be found regarding how to keep guns from reaching the hands of the wrong people, how legitimate gun owners can better protect their weapons, whether there should be a limit on the types and numbers of firearms legally owned, and other related questions. In considering the answers, it might be helpful and instructive to think back about what the framers of the Constitution, and its Second Amendment, might really have had in mind. I doubt their thinking would have extended the right to bear arms to a young student for shooting innocent fellow classmates, or an active shooter using an automatic weapon to murder unsuspecting pedestrians or fellow business employees.

What Has Happened to Our Spiritual Cornerstone and Backbone?

If the Sandburg quote about "our future if we forget our past" has validity, we need to consider one trend that should seriously concern us.

The early leaders of our democracy founded a spiritual nation that liberally referred to God, not only in their worship activities, but on their money, in opening their business and government meetings, and in most of their official writings and documents.

In my post-FBI travels I have noticed, in some of America's most historic churches, the notation that President George Washington worshiped there (Trinity Church in Boston), or identification of the pews occupied by Betsy Ross or Benjamin Franklin (Christ Church in Philadelphia). It has also been written that 70 to 80 percent of the colonists attended some church. In fact, one historic comment noted that a particular sermon at Trinity Church in Boston was heard by thirty thousand people. As late as 1954, we were still adding God to our documents, as we did that year when we inserted "under God" to the Pledge of Allegiance to our flag.

However, it seems that, in recent years, it has become politically correct to remove the reference to God in a number of documents and situations. There also appears to be ongoing pressure from other voices and elements to continue and increase the practice. For some, former greetings of "Merry Christmas" have changed to "Happy Holidays." Easter egg hunts have morphed to spring egg hunts. Religious iterations and displays containing such writings as the Ten Commandments have been removed from their previous coveted positions to other locations. During a speech in Jakarta, Indonesia, in 2010, the President of the United States, himself, mistakenly referred to the United States motto as "E Pluribus Unum," while the motto has been "In God We Trust" since 1956. Interestingly, by a vote of 396 to nine the US House of Representatives, soon after, passed a bipartisan resolution reaffirming the official US motto as "In God We Trust."

Among other actions, in 2012, the Rapid Capabilities Office of the US Air Force removed the Latin word for God from its logo. There are other examples, and the trend is real and visible to the public. Considering the inextricable connection between God and the founding fathers, one can certainly make a case that we might indeed be "forgetting where we came from and what brought us along."

Fortunately, despite the effort to minimize God in society, there are those real incidents and spiritual myths that tend to shore up and protect spiritual faith. Take the US Marine Corps War Memorial in Arlington, Virginia, which shows the six US Marines raising the American flag on Iwo Jima in 1945, where nearly sixty-eight hundred Marines gave their lives in World War II. Despite affirmation by the sculptor personally, that there are only twelve hands on the monument, many swear they have seen or, at least, firmly believe there are thirteen hands on the flagpole – number thirteen being the hand of God.

I can contribute a couple of real-life situations that, for me, went well beyond coincidence, and certainly kept me from losing my faith, strengthening it instead. We all face unexpected and difficult situations from time to time. We are usually able to cope, and resort to alternative methods to solve or resolve our predicament. I would bet that, if the truth were told, a lot of us, on some rare occasions, get placed in a difficult situation for which there appears to be no rational or reasonable solution.

Unfortunately, I faced one such predicament a few years ago in 2015, while on a law enforcement visit to Warsaw, Poland. Picked up at Frederic Chopin Airport by the Polish National Police, law enforcement attendees from throughout Europe were transported to the meeting hotel to briefly register and drop our luggage before being reloaded on a bus and transported to a large park in the suburbs of Warsaw, to network and enjoy a piano concert of Chopin music. The concert featured a professional female artist, playing a beautiful grand piano situated on a stage in a hilly area, in the far upper end of the park. The bus dropped us off at the lower end of the park. I enjoyed walking through the lower end with other attendees, enjoying its museums, a lake with fountains, and beautiful flowers, and then moved up the hill about a quarter of a mile to the concert area.

About three-quarters of the way through the concert, I decided to leave and return back down the hill to further explore the scenic park, expecting that the bus would remain at the drop-off point, and I would rejoin the group there at the conclusion of the concert. As the concert ended and the large crowd of hundreds of attendees left and walked

The park where we enjoyed a piano concert of Chopin music.

down the path toward me, I moved toward the point where the bus had been parked. It was not there! I expected the driver had moved the bus to a different required parking space and would return, so I waited. As the departing crowd thinned, I saw none of my fellow law enforcement attendees returning to the drop-off area. Suddenly, it struck me that the bus must have been moved to a point at the other end of the park near the concert site. I hurried at least twice, up and down the quarter mile, between the two sites, but never found the bus. Finally, exhausted from my earlier flight from the United States, as well as running between the two ends of the park, and with a very dry mouth and throat, I began to realize I had missed the bus and was alone.

A perfect storm of quiet panic set in, as I contemplated the problem I faced. Because of the hurried circumstances that got us to the park almost immediately upon arrival in Warsaw, I had not exchanged any currency and had no Polish money. I could not remember the name or address of the hotel. I had not yet received the name or contact number of our police host. The park was in a distant suburb of the city, surrounded by high-speed avenues from which no taxis, buses, or other vehicles could or would stop. Other than the name of the park, I had no idea of my location in the city, and it seemed no one in the area spoke English, or would admit that they could. I crossed from one side of the busy avenue to the other, several times through multitraffic lanes, in order to try to engage a taxi without any success. The sidewalks were nearly deserted now, darkness was closing in, and I was out of ideas.

Standing alone on the curb of the avenue, I suddenly heard a voice from directly behind me in perfect English, and remember the exact words: "May we help you?" Turning around, I saw a gentleman about fifty- to sixty-years-old, conservatively dressed in a business suit, with a young boy about eight- to ten-years-old holding his hand. I probably sounded a bit desperate and foolish, as I explained my plight, that I was in the city on business but didn't know my current location, the name or location of my hotel, or how to get there. Without any hesitation, the gentleman invited me to follow him and the boy, as he led me through a number of streets and alleys, ending at a streetcar or tram stop. Reaching into his jacket pocket, he produced a tram ticket and handed it to me. We then waited for at least three streetcars to stop and then proceed, as he patiently smiled and indicated "not this one." As the fourth streetcar approached, he motioned me to board and almost whispered, "Ring the bell at the third stop, get off, and you will see your hotel." The young boy spoke no words during the entire encounter – just smiled at me. I boarded the streetcar, punched the ticket at the entrance, and immediately turned around to wave thanks to my benefactors – but the platform was empty. I quickly glanced back and forth the entire length of the station platform, but there was nobody there – they had disappeared. As the third stop approached, the appearance of the hotel and the name came back to me, and I pulled the cord to exit and return to my group. Now people can believe whatever they want, and explain this episode however they wish, but I know what I believe … when I truly needed help, even though not a life-and-death situation, I got it from a higher authority.

Another odds-long and unlikely, but much less stressful, coincidence occurred for me on May 1, 2016. I had arrived the night before in Charleston, South Carolina, for a conference of state police and other state-level US criminal investigative agencies. My hotel was located in the historic section of Charleston on Meeting Street. I had planned to call an old friend, Bill Nettles, a retired FBI Agent who supervised the Charleston FBI office when I was assigned in Charlotte, North Carolina, years earlier. During my flight from Denver, I suddenly realized I had forgotten to retrieve his special telephone number in my office, and without it, would be unable to make contact during my stay in Charleston.

After breakfast the next morning, Sunday, May 1, I decided to take a walk down Meeting Street and locate the hotel that would be hosting the conference. A few blocks down Meeting Street, my attention was drawn to a beautiful church, with a number of white columns along its front and a number of steps up to its main entrance. I felt an unusual attraction to the church, but passed by for about a block until I felt the urge to go back. Back in front, I paused for a few moments, and then climbed the steps of the Trinity United Methodist Church to the entrance. A few steps through the door, and standing directly behind the last pew I suddenly came face-to-face with Bill Nettles. I stayed for the service, and afterward enjoyed a great visit with Bill, who volunteers in an unofficial security role at that church. Later, on my way down Meeting Street, I smiled at the odds of what had just happened in Charleston, whose nickname is the "Holy City" with about four hundred churches, and just knew I had gotten some high-level help for that particular meeting.

CHAPTER 26

Rays of Hope for America

TRULY, SOME SERIOUS CHALLENGES REMAIN facing us in the struggle against unacceptable violence in America. With that as a given, we need to believe as a nation that it is not too late to restore the LOVE, CARE, RESPECT, or LCR, factor, starting with the family and spreading out from there to our neighbors and the greater community. First, we need to take a look back and remember "where we came from" and "what brought us along," and then we can work to meaningfully restore the LCR factor.

Every available effort of our vast bureaucracy of government agencies and private sector organizations should be directed toward salvaging our Group B vulnerable population described in Chapter 24. They need to be rescued from homelessness, drugs, mental illness, and crime, with as many as possible restored to the Group A law-abiding and well-balanced citizens. Special attention needs to go to our youth, who are surrounded by so many violent stresses (domestic violence at home, gangs, guns, drugs, violent video games, bullying, and mental illness) and are on the verge of being swept into the Juvenile Justice system (sometimes surrendered to the court just to obtain mental health treatment not available otherwise). We need to remember our youth might represent a lesser percentage of our population at present, but they are 100 percent of our future. If Group A and Group B can interact and come together using the LCR factor, law enforcement officers would be much more effective directing their time and attention toward controlling the hopeless criminals in Group C.

Meanwhile, until the LCR factor is fully restored, Americans still need to protect their own personal safety. Crime rates will show ebbs and flows, and can probably lull some into a false sense of security. For example, some crime rates will demonstrate a lower number of homicides for a specific time period in certain cities, counties, or states, while a deeper look might show an actual increase in the number of shootings and assaults, but with fewer deaths due to an incredibly improved and advanced emergency treatment and healthcare system now available in America. I think it sufficient to conclude that the country, in many locations, remains a very dangerous place with extremely high risks. Nevertheless, it does pay to avoid being in the wrong place at the wrong time!

Another bit of advice comes from the presentation of Pence's Personal Protection Principles (PPPP), and is number one on the list – be aware of your surroundings. Americans, out of habit, seem to be woefully inattentive to individuals and events in their immediate surroundings. A recent shopping trip by my own family clearly demonstrated this. In a local strip mall, I parked at a store at one end of the mall, while my wife walked to the other end to shop at a bookstore. My business concluded, I moved the car across to a spot directly in front of the bookstore to wait for my wife. Frankly, I was not surprised when she left the store and walked right by my location without even noticing me. Perhaps we need to adopt some of the techniques of the foreign spies who operate in the country, and are always extremely aware of their surroundings. Not to recommend paranoia, but it would be a good practice to take time to notice people, vehicles, and events, and always heed the advice to "see something, say something," especially as terrorism continues to find a home in the United States.

In the unlikely event of a personal contact from a law enforcement officer, my advice to everyone is simple, clear, and direct. From everything I have seen, heard, and learned, I believe that the majority of situations that cascade into excessive-force scenarios can be easily avoided, if only residents simply and quickly, comply with a legitimate, lawful order of a duly authorized law enforcement officer.

On the gun issue, many in this country agree that the number of, and easy access to, guns are problematic. However, whether or not individuals, groups, or organizations agree about the number of guns, the divide between gun supporters and gun control advocates is seriously strong, deep, and wide. As discussed earlier, guns came with the founding of America's democracy, and certainly are not going away. Frankly, I don't see any currently effective strategy to lessen the numbers or the proliferation of guns in the country. However, I seriously believe that, in the best interest of society, common ground and an effective solution must be found to keep the guns out of the wrong hands, and particularly the wrong young hands.

On the good news side, there are hopeful and positive signs that law enforcement agencies, for their part, are employing the LCR factor inwardly, as well as externally, to better serve and protect citizens.

Sir Robert Peel was a potent force for community policing in England in the early 1800s. His work led to the creation of the Metropolitan Police Force in Britain, and his tenets and principles essentially held that the police are the people, the people are the police, and crime prevention is possible without overly abridging citizens' rights and privacy. For a number of years now, American law enforcement has taken officers back out of their patrol cars, and has them working on the barrier between "us and them" through a return to community policing.

Departments have instituted citizen academies designed to solicit cooperation from the public and better explain the role and responsibilities of law enforcement. Neighborhood Watch programs have also been helpful in getting communities involved. In an attempt to be more transparent to their public, during critical incidents law enforcement agencies are communicating more frequently through social media and press conferences. Better relations with media organizations are also allowing law enforcement to inform citizens of all the good, sometimes even heroic, efforts law enforcement personnel, in non-law-enforcement emergencies, are performing (assisting with childbirth, fires, floods, etc.).

On an organization level, public-private partnerships between law enforcement and other security and business organizations go straight to the heart of building better community relationships. A particularly valuable partnership now exists between law enforcement organizations and the American Society for Industrial Security International, which represents the corporate security world. Since corporate America's guards are responsible for security at nearly 90 percent of US critical infrastructure, they will normally be the first responders to any incident, thus making their relationship with law enforcement of paramount importance.

Aside from the external efforts, what law enforcement is working on internally is equally significant. In addition to training topics of a reactive nature, such as responding to active shooter situations or how to utilize new emerging technology, officers are learning how to de-escalate stressful situations in an attempt to lessen the need for deadly force. Training includes topics such as how to deal more effectively with offenders suffering from mental illness, including former military personnel with post-traumatic stress disorder, as well as more effective methods to deal with juveniles. In response to the extreme challenges suffered by the effects of so many officers being ambushed and assaulted, and also feeling the direct effects of the anti-law-enforcement sentiments, suicide rates are high among the law enforcement ranks. Certainly, for many, the negativity shown the officers, while they, in turn, are still expected to continue putting their lives on the line daily, has to double the stress and deepen their frustration.

To their credit, most departments are initiating training and support for employee wellness –mentally, emotionally, and physically. In fact, with the assistance of chaplains, many departments are augmenting the training to add the topic of spirituality to give officers the total support of mind, body, and spirit. The purpose here is to remind them of the vital purpose they fulfill, to the community they serve.

What the Los Angeles Police Department has been teaching officers for the past few years may be restoring the LCR factor, representing a possible prototype for the future of policing. The department is one of a number of agencies doing de-escalation training in an attempt to reduce tension and avoid using deadly force. One initiative is to consider the police as guardians of their communities, and not an occupying force of soldiers or warriors. They want to interact with their citizens and rightfully embody their motto of "to serve and protect," with more patience and empathy. Officers are instructed that perceptions of the police are formed by such habits as foul language or cursing, and even walking with a swagger, which can appear disrespectful to the people. Although considered controversial by some officers, it has been reported that there have been fewer fatal police shootings, and even fewer police weapons fired, in the years since this training commenced. The only important consideration is that de-escalation should not delay or deter an officer from resorting to deadly force, where such a delay could cost him or her their life.

Optimism and Hope

backdrop of a particular challenge and quote, I have
for America...

a French diplomat named Alexis de Tocqueville was sent
to the United States by the French government to study the prison
system. He loved what he saw in this country, and wrote what was
to become a classic called *Democracy in America*. It was published
in 1835, and remains one of the great works describing American
national policy.

About America, he wrote:

> I sought for the greatness and genius of America in her com-
> modious harbors and her ample rivers – and it was not there ... in
> her fertile fields and boundless forests – and it was not there ... in
> her rich mines and her vast world commerce – and it was not there
> ... in her democratic Congress and matchless Constitution – and
> it was not there. Not until I went into the churches of America
> and heard her pulpits aflame with righteousness did I understand
> the secret of her genius and power. America is great because she
> is good, and if America ever ceases to be good, she will cease to
> be great.

As de Tocqueville duly noted then, and is still true today, America is "good," and allows us every hope that it can stay that way and
become even "better" with the right effort. My confidence rests in the
belief that it is the very freedom that we enjoy in the United States
that offers our greatest hope for the future. Of course, freedom brings
with it some waste, inefficiency, and even corruption, but it still provides us, in this country, a life better than probably anywhere else
in the world. Americans enjoy the ability to create, innovate, and
produce, and without question, they represent the most charitable
nation on the planet. When the chips have been down, and in the face
of serious challenges with crises looming, Americans have defended
and secured our liberty, over and over, time and time again – from
the time of the American Revolution, through a series of wars, and
up to, and including, the current struggle against domestic and international terrorism.

Speaking of terrorism, on the very day of one of the worst domestic terror disasters up to that time, I witnessed an interesting example of the can-do attitude and innovative capabilities of my fellow Americans. On April 19, 1995, a truck bomb in Oklahoma City, Oklahoma, nearly leveled the Alfred P. Murrah Federal Building, killing 168 people and injuring many more. I happened to be in Dallas, Texas, at the airport, awaiting a connecting flight to Austin for a speaking engagement at the Texas Police Chiefs Association annual conference.

When the news of the bombing hit, all flights were canceled or delayed, and affairs at the airport were in near chaos. We waited nearly all day, and then early that evening an announcement was made at our gate that an airplane was available, along with a crew, but, due to the delays, the crew would be timed out to fly if the plane did not leave the gate in fifteen minutes, and there would be no further flights to Austin that evening. The airline employee then offered very little confidence that the nearly one hundred and fifty passengers could be boarded, and the gate closed in the time period remaining. That's when American ingenuity took hold, and some of us volunteered to load the plane immediately after passengers had presented their boarding passes to the gate agent.

With no complaints and total cooperation of all passengers, we boarded the last row first, first class last, with some of us expediting passengers to their seats and stowing luggage in the overhead compartments for them. Bottom line, the plane was fully boarded and passengers seated in a little over ten minutes, gate closed, and the plane pushed back from the gate, just before the fifteen minute deadline. Even minor moments like those can't help but give us confidence in America's possibilities.

A few years ago, while on business in Indianapolis, Indiana, and walking along West Ohio Street, I happened to stop at the 911 Memorial, built by Project 911 Indianapolis and dedicated on September 11, 2011. The text on the memorial resonated strongly with me, and I refer to it frequently. The text was attributed to Cheryl B. Sawyer, EdD, and portions of it are quoted here:

As the soot and dirt and ash rained down,
We became one color.

As we carried each other down the stairs of the burning building,
We became one class.

As we lit candles of waiting and hope,
We became one generation.

As the firefighters and police officers
fought their way into the inferno,
We became one gender.

As we fell to our knees in prayer for strength,
We became one faith.

As we whispered our shouted words of encouragement,
We spoke one language.

As we gave our blood in lines a mile long,
We became one body.

As we mourned together the great loss,
We became one family.

As we cried tears of grief and loss,
We became one soul.

As we retell with pride of the sacrifice of heroes,
We become one people.

We are the power of one
We are united
We are America.

As I reread the text, the main thought I always get is that the inspiration from it should not last for a day, a month, or a year, but should be burned into the spirit of every American and remembered daily. I get the same feeling from a quote attributed to the late Father Edward J. Flanagan, founder of Boys Town in Omaha, Nebraska: "Bending a knee toward the idea of Americanism will avail us little, unless we are also willing to put our hands to the job of being the kind of Americans it is our duty and privilege to be."

I will leave you with the story, from an unknown source, of an old Native American chief, who was being challenged for tribal leadership by a young aspiring brave. The brave concocted a scheme to belittle and embarrass the chief, by meeting with him carrying a small bird cupped and concealed in his hands. In front of the other tribal members, the young warrior challenged the chief: "If you are so wise, tell me if the bird in my hands is alive or dead." His plan was to open his hands and release the bird if the response was "dead," but quickly squeeze the tiny bird to death in the event of the opposite response. After a brief pause, the chief gave this brave a stern look and answered, "My son, the fate of that bird is up to you." And so in America, it is up to us, her people, to decide the fate of our country, which has given so much to so many of us.

Finally, if I could finish this book with a song, I know which one I would choose. A popular song released in 1965 and co-written by Hal David and Burt Bacharach captured it well. It is entitled *What the World Needs Now is Love*, and begins "What the World needs now is love sweet love, it's the only thing that there's just too little of…"

God Bless the United States of America.

Afterword

AS THIS IS BEING WRITTEN in the early days of June 2020, the country and even our world are in great turmoil. The world is experiencing a global virus pandemic and America is being ravaged by protests, many violent, stemming from alleged racist excessive-force practices by law enforcement. While these present immediate and direct concerns for public safety, there have been questions growing in the last few years concerning activities by some officials in one of our most important protectors of public safety – our FBI.

When Mr. Hoover accepted leadership of the FBI in 1924, he did so under the conditions that his Agents would be hired and investigations conducted on the basis of merit and facts but never politics. For nearly a century now, I believe this policy and practice have been sustained. Regretfully, for the past several months a number of allegations have gone public, on media air and in print, suggesting that certain highly placed FBI officials might have stepped over the line and engaged in political activities that would be unethical, if not illegal. Although there may be only a limited few involved, there have been some firings and retirements, and a number of inquiries are still pending.

Personally, I have no direct or firsthand knowledge, and this story is not mine to write. However, clearly my discussions with active FBI Agents about the issues have helped assure me that the vast corps of FBI personnel are not involved and that their responsibilities continue unabated and without interruption. I mention the central issue mainly to emphasize; one, how concerning it is to the hundreds of former FBI Agents who have given so much and for so long to their agency, and two, how important it is for thousands of Americans to retain their respect for the FBI. For the Bureau to slide back into any form of political shading and away from its tradition and requirement for independent fact-finding would damage irreparably the three prongs of its trident motto – Fidelity, Bravery, and Integrity.

There is every hope and wish that in the very near future all issues of possible political wrongdoing can be resolved and those proven responsible dealt with appropriately. It is vitally important that before the FBI reaches its century of existence in 2024 (as the FBI), it has fully retained its outstanding global reputation and the complete respect of our citizens.

Acknowledgments

MY SINCERE HEARTFELT THANKS are owed to so many whose contributions and support have made it possible for me to write this book. Although I have singled out some individuals throughout the book for their individual or group efforts, I need to certainly recognize and thank some others for their long standing past or contemporary contributions:

First and foremost to my wife, Irmgard, daughters Barbra and Lisa, and son, Eric, who have worried about me and tolerated so many days and nights that I have come home late or been away from home over so many years, both in and out of the country. Their support and love are cherished each and every day.

To my Special Agents in Charge (SACs), Stan Czarnecki and Ben Cooke (Louisville), who taught and supported me so well as their Assistant Special Agent in Charge (ASAC)

To all my ASACs who performed so admirably in Charlotte and Denver, especially Cecil Moses and Tom Coyle, who have both maintained close contact and friendship through the years.

To my Support Staff leaders, Carl Ross (Louisville), Craig Smith (Charlotte) and Marianna Harris (Denver) who supervised so professionally all the employees performing the administrative and logistical functions that actually make an FBI Division run efficiently

To my incredibly proficient and dedicated Secretaries, Martha Medley (Louisville), Faye Reid (Charlotte), Sharon Carson (Denver), and Pat Chancey, (FBI Headquarters), who were of invaluable assistance. Special thanks to Faye Reid who maintained close contact with me until her death in 2019, and Martha Medley, who continues to stay in frequent contact.

To a couple of FBI Agent friends who were my treasured mentors and have now passed away. George Lex and Bill Hamilton each ended up in the Washington D.C. area at the end of his career, and I was fortunate to have continued contact with each close to the end of his life journey.

To all the men and women of the FBI who worked in my day and those who work today to keep this America of ours safe from all her criminal and security threats.

To my Publisher, Bob Baron, who has become a dear friend and believed that some of my stories and adventures might be of some interest for others to read, and most especially to his Creative Director, Patty Maher, who has materially assisted and participated with me virtually every step of the way in preparing this book.

And finally for all my friends and associates who told me, at one time or another, that I should write a book and for all the attendees at one of my speaking engagements who approached afterward and asked "Where's the book?" As the saying goes, "This one's for you!"

Acronyms and Terms

AD – Assistant Director

AFL-CIO – American Federation of Labor and Congress of Industrial Organizations, the largest federation of unions in the United States

ASAC – Assistant Special Agent in Charge

ASD – Administrative Services Division

ASIS – American Society for Industrial Security

AST – Alaska State Troopers

BATF – Bureau of Alcohol, Tobacco, Firearms, and Explosives

BOI – Bureau of Investigation, precursor to the FBI

Bucars – Bureau Cars used for official FBI business

CIA – Central Intelligence Agency

CJIS – Criminal Justice Information Services

CJJ – Coalition for Juvenile Justice

COLCOR – Columbus County Corruption

COUNTERVAIL – investigation into Outlaw motorcycle gang

CROSSFIRE – investigation into cross burnings in the South

CPUSA – Communist Party, USA

CWP – Communist Workers Party

DDRP – Drug Demand Reduction Program

DID – Domestic Intelligence Division

DIPSCAM – the investigation involving the sale of phony college diplomas

DLI – Defense Language Institute

DMC – Disproportionate Minority Confinement/Contact

DNA – deoxyribonucleic acid

DNI – Director of National Intelligence

DOE – Department of Energy

DOJ – Department of Justice

DPD – Denver Police Department

EPA – Environmental Protection Agency

FBIHQ – Federal Bureau of Investigation Headquarters in Washington, D.C.
FCI – Foreign Counterintelligence
FO – Field Office

G-Men – Government men, nickname for FBI SAs
GATEWAY – investigation into drug smuggling
GSA – General Services Administration

HD – Headquarters Division
HUD – US Department of Housing and Urban Development

IA – inspector's aide
IACP – International Association of Chiefs of Police
ID – Inspection Division
IRS – Internal Revenue Service

JJDPA – Juvenile Justice and Delinquency Prevention Act
JJDP Council – Juvenile Justice and Delinquency Prevention Council
JNP – Jordan National Police

KKK – Ku Klux Klan
KSP – Kentucky State Police

LAFB – Lowry Air Force Base in Denver, Colorado
LCR Factor – Love, Care, Respect
Legat – Legal Attaché
LELC – Law Enforcement Liaison Council

MAFB – McGuire Air Force Base
MCSO – Monterey County Sheriff's Office
MIBURN – Mississippi Burning
MPCC – Monterey Peninsula Community College

NBA – National Basketball Association

NCIS – Naval Criminal Investigative Service

NOLA – New Orleans, Louisiana

NORAD – North American Aerospace Defense Command

NSA – National Security Agency

NYC – New York City

NYPD – New York Police Department

NYO – New York Office

OJJDP – Office of Juvenile Justice and Delinquency Prevention

OPCW – Organization for the Prohibition of Chemical Weapons

OSI – Office of Special Investigations

P3 – public-private partnership

PPPP – Pence's Personal Protection Principles

PRC – People's Republic of China

RA – Resident Agency

RCMP – Royal Canadian Mounted Police

ROTC – Reserve Officers' Training Corps

SA – Special Agent

SAC – Special Agent in Charge

SAG – State Advisory Group

SOG – Seat of Government (headquarters)

SRA – Senior Resident Agent

SSA – Supervisory Special Agent

STOMP – Stop Theft of Military Property

SUPERGLIDE – undercover investigation into motorcycle gang activities

UCA – Undercover Agent

UCO – Undercover Operation

WCC – White Collar Crime

WESTVOTE – investigation into voter irregularities in western North Carolina

Bibliography

Cesare, Don. *Blue • Gray • Black: My Service to Country*. Colorado Springs, CO: Rhyolite Press, 2015.

DeLoach, Cartha D. "Deke," and Jeff Riggenbach. *Hoover's FBI: The Inside Story by Hoover's Trusted Lieutenant*. Washington, DC: Regnery Publishing Inc., 1995.

Ezell, Allen, and John Bear. *Degree Mills: The Billion-Dollar Industry That Has Sold Over a Million Fake Diplomas*. Buffalo, NY: Prometheus Brooks, 2005.

Kelley, Clarence M., and James Kirkpatrick Davis. *Kelley: The Story of an FBI Director*. Kansas City, MO: Andrews McMeel, 1987.

Kennedy, Weldon L. *On Scene Commander: From Street Agent to Deputy Director of the FBI*. Lincoln, NE: Potomac Books Inc., 2007.

Massey, Morris. *What You Are Is Where You Were When … Again!* Cambridge, MA: Enterprise Media, 2006.

Overstreet, Harry Allen, and W. Bonaro. *The FBI in Our Open Society*. New York: W. W. Norton, 1969.

Index

About the Author

Bob Pence

BORN IN BROOKVILLE, Pennsylvania, Bob graduated from Dickinson College in Carlisle, Pennsylvania, in 1960, and then served as an infantry company commander in the US Army. During nearly 30 years with the FBI, he held a number of supervisory and executive positions, retiring in 1992, as the Special Agent in Charge of FBI offices in the Rocky Mountain states with headquarters in Denver, Colorado. Starting with the iconic Director J. Edgar Hoover, Bob's service extended through some of America's most turbulent eras, including the civil rights protests of the 1960s and the Vietnam War home front struggles of the 1970s.

Since retirement, he has been active as a law enforcement, media, and corporate security consultant and travels widely throughout the US and abroad. He has also served on a variety of charity, foundation, and law enforcement boards, councils, and committees. Bob co-chairs the Technical Assistance Committee for the Colorado Association of Chiefs of Police and has represented Colorado on the Federal Advisory Committee on Juvenile Justice, which advises the President, US Department of Justice, and the Congress on juvenile issues. He is a Past National Chair of the Coalition for Juvenile Justice, headquartered in Washington, D.C. On the law enforcement side, Bob is a member of the International Association of Chiefs of Police, the FBI National Executive Institute Associates, the National Sheriffs' Association, as well as the American Society for Industrial Security International, and law enforcement associations in several states.

Bob is a member of the International Speakers Network and a past member of the National Speakers Association. He resides in the US with his family in Littleton, Colorado.